DEMOKRASI

INDONESIA IN THE 21st CENTURY

Hamish McDonald

palgrave
macmillan

untuk Tukiyem, Heri,

Yon dan Fitri

DEMOKRASI

First published 2014 by Black Inc., an imprint of Schwartz Media Pty Ltd.

First Published in the United States in 2015 by PALGRAVE MACMILLAN TRADE ®—a division of St. Martin's Press LLC, 175 Fifth Avenue, New York, NY 10010.

Palgrave® and Macmillan® are registered trademarks in the United States, the United Kingdom, Europe and other countries.

ISBN 978-1-137-27999-6

Library of Congress Cataloging-in-Publication Data

McDonald, Hamish, 1948– author.
    Demokrasi : Indonesia in the 21st century / Hamish McDonald.
       pages   cm   Includes index.
    1. Indonesia—Politics and government—1998– 2. Indonesia—History. I. Title.
DS644.5.M38163   2015
959.804—dc23

2014021926

Design by Letra Libre, Inc.

First Palgrave Macmillan Trade edition: January 2015

10 9 8 7 6 5 4 3 2 1

Printed in the United States of America.

CONTENTS

AUTHOR'S NOTE

THIS BOOK IS INTENDED AS A QUICK OVERVIEW OF CONTEMPORARY INDONESIA AND, IN some aspects, has been streamlined for ease of reading. In most cases, Indonesian names are rendered in standard modern spellings, even when their owners prefer the older Dutch-era renditions. Notably, the *tj* consonant becomes *c,* and the *oe* vowel becomes *u.* Monetary amounts are given in the US dollar equivalent at the exchange rate of the time, though at times of wild fluctuations—such as in 1997–8—this can produce wide variations. Again for ease of reading, attribution to sources is given in the text where possible, rather than in footnotes. Where the US embassy or its officials are cited as sources, the material has been drawn from the vast cache of US diplomatic reports published by WikiLeaks in 2010–11.

ABBREVIATIONS

ABRI	Angkatan Bersenjata Republik Indonesia (Armed Forces of the Republic of Indonesia)
Bappenas	Badan Perencanaan Pembangunan Nasional (National Development Planning Agency)
BIN	Badan Inteligen Negara (State Intelligence Agency)
BNPT	Badan Nasional Penanggulangan Terrorisme (National Counterterrorism Agency)
Brimob	Brigade Mobil (Mobile Brigade, Indonesian National Police)
DAP	Dewan Adat Papua (Papua Traditional Council)
DPR	Dewan Perwakilan Rakyat (People's Representative Council)
FPI	Front Pembela Islam (Islamic Defenders Front)
GAM	Gerakan Aceh Merdeka (Free Aceh Movement)
Gerindra	Gerakan Indonesia Raya (Great Indonesia Movement)
Golkar	Partai Golongan Karya (Party of the Functional Groups)
IBRA	Indonesian Bank Restructuring Agency

ICMI	Ikatan Cendekiawan Muslim Indonesia (Indonesian Association of Muslim Intellectuals)
KKN	*Korupsi, Kolusi, Nepotisme* (Corruption, Collusion, Nepotism)
KNIL	Koninklijk Nederlands Indisch Leger (Royal Netherlands Indies Army)
KNIP	Komite Nasional Indonesia Pusat (Central Indonesian National Committee)
KNPB	Komite Nasional Papua Barat (National Committee for West Papua)
Komnas—HAM	Komisi Nasional Hak Asasi Manusia (National Commission on Human Rights)
Kompak	Komite Aksi Penanggulangan Akibat Krisis (Crisis Management/Prevention Committee)
Kopassus	Komando Pasukan Khusus (Special Forces Command)
Kopkamtib	Komando Operasi Pemulihan Keamanan dan Ketertiban (Operational Command for the Restoration of Security and Order)
Kosgoro	Kesatuan Organisasi Serbaguna Gotong Royong (Federation of Miscellaneous Mutual-Aid Organizations)
Kostrad	Komando Cadangan Strategis Angkatan Darat (Army Strategic Reserve Command)
KPC	Kaltim Prima Coal
KPK	Komisi Pemberantasan Korupsi (Corruption Eradication Commission)
Malari	Malapetaka Januari (January Calamity)
Masyumi	Majelis Syuro Muslimin Indonesia (Council of Indonesian Muslim Associations)

MPR	Majelis Permusyawaratan Rakyat (People's Consultative Assembly)
Mubes	Musyawarah Besar (Grand Consultation)
MUI	Majelis Ulama Indonesia (Indonesian Ulemas' Council)
Nasakom	*Nasionalisme, Agama, Komunisme* (Nationalism, Religion, Communism)
NHM	Nederlandsche Handel—Maatschappij (Netherlands Trading Company)
NU	Nahdatul Ulama (Muslim Scholars' League)
OPEC	Organization of the Petroleum Exporting Countries
OPM	Organisasi Papua Merdeka (Free Papua Movement)
Opsus	*Operasi Khusus* (Special Operations)
Otsus	*Otonomi Khusus* (Special Autonomy)
PAN	Partai Amanat Nasional (National Mandate Party)
Parmusi	Partai Muslimin Indonesia (Indonesian Muslim Party)
PD	Partai Demokrat (Democratic Party)
PDI—P	Partai Demokrasi Indonesia—Perjuangan (Democratic Party of Indonesia—Struggle)
PDI	Partai Demokrasi Indonesia (Indonesian Democratic Party)
Permesta	Piagam Perjuangan Semesta (Universal Struggle Charter)
PETA	Pembela Tanah Air (Defenders of the Homeland)
PKB	Partai Kebangkitan Bangsa (National Awakening Party)

PKI	Partai Kommunis Indonesia (Communist Party of Indonesia)
PKS	Partai Keadilan Sejahtera (Prosperous Justice Party)
PND	Partai Nasional Demokrat (National Democrat Party)
PNI	Partai Nasional Indonesia (Indonesian National Party)
PPP	Partai Persatuan Pembangunan (Development Unity Party)
PRRI	Pemerintah Revolusioner Republik Indonesia (Revolutionary Government of the Indonesian Republic)
PSI	Partai Sosialis Indonesia (Socialist Party of Indonesia)
REDD+	Reducing Emissions from Deforestation and Forest Degradation
SBY	Susilo Bambang Yudhoyono
TAVIP	*Tahun Vivere Pericoloso* (the Year of Living Dangerously)
TNI	Tentara Nasional Indonesia (Indonesian National Army)
VOC	Vereenigde Oost-Indische Compagnie (United East Indies Company)

INTRODUCTION

INDONESIA
REVISITED

"I AM ENCHANTED WITH THESE ISLANDS!" EXCLAIMS THE MAIN CHARACTER IN JOSEPH
Conrad's novel *Victory*, set in the East Indies at the start of the last
century. Many other foreign visitors continue to find magic in the
Indonesian archipelago, which spreads as wide as the United States
along the equator in Southeast Asia.

For this writer and others, it was a romantic place to start a
career as a foreign correspondent. Though the islands had been explored, occupied, and exploited by the West for centuries, the newly
emerged Indonesia was somehow outside the world's mainstream. It
had an aura of beauty, sensuality, chaos, and violence. Those who
came and stayed saw the possibility of a great but gentle nation arising here; one retiring American ambassador titled his book about
Indonesia *The Possible Dream*.

In the late 1970s, Jakarta was a city of intermittent electricity,
frequent flooding, prohibitive rents (thanks to an oil boom), limited
telephones, and taciturn officials. Yet our small house, which was
off an alleyway called Gang Sekayu, was surrounded by a welcom-
ing community. Neighbors watched over our small child. The family of the respected hajji (a returned pilgrim to Mecca) welcomed
her to Muslim ceremonies and exhibitions of *silat* (martial arts). A

housekeeper from Kediri, in East Java, became like a second mother. This woman's hometown became my case study of grassroots politics: there I met a former military commander and a venerated *kyai* (an Islamic scholar), who together had wiped out the local communists a decade earlier and who were now political enemies in the highly controlled "New Order" regime.

Indonesia had changed, old hands said. Yet it was still possible to call at the home of the president at the end of the fasting month and shake Suharto's hand. Nonetheless, my journalistic sins mounted up in the black book kept at the Ministry of Information. After three and a half years, further visa extensions were refused. I wrote a book, *Suharto's Indonesia*, which for some years became a primer on the country. A decade as persona non grata followed.

A conciliatory foreign minister, Ali Alatas, persuaded the system to relax, and in 1989 I resumed making short visits to a rapidly changing country. My book by now was out of date. At last Suharto was pushed from power in the financial crisis of 1997–8, in an almost unbelievable repudiation of what had seemed an unbreakable system. Then, in Dili, the violent side of Indonesia emerged. Back in Jakarta, we journalists waited long into the evening at the presidential palace; near midnight, the small figure of B. J. Habibie, Suharto's successor, announced the end of thirty-four years of occupation in East Timor. When I saw the grim faces of the army generals around him, it seemed impossible that this experiment with democracy would be allowed to continue. Yet it has.

Fifteen years later, Jakarta is beset with protest and bold media reports. Demonstrators mock the president in front of the palace. The city is bigger: the once-empty boulevards are choked with cars and lined with high-rise offices and shopping malls. Where a motorbike was once a luxury, now millions zoom through gaps in the traffic and along footpaths. Orderly commuters pack trains to and from the nearby towns.

There are more mosques, and their muezzin and prayers broadcast more loudly. More of the women and girls wear the hijab, either a headscarf or a cowl. A more egalitarian spirit prevails: everyone is *Bapak* (Mr.) or *Ibu* (Mrs.), rather than the graduated titles of the more hierarchical recent past. During my several months back in Jakarta, no one addressed me as *Tuan* (Master), a term of the feudal and colonial era that was often reserved for European men. Instead of the gaunt men from the villages who once waited for customers and slept in their rented *becak* (pedicabs) at street corners, there are now clusters of *ojek* (motorbike taxis) and their drivers: burlier, urban types who are full of swagger.

When I went to look at my old house, I discovered that the entire neighborhood had been razed, in preparation for a large construction project. The alleyway, Gang Sekayu, had disappeared from the map. Indonesia's own leaders were thinking bigger.

Today, analysts are forecasting Indonesia's rise to the top half-dozen economies by GDP within two decades, and the nation is being mentioned as another important strategic "counterweight" to the fast-rising China. But it remains a country that is hard to figure out. This, then, is a new attempt to provide a starting point for understanding.

1

NUSANTARA

LONG DERIDED BY INTELLECTUALS AND CRITICS OF THE SUHARTO PRESIDENCY, TAMAN Mini Indonesia Indah (meaning "Beautiful Indonesia in Miniature Park") is a surprisingly enduring memento of the military strongman's rule. The theme park was one of the earliest investments of the Suharto family after the general took power in the nation; it became the special project of his wife, Tien, and was financed by their Yayasan Harapan Kita (Our Hope Foundation), a fund that channeled donations from business tycoons anxious to remain in official favor.

Commenced in 1970, Taman Mini aimed to acquaint Indonesians with the various cultures and ethnicities of the regions of their far-flung *nusantara* (archipelago). Pavilions to represent the then twenty-six provinces (East Timor was added after its formal annexation in 1976) were constructed in the appropriate traditional styles. Dance, costumes, music, and handicrafts presented a picture of calm, harmonious societies inside scenic landscapes, all close and accessible enough to illustrate the motto on the national emblem, *Bhinneka Tunggal Ika* ("Unity in Diversity").

After some years of mounting shabbiness during which Taman Mini seemed destined to be one of the discards of the Suharto era, the theme park is now back in vigorous life. Pavilions have been added to accommodate new provinces hived off from the old. East

Timor's pavilion has been turned into a small museum chronicling its twenty-three years as part of this happy family, with few clues in the display as to why its people had opted out. A new hotel, meeting places, and a technology hall have been added to the park, along with a Disneyesque fantasy subpark. Buses bring large groups from the vast metropolis of Jakarta and the nearby regions of West Java. The park's internal roads have miniature versions of the traffic jams that afflict the city roads outside, as the middle-class patrons show off their new vehicles. Long queues of people wait to ride around the park on an elevated monorail or cable car. Once aloft, they can look down on fellow excursionists pedaling swan-shaped boats around a lake, which has mini-islands in the same array as the archipelago.

That Taman Mini thrives is a testament to the longevity of Suharto-era capitalism (the family foundation remains the owner, with the late president's eldest daughter, Siti Hardiyanti Rukmana, or Tutut, in charge) and to the growing market for organized recreation among Indonesians with time and a bit of money to spend. It reflects a continuing concern in Jakarta with national integration, one that goes back to a time well before Tien Suharto thought of building a theme park. No doubt subconsciously, as the late historian Onghokham observed, her vision mirrored that of the Orientalist scholars, artists, and officials of the later Dutch administration, who dreamed up *Mooi Indie* (Beautiful Indies). A common theme in popular art was the landscape of high mountains (the volcanoes dormant), green jungles, vivid flowers, and ripening rice paddies, which benignly support a tranquil and harmonious village life. For Dutch officials and, subliminally, their Indonesian successors, this ideal carried a message: *Roost im Ordre* (Peace and Order). Their duty was to leave this world undisturbed.

Yet violent history pushes its way onto the canvas. Echoes of the separatist rebellion that only ended in fiercely proud Aceh in 2005 can still be heard. The position of Indonesia's two Papuan provinces in western New Guinea—which could be revisited by the United Nations, should there be some change in the international balance of power and perception—remains a deeply sensitive issue in Jakarta. When a boatload of Papuan dissidents crossed the Torres Strait and gained political asylum from an embarrassed Australian government in 2006, President Susilo Bambang Yudhoyono withdrew Indonesia's ambassador from Canberra—a step not previously taken in all the years of diplomatic relations between the two countries, not even when their troops were stalking each other in the jungles of Borneo during the 1963–65 *Konfrontasi* episode. Hence the constant harping in speeches by Indonesia's politicians and military chiefs on the sanctity of the "unitary state," and the expedient homage paid by visiting foreign leaders, especially those from Australia and the South Pacific, to Indonesian sovereignty within its existing borders.

In the sweep of history, Indonesian-ness is a comparatively recent thing, and it's still under construction in the country's peripheries. The very idea of Indonesia is barely a century old. But there was much history on which to build. Indonesia's land and waters have been a wonderland for modern-era archeologists, with relics and inscriptions still being unearthed or salvaged to add to the mosaic of knowledge about the kings, warriors, queens, concubines, sailors, traders, and priests who battled and schemed in distant centuries.

The greatest early empire may have been that called Sriwijaya, which flowered from AD 683 and declined in the thirteenth century. It flourished amid a hemispheric order and trading system in which Europe was barely a peripheral extension. An empire based on control of the seas, and with its capital near present-day Palembang, Sriwijaya dominated Sumatra and the Malayan peninsula at the center of the great east-west navigation routes, which extended from China to India, and beyond to the Red Sea and Africa. The empire's sway covered the coastal areas of the islands around the Java Sea and most of Java itself. At times, Sriwijaya might have extended its power into present-day Thailand, Cambodia, Vietnam, and the Philippines. The religion of its courts alternated between Hinduism and Buddhism, evidenced by the ninth-century relics of two of its dynasties located near Yogyakarta in Central Java, the Buddhist monument of Borobudur and the Hindu temple complex of Prambanan.

Sriwijaya has been an inspiration for later peoples; for the builders of modern Indonesia, the empire's most useful legacy was its dispersal of the Malay language around the archipelago as a lingua franca. The language was used and taught by traders in rice and textiles from Java (which was the biggest producer in Southeast Asia until the nineteenth century), in pepper from Sumatra, in gold from Borneo, in cloves and nutmeg from the Moluccan Islands, in camphor and sandalwood from Timor, and in slaves and horses from the southeastern islands.

As Sriwijaya declined and its capital sank under river silt, a mighty Hindu empire arose in the center and east of Java, with its capital close to the present-day town of Mojokerto, inland from Surabaya along one of the two navigable rivers of any significance on the island, the Brantas. Majapahit flourished from 1293 until around 1500, reaching its apogee under its king Hayam Waruk (who reigned from 1350 to 1389) and his energetic and ambitious prime minister, Gajah Mada. The empire's power extended to vassal states across Sumatra, Bali, Malaya, Borneo, and the eastern islands, and its diplomacy reached the Champa kingdom in what is now Vietnam, Cambodia, Siam, the south of Burma, and China. Gajah Mada is said to have sworn an oath, referring to the *palapa,* or meat of the young coconut, not to eat delicious spicy foods until the boundaries of his empire were secure. In modern times, the legendary ambit of Majapahit has been used to support the current territorial limits of Indonesia—and sometimes to push claims beyond them. Tellingly, when Indonesia gained its first national communications satellite, Suharto named it *Palapa* after Gajah Mada's oath.

In practice, the hold of the ruler was much more tenuous than the legend suggests. The entire population of the archipelago would have been fewer than 5 million people, with most living in isolated clusters separated by seas and mountains. Even in Java, aside from the northern coastal plains that faced a placid sea, many communities could be reached only by long journeys on foot over rugged terrain. The historian M. C. Ricklefs notes that kingship would have involved the delegation of authority to regional overlords in Java and to tributary rulers in the outer islands. He concludes: "There was, therefore, constant tension within large states between regional and central interests, and all such states were fragile entities."

The techniques of maintaining power were centered on the apportionment of "rent farms," the right to levy gate tolls and other taxes on trade. Intermarriage was used to keep potential usurpers on familial terms, while a network of spies also operated. The kings imbued themselves with mystical powers as incarnations of Hindu gods. Ultimately, they had military power if all else failed. "A successful ruler stayed on top of this precarious system," observes Ricklefs, "by balancing and manipulating the interests of those below him, by demonstrating superior martial skills and by appearing to have the support of the supernatural."

In an influential essay, Cornell University's Benedict Anderson also saw that power, in Javanese tradition, was increased by the accumulation of prestige. Successful usurpers prepared themselves by withdrawing from worldly affairs and by undertaking regimes of self-discipline. A ruler would gather around himself the *pusaka* (relics) of other powerful figures, such as their weapons or regalia; he would also bring conflicting groups into agreement, demonstrate his sexual prowess by having many wives and offspring, invoke magic with invocatory words and ceremonies, and show his ease with the supernatural by bringing into his retinue "extraordinary human beings such as albinos, clowns, dwarves and fortune tellers." He demonstrated his power through his quietness, as befit someone of the utmost *halus* (refined) quality.

If this indicated that power was a simple sum of elements to be accumulated by the skillful statesman, rather than by any moral force, Onghokham pointed out that *wahyu,* or divine legitimacy, could shift at any time. Civil disorder, famine, disease, inflation, the dwindling of gold savings, or the eruption of a volcano could all be signs of a ruler losing his grip, and a new *ratu adil* (just prince) might then emerge and seize power.

While Majapahit was being built, trade was bringing in a new religion from the west. Islam became a permanent presence on the archipelago as Arab and Indian merchants took local wives and conversions grew. It came surprisingly late, some five or six centuries after the faith was founded, but it was noted as the prevailing religion in many centers along the Malacca Strait by travelers, such as Marco Polo (1292) and Ibn Battuta (1345–6). By the early fifteenth century, the religion was spreading throughout Java and into court circles. Hayam Waruk's successors were showing themselves to be clumsy in statecraft, and Majapahit's power was eclipsed by the rise of three Islamic sultanates on Java.

After less than a century under Islam, though, a new kingdom of the classic Javanese model arose. A new ratu adil, Senopati, emerged after building up his wahyu through fasting and meditation, and after communing with the vengeful goddess of the seas, Nyai Lara Kidul. In 1584 he established a new sultanate, Mataram, with its capital near present-day Yogyakarta. A successor, Sultan Agung, who reigned between 1613 and 1646, expanded the domain across central and eastern Java, with tribute exacted from rulers across the

Java Sea. As well as an Islamic identity, Mataram's practices displayed many threads of Hinduism, Indian political theory, and native Javanese spiritualism. It was a blend to be evidenced in the style of Indonesia's first two presidents.

BY THIS TIME the rulers and peoples of the archipelago had a new and even more disruptive influence to deal with. In the last years of the fifteenth century, Portuguese explorers found their way around the Cape of Good Hope to India. In 1510 the expedition of Afonso de Albuquerque seized Goa, on the west coast of India, and a year later the biggest trading sultanate on the route between India and China, Malacca.

Through an advantage in military technique, the Portuguese now had one of the key staging points in what Ricklefs calls "the greatest trading system in the world at this time." But they had no clue how to take commercial advantage. Malacca had no hinterland or resources: it was a pure entrepôt, reliant on trust and acceptable fees among the merchants who used it. With the Portuguese squeezing this commerce too hard, traders bypassed Malacca for ports such as Johor. The interest of the Portuguese moved to Japan and Macau and to the eastern spice-producing islands of the archipelago. After efforts to set up bases in Ternate and Tidore, in alliance with the local rulers, they concentrated on Ambon, where a strong Christian community developed, encouraged by a visit by the Jesuit missionary Francis Xavier in 1546–47.

The Portuguese were joined at the end of the sixteenth century by the Dutch. The first Dutch expedition, in 1595–97, was a disaster in terms of men and shipping lost but still turned enough of a profit from its cargo of pepper to set off a scramble by other adventurers. In 1602 the Dutch parliament forced the competing traders to form a single chartered enterprise, the Vereenigde Oost-Indische Compagnie (VOC, United East Indies Company), which had quasisovereign powers. It seized Ambon in 1605 but by 1619 had moved its headquarters to Jayakarta, a port on the north coast of West Java that gave it a more central position in the archipelago. It was renamed Batavia, after an ancient term for the tribes of the Netherlands.

For nearly two centuries, the VOC manipulated, often clumsily, the power of the Mataram rulers and of their internal rivals and external challengers, offering the limited military power of its few

European troops (there were only 869 such soldiers on Java in 1702) and local recruits in land campaigns, and using its much more effective naval power to control and tax trade. The company gradually extended its power to the eastern islands, forcing the English out of the nearby port of Banten. But the profitability of its trading posts declined, especially after the French stole clove seedlings and set up rival plantations in their Indian Ocean colonies. VOC officials became renowned for corruption and debauchery; "Our nation must drink or die," declared the early VOC governor-general Jan Pieterszoon Coen. And die they did, if not from excess, then from the many diseases of swampy Batavia.

A low point that almost lost Java for the Dutch came in 1740, when those in Batavia panicked about being murdered in their beds by a native and Chinese uprising. A crackdown turned into a pogrom in which 10,000 Chinese were slaughtered. Survivors fled to Central Java and laid siege to VOC forts, with help from Mataram. The uprising was narrowly overcome, and Mataram was eventually subdivided into three royal houses with less and less effective power. In 1795 Napoleon Bonaparte's armies conquered Holland and installed a friendly regime in Batavia. It dissolved the bankrupt and scandal-shrouded VOC in 1800.

The administration continued, but the East Indies were now under direct rule from The Hague. In 1808 it sent out a new governor-general, Herman Willem Daendels, who was imbued with the French revolutionary spirit. He showed no delicacy with the Javanese rulers, equating them with the ousted French aristocracy. The Indies, meanwhile, were caught up in global conflict. A new governor-general, Jan Willem Janssens, had in 1811 just installed himself after being expelled from Cape Town by the British when a massive British fleet arrived off Batavia. Janssens and his forces were pursued to defeat at Salatiga.

The new British lieutenant governor of Java, Thomas Stamford Raffles, was just as short with the Javanese royalty as Daendels had been. An encounter with one of the Mataram sultans, Hamengkubuwono II, almost turned into a fight on the spot. The discovery of plotting gave Raffles the excuse to send his British and Indian troops to sack Hamengkubuwono's lavish *kraton* (palace) and install a friendly prince from a junior royal house, the Pakualaman, across town in Yogyakarta.

The British handed back the Indies to the restored Dutch kingdom in 1816, as part of the settlement of Europe after Napoleon's final defeat at Waterloo. Along with a romantic legend, Raffles left traces of his influence: the name of Yogyakarta's main street, Malioboro (from "Marlborough"), the botanical gardens next to the old governor-general's palace in Bogor, a two-volume history of Java, and his name on a giant, foul-smelling flower of the Southeast Asian jungles. Except in Indonesia, he is better known as the founder of Singapore in 1819, the entrepôt and naval base that established British preeminence in Southeast Asia for more than a century.

Ricklefs credits Raffles with introducing, at least in theory, the notion that "native welfare" should be a concern of government and the beginnings of a land rent system for state finances. He and Daendels also tightened the administrative authority of government, making Javanese officials part of its bureaucracy, whether they liked it or not.

The uprising led by Prince Diponegoro, of the Hamengkubuwono royal house, in 1825–30 was a classic case of a ratu adil figure responding to widespread popular discontent. Diponegoro repudiated the decadence of court life, spent time in religious schools, and pursued meditation, and fought against the heavy squeeze by tax "farmers" (merchants given rights to levy road tolls and land rent on behalf of the rulers) and the leasing of land by court officials to European and Chinese planters of sugar, indigo, coffee, and other cash crops. But the Dutch wore his rebel forces down in a long campaign that cost the lives of 15,000 government soldiers and 200,000 Javanese. Ultimately, Diponegoro surrendered and was exiled to Sulawesi, where he died in 1855.

The Dutch now settled down to run Java as an extractive system. The *cultuurstelsel* (cultivation system), introduced in 1830, replaced the cash paid by villages as land rent with crops grown for export on a piece of village land set aside for this purpose. This was meant to ease the demand of turning rice into cash in order to pay the tax; in effect, it meant villagers were growing huge volumes of indigo, sugar, coffee, and so on at a set price, which the government's trading company could then export and sell from Amsterdam at a vast profit.

The population of Java, meanwhile, began growing—a result of the peace and some public health improvements—rising from about

7 million in 1830 to nearly four times that number by the end of the century. This made greater and greater demands on the rice-growing capacity of the island. The effects on the Javanese were uneven, but overall they were being squeezed. Remittances to the Dutch treasury from the Indies rose to around a third of all state revenues in the 1850s and 1860s, effectively financing the construction of railways and other infrastructure of the industrial age in Holland.

By this time, an awakening liberalism in Holland was leading to doubts about the humanity of the *cultuurstelsel,* roused in part by a novel whose effect is often likened to that of *Uncle Tom's Cabin* on the antislavery mood in the United States. *Max Havelaar,* written by Edward Douwes Dekker under the pseudonym Multatuli, described the life of an eponymous young official who had been assigned as assistant resident in a district of West Java. There, the hereditary local ruler, the *bupati,* mercilessly oppressed the population to extract coffee at ever lower prices and to obtain free labor, while Havelaar's boss, the Dutch resident, continued to provide sunny reports to the governor-general.

The book's publication in 1860 caused uproar, and the gradual abolition of the compulsory growing of government crops and the official adoption of a *Liberaal Politiek* (Liberal Policy) followed. Whether the lives of Java's villagers were greatly improved is unclear. One effect was the opening of Java to private agrarian ventures, with foreigners able to lease land. The number of European residents jumped sharply, and more and more Javanese found themselves working for European or Chinese masters. The liberal policy did lead to an extension of schooling for the people of the Indies, creating cadres of teachers, medical officers, clerks, and officials in telegraphy, the railways, and other services.

After the European accord, the Dutch moved in fits and starts to regularize their territorial control, with a treaty in 1824 giving them sway over Sumatra, in return for their acknowledgement of Britain's control over Malaya. A seventeen-year uprising in the West Sumatran homeland of the Minangkabau, influenced by the puritanical Wahhabi school of Islam (which had been encountered by pilgrims to Mecca and brought back), was finally put down in 1838; its leader, Imam Bonjol, was exiled to North Sulawesi. Campaigns continued, bringing to heel any truculent sultans or rajas around the archipelago, with the costly Aceh wars being the last great expenditure of

Dutch blood, although the Acehnese were never really subdued and random suicidal attacks by individuals against passing Dutchmen continued—these were the so-called Aceh *moort* (Aceh murders). At the other end of the Indies, Dutch officials took up station in New Guinea.

It was in Bali that a final grim tableau of Dutch imperialism played out. Bali had long offended European sensibilities—its multiple kingdoms were constantly at war, a major source of its income well into the nineteenth century was the export of slaves, and its upper classes practiced a form of Hindu *suttee*, or widow burning—but it had been left alone as it produced little of exportable value. The ransacking of ships that had run aground and the burning of a widow in 1903 finally motivated the Dutch to intervene. In 1906 the royal families of the Badung kingdom, including women and children, faced the Dutch army. Dressed in ritual white and armed only with traditional weapons, they advanced on the lines of soldiers at Denpasar and Pamecutan and were mown down with rifle and machine-gun fire. Another of these *puputan* (final battles) occurred at Klungkung in 1908.

The colonial spell that had enabled small European nations to subdue vast numbers of peoples across the world was a mixture of brutal force and deliberate demoralization. Before the American invasion of the Philippines, only about 5,000 Spaniards, of whom 4,000 were priests, had controlled the entire island system. Ricklefs points out that in 1905 the Dutch were able to hold down, if not minutely control, the 37 million people in the Indies with a relatively tiny armed force of fewer than 16,000 Europeans and 26,000 local soldiers (of whom, despite the later ill feeling, only 21 percent were Ambonese, while 68 percent were Javanese). The Dutch didn't have to divide the populace in order to rule it. A national consciousness had not yet awoken. But that was about to change.

THE INDUSTRIAL AGE ARRIVED in the Indies. A new steamship line linked the islands. Railways connected the main cities of Java, while electric trams trundled their streets. The telegraph quickly brought news from around the world. Rotary printing presses churned out newspapers for a mass readership. In 1898 a Dutch company found oil in North Sumatra and, in 1907, merged with a British company active in Borneo to form Royal Dutch Shell. The motor age set off investment in vast rubber plantations. Coal mines in Sumatra and Borneo fueled the electricity grids of the cities and towns. This aggressive enterprise, much of it in the outer islands, radiated out from the great urban centers of Singapore, Batavia, and Surabaya.

This intensified exploitation was accompanied by another turn in the official Dutch policy toward the Indies. The Liberal Policy was replaced by the *Ethische Politiek* (Ethical Policy) in 1901, reflecting the feeling in a review ordered by the young Queen Wilhelmina (who reigned between 1890 and 1948): that it was time for the Dutch to recognize a "debt of honour" and give back a measure of the benefits taken from the Indies to its peoples. The pillars of the Ethical Policy were education and a combination of investment in agriculture and migration to ameliorate the population pressure that was being experienced in Java.

With the population already expanding explosively, the latter part of the policy came too late. The promise of educational opportunity coincided with a growing consciousness among local peoples, expressed in the letters of a young woman of the Javanese aristocratic (*priyayi*) class, Raden Ajeng Kartini, which were published by a sympathetic Dutch official after her death in 1904, aged just twenty-five. In the first two decades of the twentieth century, higher levels of education were opened to students of all races, with the first tertiary college (the forerunner of the Bandung Institute of Technology) opening in 1920.

By this time, a few of the brighter sons of wealthy families were graduating from universities in the Netherlands. But the government school system was reaching only a small fraction of school-age children by the final years of Dutch rule, with adult literacy under 10 percent. Like its predecessor, the Ethical Policy in practice had its limits. A truly universal education system would have required actual financial sacrifice by the Dutch.

Political development was even more token, with the formation of an advisory body to the governor-general, the Volksraad (People's Council), whose European, Chinese, and *Inlander* (or native) representatives were elected by a narrow college of substantial citizens.

By the 1920s, however, the cities of Batavia, Bandung, and Surabaya were in ferment. The first graduates from higher schools emerged, and pamphlets and Malay-language newspapers appeared. Dutch radicals introduced militant socialist ideas, similar to those sweeping Russia and Germany. Ideas of self-government had begun stirring earlier but had not yet formed into a broad nationalism. Several hundred young Javanese priyayi formed the cultural revival association Budi Utomo (Highest Endeavor) in 1908. It drew inspiration from the Javanese empires of the past, and some members regarded Islam as an influence that had held the Javanese back. The more devout, both in Java and in the outer islands, joined the Sarekat Islam (Islamic Union), formed over 1911–12, which had a more ethnically universal base but also looked to the worldwide *ummat* (community of believers).

By the 1920s the name, "Indonesia" was coming into common use, and in 1928 young members of various cultural and political associations met in Batavia to declare the *Sumpah Pemuda* (Pledge of Youth): one fatherland, one nation, one language.

Local radicals had taken over the most active socialist organization, and in the early 1920s shaped it into the Partai Kommunis Indonesia (PKI, Communist Party of Indonesia). They then embarked on a feverish campaign of recruitment and mobilization around Java, battling with Sarekat Islam and the Dutch police. In November 1926 the PKI launched an uprising in Batavia and parts of West Java, with a follow-up revolt in Sumatra in January 1927. The insurrection was promptly smashed by the Dutch authorities, and mass arrests ensued. Some 4,500 radicals were given jail sentences, and 1,300 of them transported to a new prison settlement called Boven Digul in the farthest part of the Indies, inland from the town of Merauke in the far southeast of Dutch New Guinea.

Into the suspicious political atmosphere following the PKI uprising stepped the emerging leaders of secular Indonesian nationalism. Sukarno, born in 1901, was the son of a Javanese schoolteacher and his Balinese wife. He had flourished in the new educational system, proceeding to an engineering degree in Bandung, although he undertook much eclectic reading and dabbled in journalism along the way. In 1927 he and some fellow intellectuals founded what became the Partai Nasional Indonesia (PNI, Indonesian National Party); his idea of synthesizing Islam, Marxism, and nationalism into a single cause was already starting to form.

In the Netherlands, students from the Indies became more consciously Indonesian. In 1927 the Dutch arrested several on charges of inciting armed rebellion, among them a future vice president,

Mohammed Hatta, a Minangkabau from West Sumatra. The resulting trial gave them a platform to speak against the abuses of Dutch rule—and, to the further embarrassment of The Hague, all were acquitted.

Undeterred, Indies authorities arrested Sukarno in 1929 and put him on trial. He gave a flamboyant speech of defiance and criticism but could not avoid a sentence of four years in Bandung's Sukamiskin jail. The PNI effectively collapsed in Sukarno's absence, and although he was released in December 1931 by an act of clemency, further political organization by the parties was dangerous. With political activity seen as likely to run away beyond any control, and with the Great Depression limiting resources for any social or economic palliatives, the authorities turned their eyes away from schemes of political development, such as the steps toward internal self-government being taken or promised in British India or the American-administered Philippines.

Sukarno was again arrested in 1933 and sent into exile without trial, first to the primitive island of Flores in the southeast and then to the isolated Sumatran town of Bengkulu. Hatta and another Minangkabau intellectual, Sutan Sjahrir, returned from the Netherlands and threw their efforts into forming a cadre of future leaders. But in 1934 they too were arrested and exiled, initially to Boven Digul and then to the more salubrious but also isolated spice island of Banda.

The Netherlands East Indies refused offers of help from its people in resisting the mounting threat of Japan in return for political evolution. Hitler invaded the Netherlands in May 1940, forcing Queen Wilhelmina into exile in London, and took France the following month, allowing his Axis ally in the East to use Indochina as a springboard for its advance into Southeast Asia. Only then did belated efforts begin to expand the small Koninklijk Nederlands Indisch Leger (KNIL, Royal Netherlands Indies Army). But after Singapore surrendered in February 1942, it took only three weeks for the Indies government to do the same.

Suddenly, most of the Europeans in the Indies had been marched out of their big houses and into grim internment camps. Japanese army officers took control in Java and Sumatra, while the Japanese Imperial Navy managed the eastern islands. The Japanese military's intelligence services had built up considerable knowledge of

Indonesian political figures and religious organizations, and set out to use them to win popular backing and cooperation for Tokyo's war effort.

Released from their internal exile, Sukarno and Hatta decided to take Japan's message of Asian liberation at face value and use the occupation to advance their mobilization of the population toward independence. It was agreed that some nationalist elements, under the control of Sutan Sjahrir, would keep their distance from the Japanese and act as a second, semiunderground movement. The worldly and highly educated Hatta was more cynical about the collaboration: he knew the difference between democracy and fascism. This didn't matter so much to the more ingenuous Sukarno. On the pair's visit to Tokyo in November 1943 to be decorated by Emperor Hirohito, Sukarno's first time outside the Indies, he was much more impressed.

It was a relationship of mutual exploitation, though it became harder to disguise the one-way nature of the exploitation of Indonesia's human and natural resources, with 200,000 young men drafted into forced labor elsewhere in Southeast Asia—most would never return—and oil, rubber, and other products diverted to Japan's military-industrial machine. With the balance of the Pacific war already shifting against Japan in 1943, the occupiers promoted the organization of the population into security organizations. Tens of thousands of young men were recruited as soldiers in auxiliary forces, such as the Pembela Tanah Air (PETA, Defenders of the Homeland). Village loudspeakers relayed speeches and messages from Jakarta (as Batavia had now been renamed) and Bandung. A new mass movement in Java, the Jawa Hokokai (Java Service Association), was modeled on Japan's own neighborhood control system. Sukarno was enlisted to extend its reach and used its propaganda tours to extend his own following.

As Japan's control of the Pacific receded, the efforts to create a hostile barrier to the European powers increased. They moved to put their promises of independence into practice. In March 1945, Sukarno and many of the more mature leaders of the prewar independence movement were drafted into a preparatory committee in the old *Volksraad* building. By July the committee had finished drafting a constitution for a unitary republic with a strong presidency.

A major battle concerned the role of religion. Sukarno had finally talked Islamic leaders into accepting his *Pancasila* (Five Principles) as the philosophical basis of the new state: belief in God, national-ism, humanitarianism, social justice, and democracy. A further sop was the addendum of a "Jakarta Charter," which declared that be-lief in God carried "the obligation for followers of Islam to carry out Islamic law"—though the difficult question of how this would be enforced, by state law or not, was left to be wrangled over. Su-karno and certain other figures, but not Hatta or the more pragmatic committee members, were drawn to make a wider ambit claim for the new Indonesia, throwing in Malaya and the British territories in North Borneo.

With the atom bombs falling on Hiroshima and Nagasaki, Su-karno and Hatta took their document up to Dalat, Vietnam, for perusal by the Japanese supreme commander for southern Asia on August 11. He approved the charter, except for the inclusion of the British colonies, and the Indonesians arrived back in Jakarta on Au-gust 14, the day before Emperor Hirohito's surrender. The Japanese military was then ordered to hold the status quo until Allied forces could take over.

Restive students kidnapped Sukarno and Hatta to pressure them into an immediate announcement of Indonesia's formation. A sup-portive Japanese naval officer, Tadashi Maeda, also urged them to go ahead. On the morning of August 17, 1945, Sukarno walked out-side his house and read a forty-word declaration of independence, signed by himself and Hatta.

WITH THE ALLIED FORCES not arriving until the second half of September, the Japanese took a tolerant approach to the formation of a republi-can Indonesian government later in August, with Sukarno as presi-dent and Hatta as vice president. They insisted, however, that the Jakarta Charter would cause trouble with the substantial Christian minorities, and so it was abandoned, along with a provision that the president had to be a Muslim. An appointed Komite Nasional Indo-nesia Pusat (KNIP, Central Indonesian National Committee) stood in as a parliament, pending elections, which, as it turned out, would not happen for a decade. Governors were appointed in parts of Su-matra and Sulawesi.

It became a time of chaos. Japanese forces retreated into their cantonments. Some units assisted the Indonesian militias, while other isolated posts were overwhelmed and robbed of their weapons.

It was sometimes hard to distinguish idealistic freedom fighters from opportunistic gangsters. Ethnic groups settled old scores. The more traditional and the more devout Islamic villagers redressed perceived imbalances.

The Dutch military showed up first in the eastern islands, which were under the control of Australian forces. The British occupation force in Java and Sumatra consisted of only 6,000 soldiers, mostly Indians. Their theater commander, Admiral Louis Mountbatten, declined the impossible task of recapturing the empire for the Dutch. Instead, his men concentrated on supervising the surrender of the Japanese and on extricating the thousands of European civilians stuck in inland prison camps, which sometimes took fighting columns and air strikes to achieve. In November 1945, an operation to get internees out through Surabaya sparked a fanatical war against the foreigners, with Muslim leaders declaring it a jihad (holy war). A brigadier was torn to pieces by a mob, and the British punished the city with naval gunfire and Lancaster bombers.

The Dutch sent out their new conscripts, youths scrawny from the years of German occupation. During their journey, they'd been jeered by Arabs, who bared their bottoms at them from the banks of the Suez Canal. The wartime experience had caused no reflection among Dutch politicians and officials about the foreign rule they wished to reimpose on another people or about the change in Asians' perceptions of Europeans after their quick capitulation to Japan.

For four years the Dutch tried every possible way of breaking the independence movement, having quickly gained control of Jakarta and other cities along the north coast of Java. Sukarno and the republican government withdrew to Yogyakarta, where the progressive sultan Hamengkubuwono IX threw open part of his kraton for university students who'd been pulled out of colleges in Jakarta and Bandung. Funds came from rubber, sugar, opium, and other goods smuggled through the Dutch blockade and into Singapore. Transport aircraft bought by the Acehnese dodged the Dutch air force's Mustang fighters. While the republicans were pressed back in Java, the Dutch cultivated autonomous regional states in the outer islands, playing on fears of Islamic or Javanese domination.

Holland's diplomatic ploy was to offer recognition of the Indonesian republic in Java and Sumatra, but as part of a federated United States of Indonesia, with the Dutch queen as the symbolic head of a kind of commonwealth. This deal was encouraged by the British, who were desperate to withdraw, and it was signed by Indonesian delegates at the hill station of Linggajati in November 1946.

The Indonesians agonized about ratifying it, and Sutan Syahrir, who as prime minister had negotiated it, lost public standing. But with Sukarno and Hatta threatening otherwise to resign, it was ratified.

The Dutch soon lost patience with their own diplomacy and in July 1947 launched a "police action" designed to seize control of Java and Sumatra. Pressure in the United Nations from the United States, Britain, and Australia led to a ceasefire being called after two weeks and the dispatch of a "good offices" mission to supervise the truce. The Dutch reverted to setting up their federal states elsewhere, and the republicans struggled to feed the large numbers of troops and civilians who had retreated to Yogyakarta.

Now the conflict had been internationalized, and the Sukarno-Hatta leadership won new American favor when their Indonesian forces suppressed an uprising by the reformed PKI in Madiun, East Java, in September 1948. A second Dutch police action, in December that year, was ostensibly successful, capturing Yogyakarta and the entire republican leadership, and leaving Aceh as the only part of Indonesia under republican control. But it was a disastrous misstep, arousing worldwide condemnation and leading to a halt in American postwar reconstruction aid for the Netherlands itself.

In July 1949 the republican leadership were returned to Yogyakarta, and a gradual handover of military control to Indonesian regular units commenced. On December 27, 1949, the Netherlands transferred sovereignty over the entire Indies, minus western New Guinea, to a new Republic of the United States of Indonesia, with Sukarno and Hatta as president and vice president, respectively. Sukarno flew into Jakarta aboard a KLM Dakota that had been hastily rebadged as part of the new state airline, Garuda, and proceeded through ecstatic crowds to address the masses from the steps of the former governor-general's palace. The federal structure was abruptly swept away the following August, and a provisional constitution for a unitary state declared.

It's no wonder, in retrospect, that the very short history of Indonesian nationalism before the fall of the Dutch empire led to an intense preoccupation with nation building by the first president,

Sukarno, through his sixteen years in power (however "power" is defined). The story of his presidency is the triumph of this "solidarity-maker" over the attempts of the "administrators," such as Hatta and Sjahrir, to apply sound economic and social development policies. (The terms come from Herbert Feith's classic account of parliamentary politics and the shift to "Guided Democracy" in the 1950s, *The Decline of Constitutional Democracy in Indonesia*.) Yet Sukarno's grand solidarity-making efforts prevented the sober administrative measures that might have prevented the rebellions that shook Indonesia from 1957 to 1960, when exasperated army colonels and development-minded politicians launched the *Permesta* revolt in Sulawesi and the Pemerintah Revolusioner Republik Indonesia (PRRI, Revolutionary Government of the Indonesian Republic) in Sumatra, drawing unwise American and British covert support.

That is not to say Sukarno did not face other immediate, and entirely internal, challenges to the unity, the character, and, potentially, the territorial integrity of the Indonesian state. The Ambonese attempted to break away as the declared Republic of the South Moluccas in Indonesia's first year. In 1953 the restive Acehnese ulema (Islamic scholar) Daud Beureu'eh turned his back on the Pancasila ideology and launched a jihad to create a Negara Islam Indonesia (Islamic Indonesian State). He linked up with similar Islamists in West Java and South Sulawesi in insurgencies known generally as the Darul Islam (Abode of Islam) movement, which the Indonesian military quelled only in 1965 and which periodically erupts again in small extremist cells.

The Dutch, meanwhile, started preparing their New Guinean territory for a separate independence, which, however much it might have been justified by cultural incompatibility with Indonesia, was an objective totally suspect in Indonesian eyes, after the divisive Dutch behavior in 1945–49. But Sukarno had relatively few military resources; instead, he had to employ the symbolic demonstrations of power noted by Benedict Anderson: his ability to hold vast crowds spellbound with rhetoric and incantations (such as the TAVIP, from Tahun Vivere Pericoloso, the Year of Living Dangerously, which he declared in 1964 to explain his alignment against the Western powers and their economic prescriptions), his semipublic sexual life, his welding together of disparate political forces. His triumph was to drive the Dutch out of New Guinea in 1963 by a combination of rhetorical insistence, symbolic military sacrifice, and adroit balancing of strategic Cold War concerns.

It was all very precarious. Half a century later, unrest still simmers and builds in Papua. The defeat of Daud Beureu'eh was not the end of rebellion in Aceh. The termination of the Konfrontasi with Malaysia was handled graciously by the British in the wider interests of the times, but the ignominious withdrawal from East Timor gave the Indonesian military and political establishment a humiliating rebuke. Solidarity-making remains a core preoccupation of the Indonesian state to this day.

2

THE CROCODILE HOLE

NOT FAR FROM THE CHEERINESS OF TAMAN MINI IS ANOTHER MEMENTO OF THE SU-
harto era, quite different in tone. The name of the place, Lubang
Buaya (meaning "Crocodile Hole"), preceded the grim events that
took place there on October 1, 1965, but no propagandist could have
devised a more sinister one. It was here that three abducted army
generals, the bodies of three others, and an aide mistaken for the
army chief, General Abdul Haris Nasution, were taken by mutinous
troops.

Visitors to the Crocodile Hole peer through the windows of the
hut at a life-size tableau of the living captives, bloodied and tied to
chairs as frenzied interrogators in red scarves stand over them with
raised rifle butts. They look at the well, where the seven bodies were
dumped that day; fake blood drips down its rim. They walk across
to a large monument: a vast bronze *garuda*—a mythical eagle, the
national symbol—soaring over the defiant figures of the murdered
officers.

This is the defining story, the creation myth, of the New Order
regime, which had its origins in steps taken after that day by Suharto
and the military. The army leaders, the story goes, men defending
the nation and following their president's directives, were callously

murdered during a coup instigated by the PKI, which was fortuitously foiled because the conspirators had failed to target the little-
known General Suharto, who then stepped up to take control.

To emphasize that this atrocity was not an aberration, an adjacent Museum of PKI Treachery has forty-two dioramas that depict
various episodes, such as the Madiun uprising, in which communists
tried to overturn the course of the Indonesian nation and its values.
The PKI's uprising against the Dutch in 1926 is not mentioned.

The story has been picked apart by scholars outside Indonesia,
as we shall see, along with the portrayal of the subsequent mass killings and arrests of the PKI membership, and its characterization as
something like a natural disaster, a volcanic eruption or a tsunami
that resulted in a kind of catharsis. The surprising thing is that—
fifteen years after the repudiation of Suharto, the embrace of *reformasi* (reformation), and the return to electoral democracy—the myth
survives largely uncontested within Indonesia. Busloads of children
still arrive at Lubang Buaya for indoctrination, and every year on
October 1, the president and senior officials still come here to hold a
solemn commemoration.

IT IS NOT HARD TO SEE why the events of 1965–66 were seen as the virtually inevitable consequence of what had happened since independence, a result of the behavior of narrowly experienced politicians
and their followers, all striving for survival and advantage in a system that constantly changed shape, wherever it had much shape at
all. Nor is it hard to see why Indonesia's new government and its
Western and regional supporters would have largely accepted that
notion of inevitability and avoided blame, immediately looking to
the future.

Later writings about the 1950s certainly have the note of failure
and retreat, from Feith's *The Decline of Constitutional Democracy
in Indonesia,* the definitive study of the country's politics, to *Twi-
light in Jakarta,* a novel by the periodically detained newspaper editor Mochtar Lubis, which was published abroad in 1963.

But it started out optimistically, with the 1945 generation of leaders and foreign volunteers, like Feith, who were out to show that an
independent Indonesia could work. The 1945 constitution had been
hastily proclaimed in emergency conditions, and it was replaced by
a new provisional constitution that set out a government responsible

to a parliament, the Dewan Perwakilan Rakyat (DPR, People's Representative Council), and a president whose role would be largely ceremonial, aside from inviting party leaders in the DPR to form governments. It resembled, perhaps unconsciously, the Dutch parliamentary system, with Sukarno reluctantly filling the role of Queen Juliana.

Membership of the parliament was allocated on a notional estimate of relative popular support, with the largest blocks given to Masyumi, the Islamist party of the more devout, and the PNI, the perceived inheritor of the Sukarnoist nationalist tradition, which, with Sukarno now standing aloof from party politics, was being led by Javanese priyayi figures. The Partai Sosialis Indonesia (PSI, Socialist Party of Indonesia), led by Sutan Syahrir and supported by many intellectuals, and the PKI, which was reforming itself after the Madiun setback, had smaller blocks, and a large quota was shared among many smaller parties and prominent individuals.

A rotation of governments followed, which formed around leaders from Masyumi or the PNI. Suspicious of the international economic order, they wrestled with attempts to put more substance into independence, given that big American and Anglo-Dutch companies ran the oilfields, Dutch enterprises owned and ran the banks, plantations, and factories, and ethnic Chinese dominated the middle strata of commerce. Schemes to promote indigenous entrepreneurship were subverted by "Ali Baba," or dummy, partnerships, which had a *pribumi* (ethnic Indonesian) as a front man in order to hide a Chinese operation.

It was a heady time and today is viewed with much nostalgia. The new elite moved into the large houses vacated by the Dutch, as protected tenants on rents that became low over time. The round of cocktail parties and dinners resumed, with foreign embassies competing for influence and cachet. The formation and disintegration of coalitions, the maneuverings of army factions, and the schemes and love life of Sukarno all provided endless material for gossip. The ruling coalitions packed the civil service with their clients, who worked alongside the newly educated and the demobilized freedom fighters. There was no money to pay adequate salaries, and petty corruption exploded. Jakarta financed itself by printing money.

The armed forces remained barely under the control either of the civilian government, being chiefly loyal to Sukarno or to Sultan

Hamengkubuwono IX during his spell as defense minister, or of their own commanders. In 1952 General Nasution pushed a scheme to halve the army's numbers to 100,000 men and rashly mounted a show of force outside the presidential palace to press the argument. Sukarno suspended him for three years. In 1956 Nasution was back in command and forestalled a march on Jakarta by his deputy, Lieutenant Colonel Zulkifli Lubis, the head of a column of the new Special Forces. In 1960 an air force officer, Evie Mauker, outraged by Sukarno's advances to his sister during a lineup of beauties in regional costumes (known in Jakarta circles as the "*Bhinneka Tunggal Ika* routine," suggesting that the president would choose "one from many"), took off in his MiG-17 jet and strafed the presidential palaces in Jakarta and Bogor.

It was not entirely a lost era in terms of social progress. The numbers of children getting at least a few years of education grew, and by 1961 the literacy rate for the population over ten years of age had reached nearly 47 percent, in contrast to the 7.4 percent adult literacy rate last recorded by the Dutch. Newspaper circulations also grew strongly, some of which served as party or institutional mouthpieces, while others reflected broader political and social attitudes.

In the background, though, was a population growing so rapidly that it threatened to overwhelm any gains. Rural poverty deepened in Java as villagers shared farming resources in what became known as "involution": more and more minute subdivisions of land, as described by the American anthropologist Clifford Geertz. Landlessness grew, and the landless moved into cities, living in squatter settlements and eking out a living as peddlers, coolies, pedicab drivers, domestic servants, touts, and prostitutes. Jakarta's population grew from under 1 million at independence to 3 million in the early 1960s.

THE PARLIAMENT EVENTUALLY got around to holding Indonesia's first elections in September 1955, and another vote for a new constituent assembly followed in November that year. The electorate was widely divided. The PNI gained the largest vote, but that still only amounted to 22.3 percent. Masyumi was next with 20.9 percent, while a second Muslim group, the Nahdatul Ulama (NU, Muslim Scholars' League), a mass organization appealing to conservative Muslims in rural Java, gained 18.4 percent. Among the "modernizers," the shock was the rise of the PKI, which gained 16.4 percent of the vote, and the small following, just 2 percent, of the Socialists, the party seen (outside Indonesia, at least) as being the most pragmatic and as having "realistic" economic thinkers. When provincial assembly elections were held in 1957, the PKI emerged as the biggest party in central and eastern Java, winning 34 percent of the vote.

The inflation set off by Jakarta's deficit financing, along with the reliance on an artificially high exchange rate to help imports keep flowing into the elite circles of Java, was increasing the economic stress on the more export-oriented outer island regions. Many military commanders and their local business circles traded commodities directly into Singapore and Manila. An attempt by General Nasution to crack down on such freelance business and to reassign suspect officers led in December 1956 to a rebellious colonel, Maludin Simbolon, seizing control of North Sumatra and its rich oilfields. In March 1957 the commander of the East Indonesia military region, Lieutenant Colonel H. N. V. Samual, declared martial law and proclaimed a "Universal Struggle Charter" (known as *Permesta,* its Indonesian acronym) to "complete" the Indonesian revolution.

This defiance of Jakarta might have been subdued had Sukarno heeded the calls of Nasution, Masyumi, and other groups and installed the respected Hatta, who had recently resigned from the vice presidency in a sign of displeasure, to lead a new nonparty government and begin the reform process. Instead, the rebellion expanded, and in February 1958 its leaders proclaimed the PRRI, or Revolutionary Government of the Republic of Indonesia, with its headquarters in Bukkittinggi, West Sumatra.

The Sulawesi rebels linked up, and noted figures from Masyumi, such as Mohammed Natsir, and the economics professor Sumitro Djojohadikusumo of the Socialists joined its cabinet. The United States' Central Intelligence Agency (CIA) was tempted by the chance to divide an Indonesia it saw as drifting into communist hands and began covertly supporting the rebels, shipping in arms and trainers from the British base in Singapore and from its own bases in the Philippines, Guam, and Taiwan. An air wing with mercenary pilots flying B-26 strike bombers operated out of rebel-held Manado in the north of Sulawesi, although its cover was blown when an American pilot was shot down over Ambon in May 1958.

The Indonesian military had reacted to the declaration of the PRRI with ferocity and efficiency and within a few weeks had seized the Sumatran oilfields by means of parachute and marine landings. The rebellion simmered on until its commanders surrendered in 1961.

Sukarno, meanwhile, had been voicing his dissatisfaction with the parliamentary system and floated his idea of a turn to *Demokrasi Terpimpin* (Guided Democracy), in order to restore what he saw as a more acceptable and culturally suitable process of consultation and mutual self-help. Indonesia's failure to win a UN vote calling on the Netherlands to negotiate the "return" of New Guinea sparked a nationalist backlash. Indonesian workers seized Dutch enterprises and plantations, and thousands of Dutch citizens still working in Indonesia were ordered to leave.

This provided a means for Sukarno and the army to move to the center of power. Nasution installed army officers to run the seized Dutch enterprises, creating an independent revenue base. He announced a new "middle way" doctrine for the military's relationship with the state: it would be involved in political and administrative affairs but would not take over government, per se. Sukarno's decision to take New Guinea by force led to the acceptance of a massive credit from the Soviet Union to buy tanks, warships, submarines, and advanced combat aircraft.

Nasution had also urged Sukarno to cut through the muddled parliament and constituent assembly, which was still bogged down in arguments over Pancasila and the Jakarta Charter, and to do this by restoring the revolutionary constitution of August 1945. Sukarno was receptive and did this in June 1959 by proclamation, giving himself sweeping presidential powers that accorded well with his notion of Guided Democracy. The constituent assembly was dissolved. The parliament helped seal its own fate by agreeing to postpone elections due that year, and it, too, was wound up in 1960, replaced by a selected echo chamber. The two parties that had been most supportive of conventional mixed public-private economic policy, Masyumi and the PSI, were banned outright because of their involvement with the PRRI/Permesta revolt.

Sukarno was again hammering the theme of his Bandung days in the 1920s: the synthesis of nationalism, religion, and communism that he called *Nasakom* (from *nasionalisme*, nationalism; *agama*,

religion; and *komunisme,* communism). As we have seen, his leadership was understood to be harking back, whether consciously or
not, to precolonial patterns of kingly rule. Energetic sculptures of
protean figures grasping fire went up around Jakarta. The money
from Japanese war reparation funds—which also resulted in a new
Japanese wife for Sukarno as a deal sweetener—was spent on building luxury hotels in Jakarta and Bali.

The American scholars who had studied the emerging nation
since the 1940s were inclined to be forgiving. "Perhaps our basic
error all along has been to examine Indonesia with Western eyes,"
mused Harry J. Benda in 1964. Specialists had fallen into asking,
"What's wrong with Indonesia?" and were conducting an "ago-
nising search" for the entrepreneurial middle classes in Southeast
Asia and for "problem-solvers" in general. But "solidarity-makers"
seemed to represent a specifically Javanese culture; their "Hindu-
Javanese world" looked remarkably resilient. Instead of asking why
democracy failed in Indonesia, the question should have been "Why
should it have survived?"

Another scholar, David Levine, wrote that, in fact, nothing had
"gone wrong" in Indonesia: "Given the colonial legacy and the lack
of a true social revolution, things could hardly have gone any other
way." Even Feith, the author of what seemed a lament for constitutional democracy, noted that American scholarship had tended to
look with favor on figures like Hatta and Syahrir as pragmatic, realistic, and forward thinking, and more critically at Sukarno as nativ-
ist, demagogic, and a diversion from the country's real problems.

Less sympathetically, there were questions about the Indonesian
leaders' three years of tutelage under Japan. Had its version of fascism, nestled within the imperial cult, not encouraged the drafters of
Indonesia's constitution to think in terms of the national "family,"
national "spirit," and consensus formation, rather than paying attention to outright argument and to the checks and balances of power?
Even so, and despite the banning of the more reform-minded parties
and the jailing of individual critics, such as Mochtar Lubis, Sukarno's Guided Democracy was seen as essentially pluralistic. And with
the communists apparently headed for greater success at the polls,
Washington's support for electoral democracy was waning.

But the elements supporting Nasakom and Sukarno were polar-
izing. The military had used its Soviet equipment to needle the Dutch

forces in New Guinea. Strings of commandos had been dropped in the jungles, though many of them were rounded up by unsympathetic Papuans; the rest were struggling to survive. It appeared that Moscow and Beijing were winning the international competition for influence over a country that sat at the gateway of Southeast Asia.

The new administration of John F. Kennedy jumped into the fray, telling the Dutch that they couldn't win in the long run—a repeat of the US pressure in 1949. The Dutch agreed to leave in October 1962: after a face-saving UN interregnum of seven months, the territory would be turned over to Indonesia on May 1, 1963, with Jakarta promising to conduct an "act of free choice" among the Papuans by the end of 1969, in which they could decide whether to stay part of Indonesia or become independent.

After the debacle of the CIA's support for the PRRI/Permesta rebellion, the policy makers in Washington decided it was pointless to promote a division in the Indonesian army, which had anticommunists on both sides. Nasution's new *Dwifungsi* (Dual Function) doctrine accorded with the evolving US Army scheme of "civic action," whereby third-world armies would be encouraged and trained to carry out village-level development works, in order to counter the grassroots mobilization of the population by local communist cadres. Their senior officers would be encouraged to undertake broader nonmilitary education, in subjects such as economics and international relations, to prepare them for roles in government. The United States began a program that aimed to educate the Indonesian military in its way of thinking, bringing some 2,800 Indonesian army officers—more than a fifth of the officer corps—to Fort Benning and Fort Leavenworth for long residential courses. One American-trained officer, Colonel Suwarto, took this indoctrination back to the Indonesian army's senior staff college in Bandung, known as *Seskoad*, where it was integrated into the studies of middle-ranking officers headed for senior commands.

But it was a hard game to play. In 1963 Sukarno's government announced that the big foreign oil producers—Caltex, Stanvac, and Royal Dutch Shell—that had been left out of earlier localization policies would henceforth be contractors to one of three state oil companies. The existing fifty-fifty split of profits would change to sixty-forty in Indonesia's favor, and restrictions would be placed on local product distribution. New concessions to small independent oil companies upped the ante, and the threat of outright appropriation was voiced. The squeeze was seen as a crisis of the relationship at the highest levels in Washington, but eventually strategic considerations outweighed the corporate pain. The oil companies signed up.

Meanwhile, Sukarno had signed off, from Tokyo, on a package of fiscal austerity that was meant to prepare Indonesia to receive large amounts of aid from the International Monetary Fund, the United States, and whatever other allies it could bring into the arrangement. It was the conventional "structural adjustment": reduction of price controls and subsidies, removal of export taxes, a realistic exchange rate, and budget cuts. The measures set off price increases that ranged from 200 to 500 percent in many staple items, resulting in protests from many quarters.

Just as this painful preparation for the aid package set in, Sukarno embarked on a fresh campaign, his Konfrontasi (Confrontation) of the new Malaysian federation being formed by Britain out of its various protectorates and colonies in Southeast Asia. There had been the idea of a UN consultation in North Borneo about their peoples' agreement with the idea, which might have placated Sukarno's suspicions about a *Nekolim* (neocolonialist and imperialist) maneuver. But the British, anxious to reduce their military burden east of Suez, and the headstrong leaders of Malaya and Singapore (Tunku Abdul Rahman and Lee Kuan Yew, respectively) made it clear they were going ahead anyway. When Abdul Rahman declared the new federation on September 16, 1963, officially organized rioters in Jakarta promptly burned down the British embassy, while Sukarno banned all dealings with Malaysia (which then included Singapore, Indonesia's main trade gateway). Kennedy's aid initiative foundered, although limited programs of assistance to the Indonesian military continued.

SUKARNO'S GUIDED DEMOCRACY now careered around the international skies like a missile with its gyroscope disabled. Infiltration and raids into Malaysia stepped up, drawing countercampaigns from Britain and its commonwealth partners. Sukarno proclaimed a new power axis with China, Cambodia, North Vietnam, and North Korea. He told the United States, in front of an audience that included the US ambassador, Howard Jones, to "go to hell with your aid." After China exploded its first nuclear device in 1964, he suggested that Indonesia might soon do the same.

The PKI's leadership, under Dipa Nusantara Aidit, was stepping out from under the Nasakom umbrella. Its artistic organization, Lekra, hounded intellectuals of a liberal persuasion who were deemed insufficiently revolutionary. The PNI was persuaded to purge its conservative elements. In 1964 the PKI launched its *aksi sepihak* (unilateral action) campaign to implement a land reform law that had been passed in 1960. The law mandated the transfer of landholdings above a certain size to the landless and put a limit on the portion of crop payable to landlords.

The occupation of large landholdings and parts of plantations brought the PKI's mass organization, Barisan Tani Indonesia (the Indonesian Peasants' Front), into direct conflict with a rural class of landowners in Java and the army managers of plantations. That most PKI followers in Central Java and East Java were from the *abangan* (fairly nominal) stream of Islam, while the landlords were often from the *santri* (devout) stratum, if not members of the local *pesantren* (Koranic schools), sharpened the conflict. The backlash against the "godless" communists turned violent.

Sukarno stepped in at the end of 1964 to moderate the rural conflict. But the UN General Assembly's election of Malaysia to a seat on its security council sent Sukarno to a new level of fury in January 1965. He withdrew Indonesia from the United Nations and approved the training and arming of a "fifth force" of civilian volunteers (in addition to the army, navy, air force, and police).

The Year of Living Dangerously, which Sukarno had announced on Indonesia's national day in August 1964, was becoming just that. Events were taking a dramatic, deadly turn; nearly fifty years later, historians and even the surviving participants are still trying to untangle them. In two nights in Jakarta, a series of abductions, murders, troop maneuvers, radio broadcasts, arrests, threats, and bluffs changed the strategic settings of the biggest country in Southeast Asia. Like the sprawling city at the time, which was mostly lit dimly by kerosene lamps and an unreliable electricity supply, the shadowy period has spawned all kinds of theories and conspiracies. Was the pivotal event an attempted communist coup, a fake one, or neither? Were the key participants idealists, dummies, or dupes? Was the instigator working for the PKI or for the army? How was it that the senior general who had been left off the hit list reacted with such "uncanny efficiency" to take power? Was it all planned?

From all the records, including declassified diplomatic archives in Washington and London, the events of January 1965 had inspired the Indonesian army to intensively plan for a showdown with the PKI. In response to the threat of Sukarno's "fifth force" to their monopoly of armed force, the US-trained army chief, General Achmad Yani, and four of his senior generals, all strongly anticommunist, began discussing how to meet the looming PKI challenge. Over the next two months, their plan took firm shape. The army would not mount a crude coup d'état against Sukarno: he was simply too popular. Nor would it strike preemptively against the PKI, which would risk Sukarno's opposition. Instead, as American and allied diplomats reported, the generals' plan was to be ready with a countercoup if and when the PKI made a move—as the army hoped it would.

By May, rumors of a pro-Western "Council of Generals" reached Sukarno, and he called in Yani to explain. The general said the rumors must be referring to a promotions committee. Midyear, the foreign minister, Subandrio, brandished an intercepted telegram said to be from the British ambassador, which referred to "our local army friends" and some unspecified secret "enterprise."

According to a highly plausible reconstruction of events by an American scholar, John Roosa, the PKI's chairman, D. N. Aidit, around this time called in his chief secret agent. Kamaruzaman, then aged forty-one and known generally as Sjam, was a man of Arab descent from the North Java coast; after a comparatively good education, he had been a trade union organizer on the Jakarta docks following independence. Aidit, who had emerged from hiding in 1951 and taken the PKI leadership, assigned Sjam to what became the PKI's special bureau, keeping watch on the army. Sjam took up cover as a small businessman. He reported directly and only to Aidit.

By August 1965, Sjam was reporting that Yani and his right-wing generals were planning a coup. The annual Armed Forces' Day parade in Jakarta on October 5, when battalions and tanks were assembled in the capital, loomed as an obvious occasion on which it might be launched. Sjam had also identified and made contact with a number of middle-ranking officers who were alarmed at this prospect. Aidit grew increasingly attracted to the idea of an internal army putsch by these officers to remove the plotting generals. The move would not be seen as a PKI operation and would, he hoped, be endorsed by Sukarno and might result in a new, more "progressive" army leadership.

So the plot for the 30 September Movement was hatched between the left-wing officers and the PKI spy. Sjam assured Aidit of its sound military planning and gave the officers the impression that high-ranking officials of the PKI had decided on a decisive blow. Both claims were incorrect.

The officers moved late on the night of September 30, assembling small numbers of troops at Lubang Buaya, then an unpopulated stretch of rubber trees on the edge of the Halim air force base. In a camp there over the previous six months, several hundred members of the PKI women's movement, Gerwani, and its youth wing, Pemuda Rakyat, had been given some basic military training by the air force as part of efforts to create the "fifth force." Sjam, another member of the PKI special bureau, and the three leading rebel officers made their headquarters at the house of an air force sergeant at the air base. Aidit and his immediate PKI staff awaited developments in another house on the base, half a kilometer away.

At about 3:15 on the morning of October 1, trucks containing seven teams of soldiers left Lubang Buaya and headed into the city, storming into the homes of the sleeping generals who had been identified as members of the coup-plotting council. Resistance came at the houses of Yani and two other generals, and they were shot dead. The defense minister, Nasution, jumped over the back wall of his garden and managed to hide. A bullet killed his five-year-old daughter, and an aide was mistakenly arrested in his place. Three other generals were taken alive. By about 5:30 a.m. the bodies and the captives were back at Lubang Buaya.

Meanwhile, two army battalions, which had been called in from East Java and Central Java to take part in the upcoming Armed Forces' Day parade, were ordered out of their temporary camps by middle-ranking officers and deployed around Merdeka Square, the vast park in the center of Jakarta's government district. They took up positions on three sides of the square, controlling the presidential palace, the national broadcaster, Radio Republic Indonesia, and the central telephone and telegraph exchange. Dozens of PKI youth were called in to assist.

At 7:15 a.m. the radio station broadcast an announcement: the 30 September Movement, led by a commander of the presidential guard and well-known hero of the New Guinea campaign, Lieutenant Colonel Untung, had arrested several generals, known for their dissolute lifestyles, in order to preempt a "counterrevolutionary" coup that was planned for October 5. The aim was to protect Sukarno and his goals.

But the operation was already unraveling. Roosa has argued that the generals were not meant to be killed but to be paraded and humiliated in front of Sukarno, in the manner of the patriotic kidnappings of wavering leaders during the independence struggle—including of Sukarno and Hatta themselves in August 1945. Instead, the 30 September Movement had the bloodied bodies of Yani and two others. At some point, it was decided to execute the four captives, as well, and dump all the bodies in the well at Lubang Buaya.

Outside Jakarta, the only military units to join the movement later in the morning were from the Central Java command, where middle-ranking officers seized control in Semarang, Yogyakarta, Solo, and Salatiga. Only in Yogyakarta did PKI organizations turn out in support.

In addition, the president was missing—he was not at the palace. After a long speech the previous evening, he'd gone to spend the night at the home of his third wife, the Japanese-born Dewi. When he woke the next morning, aides told him of unidentified troops around the palace. Sukarno moved to the house of his fourth wife, Harjati, and then, toward midmorning, to the Halim airfield—not because he knew it was the 30 September Movement's base but because it was his default place of retreat in times of crisis, since a special aircraft was always at his disposal.

At the house of the base commander, Sukarno learned more about the events of the day from the most senior officer involved, Brigadier General Supardjo, a late addition to the movement. The air force chief, Marshal Omar Dani, had meanwhile spent the night at the base trying to find out what was going on. He and other air force officers, from a service known for its sympathies with Sukarno's anti-Western policies, had cheered the radio announcement.

By early afternoon, according to testimony by Supardjo and Omar Dani at their trials, Sukarno had deduced that the generals were dead. He asked Supardjo to call the movement off, fearing a left-right conflict that would open Indonesia up to dismemberment by neocolonialist forces.

The coup leaders debated what to do. The army officers deferred to Sjam, assuming that he was part of a bigger scheme. Sjam himself desperately tried to keep his collapsing movement together. Possibly he was the instigator of three further radio broadcasts, which dissolved the existing cabinet under Sukarno, announced the membership of a broad-based revolutionary council, and, bizarrely, abolished all military ranks above lieutenant colonel.

The commander of the army's strategic reserve, or *Kostrad,* Major General Suharto, was not targeted, even though he usually stood in as acting army chief when Yani was aboard. Nor was the Kostrad headquarters, which was located on the fourth side of Merdeka Square, seized.

By 6:30 on the morning of October 1, Suharto was at Kostrad, assessing the reports of shooting and spilled blood at the missing generals' homes in the nearby suburb of Menteng. He concluded that Yani was dead and took over his position, with the assent of other generals who had made contact during the morning. However, he had ignored a verbal message from Sukarno appointing another general as army chief and prevented that general from going to see the president.

In the early afternoon, Suharto sent an ultimatum to the troops across the square to surrender or face attack. The East Java battalion came over to Kostrad, while the Central Java battalion boarded trucks and retreated to Halim. By early evening the square was in Suharto's control, and the radio station was playing his message that the 30 September Movement had been put down. The army's best-trained troops, the Special Forces, were sent to seize control of the Halim air base and its surrounds.

At 8 p.m. Suharto advised the president to leave the base for his own safety; Sukarno drove off to the palace at Bogor, the town at the foot of mountains just south of Jakarta. The leaders of the 30 September Movement sneaked away during the night. Sjam, Colonel Abdul Latief, and Supardjo went into hiding in Jakarta. Untung took a train to Central Java. Aidit was given an air force plane to reach Yogyakarta. When the Special Forces, under their fiercely anticommunist commander, Colonel Sarwo Edhie Wibowo, arrived at Halim and Lubang Buaya in the early hours of October 2, they met only desultory resistance from leaderless troops and civilians.

A rising smell from the sealed-off well and interrogation of captives at Lubang Buaya soon indicated where the generals' bodies were. Suharto came out in person to supervise the retrieval. By then he'd gotten a signed instruction from Sukarno to restore order. The Armed Forces' Day parade was replaced by a grim funeral procession through Jakarta.

THAT SAME DAY, Suharto and the other generals decided that this was all the excuse they needed to smash the PKI—to the relief of the CIA station chief, Hugh Tovar, who'd been worried that the army might miss the opportunity.

The campaign did not visibly get started until mid-October, by which time it was quite clear that the PKI had not even tried to call out its supporters en masse. The civilian PKI involvement in the 30 September Movement had been limited to the few hundred Gerwani and Pemuda Rakyat members at Lubang Buaya and the communications facility on Merdeka Square, as well as those who had rallied in Yogyakarta. The PKI's top leadership was nowhere to be seen. The party's newspaper, *Harian Rakyat*, had cautiously backed the movement in its last edition, printed in the night of October 1, but painted it as part of an internal struggle within the army.

As soon as the generals' bodies were brought to the surface on October 2, the propaganda writers on Suharto's intelligence staff swung into action. The generals had been tortured, emasculated, and killed by naked, frenzied Gerwani members, who, during the training at Lubang Buaya, had been given stimulant drugs and encouraged to take part in sexual orgies by their PKI superiors. Autopsies later tabled in trials showed no evidence of this, but the misinformation and "psywar" created the impression that the PKI's perfidy and inversion of the natural order extended down to its rank-and-file members.

Across Indonesia, district army commanders called in PKI members and mass organizations, and went around to houses with lists. Leaders were put in trucks, taken to fields, and shot on the edges of mass graves. Hundreds of thousands of others were taken to temporary prison camps.

In Central Java, senior commanders had rallied powerful armored and other units against the 30 September Movement and

smashed its grip on the major cities by October 5. Sarwo Edhie Wibowo arrived in Semarang with commandos of the Special Forces.
They quickly put down a strike by railway workers and then drove
their armored cars and trucks into Central Java, machine-gunning
any protesting PKI supporters. In Solo, where PKI supporters continued to come out in protest, Sarwo Edhie's troops ran quick training
courses so that army-friendly groups could make arrests and per-
form executions. Elsewhere in Java, the Muslim organization that
had battled the PKI over land reallocation the previous year was
given the green light to begin sweeps against party supporters. The
santri (devout) young men who walked through their villages to the
mosque in green sarongs and black fez-type caps became members
of death squads at night, calling their mostly abangan (nominally
Muslim) PKI neighbors out to local fields or river banks and then
killing them with knives and blows.

Colonel Kemal Idris, the army's anti-Malaysia commander
based in Medan, North Sumatra, had begun rounding up and ex-
ecuting known PKI leaders in the region almost as soon as he heard
the Untung broadcast. Here, the army subcontracted some of the
killings of the PKI's rank and file to members of an army-sponsored
youth movement, Pemuda Pancasila (Pancasila Youth), which was
headed by a former boxer, Effendi Nasution. Many of its city members were street thugs who made money from systematic ticket
scalping at Medan's cinemas. Across the street from the movies, they
began butchering actual or suspected PKI members. In Bali, the killing started on a large scale after the arrival of Sarwo Edhie's Special Forces in December 1965 and at times took on the character of
Hindu ritual sacrifice.

That month, Sukarno spoke out against the killings, which he
put at 78,000, berating his people for "running amok like monkeys
caught in the dark." But the "mouthpiece of the revolution" was cut
off from the microphones and radio stations on which he was a spell-
binder, and the newspapers were being told to downplay anything he
said. The killings went on. The rivers of Java choked with bodies.

Nor were the Western powers interested. The killings were just
what they wanted. It was a turn in the tide in Southeast Asia, the
"best news" for a long time, as *Time* magazine commented. In mid-
October the army was helpfully advised that the British would not
attack while it was otherwise engaged with the PKI. On November

4, 1965, Ambassador Marshall Green reported to the US State Department that even the PKI "smaller fry" were being "systematically arrested and jailed or executed." Green had assured the army that America was "generally sympathetic with and admiring of what they were doing."

British operatives in Singapore stepped up "black propaganda," spreading stories in the media about caches of arms smuggled in from China to the PKI. The US embassy's political section handed the Indonesian army a list of several thousand names, all members of PKI cadres. Partly thanks to a radio communications network rushed out to help the Indonesian army, US intelligence was able to listen in to commands from Suharto's intelligence section about which PKI members were to be executed on the spot and which were to be brought in alive. Almost certainly, an instruction would have come to execute Aidit, who was shot after being captured in a village on the slopes of Mount Merapi in November, thus removing both the PKI's most charismatic figure and his testimony.

The wave of killings abated around March 1966. By then, the few American and other journalists allowed to travel around Java and Bali were putting their estimates of the dead at about 400,000. Others thought that conservative, and a later tally by the army's internal security command put the number across Indonesia at 1 million killed. More than 600,000 had been arrested. The West still didn't care—the massacre was put down to the irrational Malay tendency to run amok or the inevitable collision of santri and abangan social groups in a time of political change. The role of the army in stirring up the violence, and in directing and sustaining the killings, was played down. "With 500,000 to one million communist sympathisers knocked off, I think it is safe to say a reorientation has taken place," the Australian prime minister, Harold Holt, noted with evident satisfaction in July 1966.

THE SURVIVING SENIOR LEADERSHIP of the PKI and the leaders of the 30 September Movement were put through show trials in an "Extraordinary Military Court." None was acquitted. Death sentences were handed down and promptly carried out by firing squads.

Strangely, the mysterious Sjam and two other PKI Special Bureau operatives were kept on death row until 1986: Sjam still hoped he could spin out his story to stay alive but was eventually executed.

Other senior figures, such as Abdul Latief and Subandrio, emerged from imprisonment toward the turn of the century, adding little new to the story—except Latief's assertion that he'd told Suharto about the plot beforehand and believed he'd assented. The very elderly Subandrio claimed that Untung hoped to the end that Suharto would save him.

The conspiracy theories persisted even beyond Suharto's eventual removal from power. Untung had been close to Suharto. Was he an agent provocateur, perhaps unwittingly? Was Sjam a double agent for the army, pretending to be Aidit's spy? But why would the army chiefs put their own lives on the line? Suharto later emerged as a masterly political figure, but could he and his staff, at that time, really have conceived and executed a plot so diabolically clever?

Unless some confession emerges unexpectedly from the Suharto group, John Roosa's thesis and parallel work by Bradley A. Simpson, drawing on US and British archives, suggests that Suharto was versed in the army's countercoup planning and promptly put it into action on October 1. Though not trained in America, Suharto would have been fully briefed on Yani's plans. Before moving into senior commands, he had gone through the indoctrination on civic action and governmental roles under Colonel Suwarto at the staff college in Bandung. He stepped up and pushed Nasution aside.

By March 1966 Suharto had finessed his political master, Sukarno. On October 2, 1965, he went to meet Sukarno and addressed the army leadership issue head-on. He offered to unwind all the measures he'd taken since the previous morning. Sukarno demurred. The other, less anticommunist general Sukarno had preferred, Pranoto, was given an administrative command (and was later jailed for twelve years by Suharto); Sukarno gave Suharto written orders to "restore order." It became the mandate he was looking for.

Backed by student protests organized by the army, Suharto faced down Sukarno and his cabinet at critical points. When ministers met to discuss nationalizing the oil industry in December 1965, Suharto arrived by helicopter, strode in, and warned them against making "precipitous" decisions. In January 1966, under the watchful eye of the Special Forces, the American-educated economists of the University of Indonesia held a seminar over several days outlining their plan to rescue the economy from its collapse. Sukarno responded by announcing his own new cabinet. Demonstrations and counterprotests swept the city, with foreign embassies under attack from different sides. It was orchestrated chaos.

Sukarno retreated to his palace at Bogor. On March 11, 1966, three of Suharto's senior generals arrived and handed him a draft letter of decision, transferring all executive powers to Suharto. The terms of the discussion have not been revealed—at least, not in any credible sense. It was what the political scientist Harold Crouch identified as a "disguised coup," and others as the culmination of a "creeping" encirclement of Sukarno.

After that, Suharto moved quickly. He banned the PKI formally on March 13 and followed up by arresting fifteen of Sukarno's ministers, including the most senior, the foreign minister, Subandrio. Sultan Hamengkubuwono IX and the wily anticommunist Adam Malik were drafted into an emergency cabinet.

Through the year, Suharto wound back Sukarnoism. In August he sent word to Malaysia that Konfrontasi was over. A trial of the central bank governor gave him a platform from which to reveal the hidden costs to the state of the president's amours. The cabinet was broadened to include the University of Indonesia economists, under their former dean, Widjojo Nitisastro. In early 1967 pressure was stepped up to force Sukarno out.

In March, a thoroughly intimidated and controlled Majelis Permusyawaratan Rakyat (MPR, People's Consultative Assembly), the repository of sovereign power in the Indonesian system, transferred authority to Suharto as acting president. A year later, the same body voted him into a full presidential term of five years.

Sukarno was sent into a bitter and lonely retirement. The withdrawal of public attention and contact with crowds, not to mention the four-month separation from his family during a period of interrogation in about 1965—the *kesepian,* or isolation, that can be a cultural torment for the Javanese—saw his spirit wilt and his body succumb to illness three years later.

After a terrible transition, which was quickly pushed to the back of their consciousness, the pragmatists, the realists, the exporters, and their Western backers had finally got the kind of leadership for Indonesia they had long wanted.

3

THE NEW ORDER

AS THE CHARACTER OF THE NEW REGIME BEGAN TO EMERGE FOLLOWING THE IMPOSITION of control, the model of Javanese kingship was cast aside by analysts (at least during its early years), and a more recent one applied. As the scholar Ruth McVey has argued, this was the *Beamtenstaat*, the efficient bureaucratic machine of the later Dutch administration. Replace the titles, and Indonesia's New Order looked quite like that system: an all-powerful governor-general, an ineffective appointed people's council, a ruthless military and police, a bureaucracy given a share of the tax farm, a view of the villagers as a passive mass, and an economy geared to exploit extractive export industries in the outer islands.

From the beginning, Suharto and his generals privately made it clear that there would be no early transfer of power back to civilians, whose messy politics were blamed for the diversion of the revolutionary spirit. But civilian expertise would be enlisted. Sukarno's incantations were replaced by new, technocratic slogans: "stabilization," "rehabilitation," "dynamic stability," and "twenty-five years of accelerated modernization."

Initially, the effort was to stop Indonesia from going into complete economic collapse. Hamengkubuwono IX, the economic expert on Suharto's initial team, revealed in April 1966 that the nation's foreign debt service obligations for the year exceeded its expected export earnings. He and Adam Malik toured world capitals to seek new credit and a moratorium on repayments, with some success: lenders either had few prospects of otherwise recovering their money or had strategic interests in helping the new government. The International Monetary Fund set up an office in the central bank, and in February 1967 it, the World Bank, and the Asian Development Bank began loan programs.

Hamengkubuwono's team of advisers included the University of Indonesia economists who had run the army-sponsored seminar in January 1966 and, earlier, been guest lecturers at Seskoad, the army's staff college in Bandung. Their senior member, Widjojo Nitisastro, and two others, Ali Wardhana and Emil Salim, had all gained their doctorates at the University of California, Berkeley. Others, including J. B. Sumarlin, Subroto, Mohammad Sadli, Radius Prawiro, Frans Seda, and Rachmat Saleh, had done their higher studies elsewhere. But "the Berkeley Mafia" became one sobriquet for this group, who were also known as "the technocrats." All were to move up into key economic and planning positions. In 1967 they were joined in the government by the former economics dean and PSI politician Sumitro Djojohadikusumo, who had pursued business interests in Singapore and Malaysia after retreating from the 1958 rebellion in Sumatra.

Through careful control of government spending, credit growth, and the allocation of foreign exchange to industries strangled by a lack of replacement parts and inputs, the technocrats were able to re-expand the economy and rein in inflation. By 1969 real per capita income had gone past the best level previously attained, in the early 1950s. Inflation, which had hit 640 percent over 1966, fell to 10 percent in 1969.

The regime change also sparked a stampede into Jakarta by foreign banks, oil companies, and miners, manufacturers, and traders. The new ministers were not going to delay things with due diligence or outside policy advice. The New Orleans–based Freeport Minerals virtually wrote its own contract for a copper-gold deposit on a mountaintop in New Guinea, which it had spotted in Dutch geological records. A dozen oil explorers signed production-sharing contracts with the emerging state oil giant Pertamina for the first wells in the Java Sea, and Japanese companies opened textile and car-assembly plants.

In 1969 Suharto launched the first of successive five-year plans that put special emphasis on improving rice yields, through the introduction of high-yielding varieties and the provision of subsidized urea fertilizer. Another initiative was a family-planning scheme that employed middle-aged women to introduce young village women to contraceptive pills and intrauterine devices. A moribund program of *transmigrasi* was revived, to ship landless villagers from Java to cleared jungle areas in Kalimantan, Sumatra, and New Guinea. Through these programs, Suharto began working on the problems neglected by the Ethical Policy of the Dutch. Along with anticommunism, "development" became the second mission and proclaimed base of legitimacy for the New Order.

BUT IT WAS NOT ALL ECONOMICS: there was also some clever manipulation of the Javanese courtly tradition and oral literature. The March 11, 1966 letter extracted from Sukarno was given the abbreviated title of *Supersemar* (an acronym from the Indonesian for "Letter of Decision, 11 March"). This was also a reference to the peasant figure named Semar, introduced by the Javanese as comic counterpoint in their versions of the Hindu epics, the *Ramayana* and *Mahabharata*. Along with his sons Gareng, Petruk, and Bagong, the clownish Semar is the repository of great wisdom and common sense, his interventions solving conflicts that baffle the more elevated characters.

Suharto thus positioned himself as a Semar-like figure, an adviser who did not aspire to compete with Sukarno in charisma or worldliness. He seemed made for the role. Born in June 1921 in a small and impoverished village called Kemusuk, about 12 kilometers west of Yogyakarta, his credentials as a man of the masses were impeccable. His father was a village irrigation official, and his mother a village woman, though she may have descended from a royal concubine at the kraton in Yogyakarta.

A difficult childhood turned Suharto into an exceptionally withdrawn and scheming character. Only forty days after his birth, his mother disappeared; she was found three days later carrying out a ritual fast in a rice storage shed, suggesting severe postnatal depression. The baby was given to a foster home in the village, and his parents separated and started new families. The boy Suharto went through a childhood in which he was grabbed alternately by his mother's new household in Kemusuk and that of his father's sister in a village south of Solo, a day's journey away. As a teenager, he was placed in the household of a *dukun,* a practitioner and teacher of Javanese mystical arts and faith healing.

Even in a Javanese society in which divorce, remarriage, adoption of children, and change of name was common, it was a remarkably disrupted childhood. It created a persona marked by intense self-control of emotion, to avoid shock and suppress pain. By the age of twelve, Suharto was later to assert, he had adopted the attitude of *aja kagetan, aja gumunan, aja dumeh* (don't be startled, don't feel overwhelmed by anything, don't feel superior). He also became immersed in the mystical practices of Java, a mixture of animism and Hinduism, although his limited formal schooling—to middle grades—came from the modernist Islamic organization Muhammadiyah. Thus, he knew the legends of Java inside out.

Behind a normally stern countenance, broken by a wide smile when trying to win support in small group settings, Suharto was intelligent and tough. After a spell as a bank employee, he signed up for the Royal Netherlands East Indies Army in June 1940, when it stepped up recruiting in the face of the Japanese, and rose to the rank of sergeant. After the Dutch collapse, he joined the Japanese auxiliary force, PETA, rising to become one of its trusted officers at the company-commander level by 1945.

In Yogyakarta after the surrender, Suharto was made a battalion commander in the new Indonesian republican forces. His reputation as a fighting soldier grew after clashes with the British forces trying to extricate European civilian ex-internees. A marriage was arranged with Siti Hartinah, known as Tien, who came from the lower echelons of the priyayi class, thanks to descent from Solo's junior royal house, the Mangkunegaran. In December 1948, when the Dutch army seized Yogyakarta in its second police action, Suharto withdrew his troops south of the city. He is said to have meditated in the caves frequented over a century earlier by the rebel prince Diponegoro, imbibing his spirit, and to have slipped into the city incognito to note the Dutch positions and to contact the sultan, Hamengkubuwono, the only republican leader not arrested by the Dutch.

On March 1, 1949, Suharto led his troops in a surprise attack on the city at 6:00 a.m., holding central positions for six hours until pushed out by Dutch reinforcements. His "six hours in Yogya" would later become the stuff of hagiography, in writing and in film, its importance in the independence struggle inflated.

In the postindependence army, Suharto had risen steadily to command the Central Java division, which had its headquarters in Semarang. After a short career interruption in 1959, when his commodity-smuggling activities in alliance with local Chinese merchants got him pulled out to the Bandung staff college during a crackdown by General Nasution, he rose steadily through higher commands. His roles in the military side of the New Guinea campaign and in running the army's ambivalent involvement in Konfrontasi helped him build a body of loyal and pragmatic officers, who followed him into Kostrad and then into building the political-security side of the New Order. They included his intelligence chief, Yoga Sugama, and Ali Murtopo, the head of a political warfare unit called Opsus (from Operasi Khusus, or Special Operations), the young special forces officer Benny Murdani, the navy officer Sudomo, and a paymaster with mystical inclinations, Sujono Humardhani.

HAVING CLOAKED ALL HIS MANEUVERS against Sukarno with "constitutionality," Suharto was left with little choice but to keep the existing political institutions and move ahead with the long-delayed elections. The 1945 constitution provided an excellent setting for authoritarian rule, particularly as it was quite vague about the electoral process and composition of the legislatures. Through an election law passed in 1969, the numbers in the standing parliament, the DPR, were set at 360 elected members and one hundred appointees, and of the latter seventy-five from the military. These were included in the higher assembly, the MPR, which made the presidential appointment and which had more presidential appointees within its 460 members. Elections were now set for 1971.

As well as pursuing a quiet détente with Malaysia, and later orchestrating the "Act of Free Choice" in New Guinea, Opsus, with its mixture of former Special Forces officers and civilian operatives, turned its attention to bringing the noncommunist parties into line.

A manipulated congress of the PNI in April 1966 saw the old left-wing Sukarnoist leadership of former prime minister Ali Sastroamidjojo replaced by a highly conservative one that included an old Suharto ally and business partner from Semarang, the city's former mayor Hadisubeno Sosrowerdojo. At a PNI convention three years later in Semarang, delegates were warned beforehand by their local military commanders to vote Hadisubeno into the chairmanship, with Ali Murtopo and his operatives directing the event from a nearby "command center." Hadisubeno was duly elected.

The modernist Muslims regrouped under a new party, Partai Muslimin Indonesia (Parmusi, Indonesian Muslim Party), but leading figures from the old Majelis Syuro Muslimin Indonesia (Masyumi, Council of Indonesian Muslim Associations) remained banned from political life. In 1970 Parmusi also came in for Murtopo's attention, getting his associate John Naro and a contentious Suharto minister, Mintaredja, installed as leaders. They promptly watered down the party's policies, abandoning support for the Jakarta Charter requiring Muslims to follow *Syari'ah* law. A third intervention saw a government-supported ticket under the nationalist publisher B. M. Diah installed to head the Indonesian Journalists' Association, pushing out a team of editors who advocated a more independent role for the press as a fourth estate of the polity.

The New Order now required its own political vehicle to enter the contest. It found it in the idea of a *golongan karya* (functional group), first floated by Sukarno in 1957 in his search for something to augment or replace the squabbling parties. Instead of one class striving to dominate another through political parties, or the constant adversarial clashes of the "Western" political process, Indonesia was more suited to an "organic" system, in which each class and occupational group was respected and content in its position, and each contributed to the overall good.

The army, under Nasution, had responded enthusiastically to the idea, to the point that Sukarno himself backpedaled, but Nasution had persisted. In the plantations and factories it controlled, the army-sponsored Golongan Karya (Golkar, Functional Groups) movement promoted an alternative labor organization, using the term *karyawan* (staff) rather than *buruh* (worker) to suggest that managers and employees had a common interest. It moved into a niche between capitalism and the state, forming ties with the cooperative movement Kosgoro (Kesatuan Organisasi Serbaguna Gotong Royong, Federation of Miscellaneous Mutual-Aid Organizations).

The idea of a movement based on dutiful participation, rather than activism, appealed to the "small-town Java" and military mindset of Suharto's inner group. It also drew in some of the former

Catholic student activists who had joined the struggle to overthrow Sukarno and the PKI. The "corporatist" idea of the state as a family had been a strong element of political thinking in Rome since the late nineteenth century. In 1970 the government ruled that all state employees had to observe "monoloyalty" to Golkar. Effectively, this meant the entire bureaucratic apparatus was a contestant in elections, which it was supposed to run fairly.

An additional buttress came from the military, even though it was meant to be apolitical and had its own appointees to the DPR and MPR. The military's "territorial" structure had been extended under Suharto, all the way down to the posting of sergeants in villages. Over two-thirds of provincial governors and half of all *bupati* (heads of regencies or large rural districts) and city mayors were military officers.

The relentless official support and lavish resources, plus some positive appeal as the vehicle of modernization and development, gained Golkar 62.8 percent of the vote in the 1971 elections. The PNI won just 6.9 percent, and Parmusi less than 5 percent. The unreconstructed NU, the league of traditional Javanese Muslims, was the rock of resistance, gaining 18.4 percent of the vote—almost the same as its result in the only previous election, in 1955.

The New Order's political strategists moved to tidy up further. One of Suharto's more thoughtful loyalist generals, Widodo, came up with the concept that the population should be a "floating mass" between elections, going about the hard work of development without distraction from parties. A law in 1975 put this into effect, banning parties from organizing below regency level. Another fiat in 1973 had already railroaded the non-Golkar parties into two new "factions." The PNI was amalgamated with several smaller nationalist and Christian parties into the Partai Demokrasi Indonesia (PDI, Indonesian Democratic Party), and the Muslim parties, including the NU, into the Partai Persatuan Pembangunan (PPP, Development Unity Party).

A pattern of manipulated electoral democracy was established for the remainder of the New Order, with the Golkar majority varying, mostly upward, from the level set in 1971. Candidates were screened by government panels for "subversive" tendencies. The military's internal security command, known as *Kopkamtib*, wielded unchecked powers of arrest and detention. The parliament became an echo chamber, in a system that one Golkar founder likened to the Vatican: the pope chooses the cardinals, and the cardinals choose the pope.

Communism in Indonesia had vanished. The army had quickly detected attempts by PKI remnants to regroup and wage "people's war" from remote rural areas of East Java. All were quelled by 1968. In West Kalimantan, party elements merged into the substantial population of Chinese gold miners, timber and rubber traders, and other settlers. The army stirred up a racial vendetta among the indigenous Dayaks, who slaughtered hundreds of Chinese and drove 50,000 into the towns, thus removing the population in which guerrillas had operated. Until 1979, the army kept some 30,000 former sympathizers of the PKI, including intellectuals like the novelist Pramoedya Ananta Toer, in prison settlements on Buru, an island in the Moluccas, and on Nusakambangan, an island close to the south coast of Java. They and hundreds of thousands of others remained noncitizens, barred from political activity and voting.

By the early 1970s, many of the former students of 1965–66 and many older proponents of open democracy and free speech were parting company with the government. Protests and newspaper articles criticized the patrimonial style of Suharto's rule, his links to ethnic Chinese businessmen dubbed *cukong* (from a Fujian word for "boss"), his reliance on foreign investors, and the enrichment of his family circle through government favors. In 1971 he responded by saying that the campaign was aimed at kicking the military back to the barracks. His response would be the same as in 1965: to "smash" any opposition.

In late 1973 the chief of Kopkamtib, General Sumitro, undertook a dialogue with the critics, which seemed to Suharto loyalists to be the start of a campaign to undermine the president. As Ali Murtopo and another presidential adviser, the financier-cum-mystic Sujono Humardhani, were also being criticized (the latter for his links with Japanese investors), this dialogue became intensely personal for Murtopo's people. A visit by the Japanese prime minister Kakuei Tanaka in January 1974 brought matters to a head. Protests erupted into rioting across Jakarta, with the Toyota dealership and other Japanese symbols set ablaze.

The Malari affair, as it became known (from Malapetaka Januari, or "January Calamity"), was the moment when Suharto showed his authoritarian colors for good. Sumitro was replaced as Kopka-mtib chief by the longtime naval aide Sudomo, now holding admiral's rank. Several liberal newspapers were closed, and their editors barred from practicing journalism under the licensing system run by the Information Ministry. Among the hundreds arrested were the lawyer Adnan Buyung Nasution and the editor Mochtar Lubis.

This political crisis was followed within a year by a new economic one, when it was discovered that the state oil corporation, Pertamina, had run up $10 billion in debt, much of it in short-term loans, and also had contingent liabilities in oil tanker charters, commissioning of petrochemical works, and a new industrial base at Batam Island. That was equivalent to a third of the nation's gross domestic product (GDP) at the time. Pertamina's entrepreneurial chief, Lieut-General Ibnu Sutowo, was sacked in 1976, and Suharto squeezed Caltex and other oil companies for a higher split of production.

That year Suharto also faced an unexpected challenge from a quarter he had long regarded as his own resource, the stream of Javanese mysticism known as *Kepercayaan* (belief) or *Kebatinan* (inwardness). The son-in-law of a retired police general running the official organization for Kebatinan followers, and by then a middle-aged official in the Ministry of Agriculture, Sawito Kartowibowo had been touring the places in Java where mystical forces are said to be concentrated. After a night's meditation on a sacred mountain, he claimed to have found a stone engraved with his image, convincing him that the wahyu was descending to make him a new ratu adil.

In 1976 Sawito made a series of calls on eminent figures, including the former vice president Hatta, the Catholic cardinal for Indonesia, a well-known general heading the council of the Protestant church, and a police general, Hugeng, who was widely known as having been sacked in 1971 for busting a well-connected smuggling operation at Tanjung Priok, Jakarta's port (as well as enormously popular for his ukulele band, the Hawaiian Seniors). Sawito got many of these figures to sign a petition, titled "Toward Salvation," criticizing the moral decay of the government. To this, Sawito attached his own call for Suharto to hand power to Hatta.

The episode gave Jakarta journalists and the scholar Ong-hokham an opening to explore Javanese mysticism and Suharto's use and abuse of it. On the government side, it was all taken very seriously, and Sawito was given eight years in jail. "From the rational point of view the Sawito case is just a comedy," Ali Murtopo observed. "However, from the irrational point of view . . ."

The 1965 alliance of army and rural Muslims against the PKI was long over. Mosques and *pesantren* remained the only local centers of power the government could not fully control, though they were kept under constant watch and their activists frequently arrested and beaten. Ahead of the 1977 elections, Opsus undertook a spoiling action, following an agent-provocateur strategy inspired by the 1965 events and by the agency's successful fomenting of civil war in Portuguese Timor in 1975.

One of its top operatives, Colonel Pitut Suharto, had long cultivated the remnants of the Darul Islam movement in West Java. He may have helped kindle the flames of the Malari fires, as truckloads of young Muslim hotheads from West Java were seen joining the riots. In late 1976 and early 1977, there were explosions at a Baptist hospital in West Sumatra and at nightclubs in Medan. Threats and attacks were made against the PPP. The arrest of a Jakarta student for allegedly preparing an incendiary device for use against officially tolerated dens of sin was the forerunner of a wave of arrests in the weeks before the elections. Those arrested were said to be members of a new organization, Komando Jihad (Holy War Command), which was set on reviving the Darul Islam campaign for an Islamic state. The hands of Pitut Suharto and Opsus could be seen.

The 1977 election was a repeat of the Golkar victory, with its vote down slightly to 62.1 percent. The PDI won just 8.9 percent, and the PPP a sizeable 29.3 percent, thanks to the inclusion of the NU. In 1978 Suharto was duly sworn in for a third five-year term, amid student protests that were quelled with ease.

Many of the president's former allies had now distanced themselves. Sultan Hamengkubuwono IX declined a second term as vice president. Liberal-democratic figures and Western-minded generals had been bought off with ambassadorships or other posts, or simply frozen out. Suharto didn't care. He had survived the Malari challenge, kept the Islamists in a box, handled the Pertamina crisis, and brought Portuguese Timor into the nation. He'd also come through a prostate operation in the United States. High oil prices were sustaining Indonesia's economic growth at close to 8 percent a year. When unusually bold foreign visitors asked about succession plans or the regime's evolution, Suharto appeared baffled by how anyone could think of such things.

THE CONTINUING HIGH OIL PRICES allowed a reassertion of domestic business empire building. In the state sector, it came from the Ministry of Industries, usually headed by an army general rather than an economist, and from a new figure in the Suharto entourage, technology minister Bacharuddin Jusuf Habibie.

As a young teenager, the half-Makassarese, half-Javanese Habibie had become a protégé of Suharto while the general was on assignment in South Sulawesi. He had gone on to study aeronautical engineering in Germany and had risen high in the aircraft manufacturer Messcherschmidt-Bölkow-Blohm's (MBB) ranks. In the mid-1970s Suharto and Pertamina's Ibnu Sutowo enticed him home with the promise of whatever resources he needed for new ventures. Habibie started with an aircraft factory, building a twin-engine turboprop transport of Spanish design and an MBB-designed helicopter. The aircraft were flyable but much more expensive than direct imports from the original makers, as the local civil and military customers grumbled. They had little choice, however, as did the Ministry of Finance, which was pumping money into Habibie's venture. "First we have to pay him to build the aircraft," the economic minister, Radius Prawiro, was wont to comment. "Then we have to pay the full price for it." Habibie would also take over the money-hemorrhaging state steel enterprise, Krakatau, built by a German industrial group under corruption-shrouded contracts.

Suharto's circle of relatives, the army, and business allies from Semarang had flourished from the start of the New Order. The army's holding company, Tri Usaha Bhakti, was given control of forests in Kalimantan, where it granted logging leases in return for 35 percent equity as a sleeping partner. Other companies and foundations belonging to the various armed services and their divisions became partners in hotels, construction, and automobile assembly. Government contracts were inflated to allow generous kickbacks to figures in the regime.

Liem Sioe Liong, who had migrated from Fujian in southern China in 1938 to become a trader in Semarang, was the most notorious of the cukong around Suharto, try as he might to dispel hostility by taking an Indonesian name, Sudono Salim. His two banks in the Chinese-dominated commercial sector of Jakarta, known as *Kota* (notably Bank Central Asia), became the core of a rapidly expanding conglomerate.

Smuggling across Dutch and civil-war lines in the 1940s and 1950s had given Salim a keen appreciation of Indonesians' addiction to the clove-flavored cigarettes known as *kretek,* the most popular brands of which were manufactured in towns near Semarang. With domestic production in a shambles, in 1968 the government gave control of clove imports from Zanzibar and Madagascar to a firm owned by Salim and to another owned by Suharto's younger half-brother Probosutedjo. The domestic selling price to kretek factories was set at about twice the buying price in the Indian Ocean islands. In 1970 Salim's company, Bogasari, gained exclusive rights to flour milling and wholesaling in Java, Sumatra, and the southeastern islands, and he later pioneered a global instant-noodle market through the brand Indomie. A cousin of Suharto, Sudwikatmono, gained a small shareholding in Bogosari.

Salim now expanded into other sectors, like cement and property, in partnership with other canny migrants from Fujian. In return for import protection and domestic monopolies, he was expected to put his money into various state projects favored by Suharto, including a steel-rolling mill attached to Krakatau, and expansion of sugar and rice production. When his businesses ran into short-term difficulties from time to time, state banks were ready with capital injections. The symbiotic relationship of Suharto and Salim—business acumen provided by one partner, political clearances and protection by the other—became the model for similar relationships between military commanders and local ethnic Chinese businessmen down the line.

The genteel enterprises of Suharto's wife (which gained her the widespread and probably unfair nickname "Madame Ten Percent"), the placement of Mangkunegaran-connected figures in various high offices, and the cuts given to Suharto's brother and cousin were overtaken by the business activities of the six Suharto children. An early starter was the eldest son, Sigit Haryoyudanto, who emerged as partner in a cargo airline, Bayu Air, financed by a 5 percent levy on all air cargo shipments in and out of Indonesia. In 1982 the second son, Bambang Trihatmodjo, set up his Bimantara group with lucrative contracts from Pertamina. The two brothers gained an import monopoly on the import of plastics in 1984.

The oldest of the sisters, Siti Hardijanti Rukmana, or Tutut, set up the Citra Lamtoro Gung group with her husband and two younger sisters in 1983, later gaining a share of the cash flow from Java's burgeoning toll-road network and its first private television license. The brash youngest son, Hutomo Mandala Putra, or Tommy, set up his Humpuss group at age twenty-two in 1984, with the help of exclusive trading rights for certain key petrochemical products. With another ethnic Chinese businessman from Semarang, the timber and plywood tycoon Mohamad "Bob" Hasan, Tommy later gained the first private airline license, among many other ventures.

The collapse of oil prices in the mid-1980s strengthened the hand of the technocrats in rolling back some of the more egregious monopolies and price-fixing, which was sending a cascade of cost increases through the economy. Indonesia had to diversify its exports quickly, especially into manufacturing and agribusiness. In 1988 the government announced sweeping reforms to open up banking and the stock market, liberalized steel imports and interisland shipping, and most dramatically removed the plastics import monopoly enjoyed by a firm controlled by Suharto's cousin Sudwikatmono and sons Sigit and Bambang. This had been raising the cost of inputs to local manufacturers by 15 to 20 percent, without any clear reason beyond enriching the family members. The reforms quickly galvanized investment in manufacturing, making Indonesia an important base for global supply chains in items such as shoes, clothing, and luggage.

THE NEW ORDER POLITICAL SYSTEM continued its five-year election ritual, with Suharto standing again and again for the presidency. But while the official Muslim party was even more dispirited after being forced to abandon its potent symbol of the *Ka'abah,* the black granite focus of worship at the center of Mecca, the broader *ummat* was stirring across Indonesia.

The post-1965 political suppression had turned religious activists to *dakwah,* the spreading and deepening of faith and Islamic study. Many thousands of new mosques and religious schools appeared. People were turning to religion for moral guidance in their rapidly changing lives, taking on the outward symbols of faith, like prayer caps and headscarves, and peppering their speech with Koranic phrases. A similar thing was happening in the Christian churches, in some cases involving people who might earlier have had national- ist or communist involvement. Suharto himself quietly abandoned his identification with Kebatinan and became more Islamic in style, making the minor pilgrimage to Mecca in 1977.

Muslim thinkers and proselytizers were now becoming more as- sertive. In 1984 an alleged intrusion by soldiers wearing their boots into a mosque at Tanjung Priok started a protest, which was fired on by army troops, killing dozens of people and sparking riots. In 1989 the army viewed a group that was protesting land grabs in Lampung, South Sumatra, as a secret fundamentalist camp and massacred one hundred men, women, and children in a raid.

The president adopted a familiar strategy of cooption, though his master at the game, Ali Murtopo, had died in 1984. In 1990 Suharto commissioned Habibie to set up the Ikatan Cendekiawan Muslim Indonesia (ICMI, Indonesian Association of Muslim Intel- lectuals), which had free rein to canvass views on how to insert an Islamic perspective into state policies, with the help of a well-funded think tank and a new newspaper, *Republika*. Who was using whom was a moot question, as Muslim activists, like others, were becom- ing conscious of Suharto's advancing years.

The president showed no sign of bowing out, however, gaining reelection in 1993. Having made the full pilgrimage to Mecca in 1991, he now presented himself as Hajji Mohammed Suharto, and his daughters began appearing in headscarves. There was no modifi- cation of his defense of the family businesses: they had as much right as anyone else to engage in commerce, not mentioning the unique favors they enjoyed.

Benny Murdani, the former Special Forces hero, had been pro- moted to armed forces chief in 1983. Murdani warned Suharto in 1988 about the effect on public opinion of the children's activities, counting on what he thought was an intimate, decades-old friend- ship. He was promptly sidelined to a powerless position, and the Centre for Strategic and International Studies, the Jakarta think tank whose sponsorship he had inherited from Ali Murtopo, lost its former direct influence.

In 1992 Suharto forced the Netherlands out of a foreign aid consortium, the Inter-Governmental Group on Indonesia, after its government reacted to the Santa Cruz massacre of protesters in East Timor the previous year by insisting on new human rights standards as a condition of aid. The other donors meekly acquiesced.

In 1993 the president abruptly dropped Prawiro, Sumarlin, and Mooy, three of the top technocrats who had been with him since 1966, putting a Japanese-trained engineer and economic nationalist, Ginanjar Kartasasmita, at the head of the agency at the center of the technocrats' policy making, Bappenas, the National Development Planning Agency. They departed without thanks. In a new ghost-written autobiography, Suharto was similarly ungraceful to other former supporters. Sultan Hamengkubuwono IX was written out of the story of the March 1, 1949, "general attack" in Yogyakarta. The late assistant Sujono Humardhani was dismissed as a source of spiritual counsel: Suharto had in fact been the guru in the relationship. Habibie praised Suharto's mastery of Arabic and Islamic teaching: it was worth three doctorates, he said. Suharto's style of rule was now widely described as "sultanistic."

The armed forces came under the leadership of a younger breed of commanders, many of whom, including General Feisal Tanjung, were from the Special Forces. They were known for applying harsh, aggressive methods during counterinsurgencies in Aceh, Papua, and Timor. In 1983–85, the Kopassus (Special Forces) carried out summary executions of street thugs who, Suharto felt, had been getting out of hand. The commandos killed about 5,000 of these *preman* (a word derived from the Dutch for "free man," referring to masterless people allowed to stay in Batavia) and left the bodies for the public to view. At the time, these were officially *petrus* (from the Indonesian for "mysterious killings"); years later, Suharto admitted they were "treatment" for rampant crime that he had approved.

Some of the army officer corps were being tinged as a "green" (or Islamic) faction, while others inclined to an early leadership succession. Suharto felt it wise to keep key positions in family hands. He made a brother-in-law, General Wismoyo Arismunandar, the army chief, while his son-in-law Prabowo Subianto (a son of the former trade minister Sumitro Djojohadikusumo) gained rapid promotion to head Kopassus and then Kostrad. His former palace aides-de-camp, Generals Try Sutrisno, Hartono, and Wiranto, also moved into the top commands (and later, in Try's case, the vice presidency). In 1993 Suharto's longtime information minister, Harmoko, was made head of Golkar, with the president's daughter, Tutut, as one of his deputies and son Bambang as treasurer.

Indonesia entered a period of excess. Tommy Suharto, after winning a stunningly destructive new monopoly over domestic and foreign clove supplies, was granted approval to start a new "national car" project, which turned out to be nothing more than the low-duty import of fully assembled Kia cars from South Korea. Habibie's newest high-tech enterprise was to develop a naval shipbuilding capability by buying up the entire navy of the defunct East German state and bringing it back for refurbishment in Surabaya. Despite the reluctance of the Indonesian navy to have its funding spent on unsuitable ships, Suharto gave the venture tax-exempt status. The new banking and stock market freedom, in the absence of sound credit controls, set off a borrowing spree in foreign currencies for speculative property investments in shopping malls and apartments and for company takeovers.

FROM THIS FEBRILE POLITICAL SETTING, two figures emerged as poles of independent political influence. Both inherited the mantles of famous fathers who'd held important places in Indonesia's short history and their deep-rooted constituencies.

Abdurrahman Wahid, known widely as "Gus Dur," was the son of the republic's first minister for religious affairs, Wahid Hasyim, and grandson of the NU's founder. After returning from studying in Cairo and Baghdad during the 1960s, Wahid had moved—by natural succession, it seemed—into the NU leadership (hence the first part of his nickname, a diminution of the Javanese title for a prince). From his wide reading and education under the liberal remnants of Ottoman religious scholarship, Wahid displayed a pluralistic outlook to religious affairs and a highly flexible approach to politics, and was alternately inside and outside the Suharto tent.

In 1984 Wahid led the NU out of the umbrella Muslim party, saying it was returning to its roots as a social and religious organization. The PPP's share of the vote would consequently plummet—from 28 percent in 1982 to just 16 percent in 1987. Later in 1984, when the government announced that all parties would have to take the Pancasila as their ideological foundation, Wahid rode with the new rule, declaring that Pancasila was a "noble compromise" for Muslims.

When the government set up the Muslim intellectuals' group ICMI in 1990, Wahid responded by calling together a Democracy Forum, which included several leading secular figures and a number of well-known Christian thinkers. He became a firm critic of the ICMI, consistently arguing that it overemphasized the alleged backwardness of the Muslim community and advantages of other religious groups, and thus tended to promote an intolerant version of Islam that would ultimately lead to calls for an Islamic state. In March 1992, ahead of that year's parliamentary elections, Wahid mounted a mass rally of NU members in Jakarta itself. It was attended by hundreds of thousands, even though army roadblocks prevented many from reaching the capital.

Later, Wahid was bluntly warned by Prabowo Subianto, the president's son-in-law and then commander of one of the four Kopassus combat groups, to endorse a new term for Suharto. Wahid demurred and later let it be known he might resign the NU leadership instead—a prospect that threatened turmoil across Java. The government backed off but in 1994 promoted an opposition group within the NU that got a rival board elected. Yet Wahid remained the authentic voice of the organization in most eyes.

The PDI, meanwhile, was proving more difficult to control. Its government-approved leader, Suryadi, ran a more inspired campaign in 1992, calling for a constitutional limit on the number of presidential terms and portraying his party as the inheritor of Sukarno's concern for the common man, epitomized in the founding president's epiphany upon meeting a Sundanese peasant named Marhaen.

Sukarno's daughter Megawati Sukarnoputri had been brought into the party's parliamentary ranks in 1987, along with her husband, Taufik Kiemas, and they proved a great crowd puller. In 1992 they were joined as candidates by her younger brother, Guruh Sukarnoputra, by then a well-known choreographer and leader of the rock band Swara Mahardhika (Voice of Freedom). That Suharto had generously provided for the Megawati-Taufik household by allocating them a chain of Pertamina petrol stations did not abate their criticism of the president's nepotistic practices.

At that year's parliamentary elections, the PDI vote jumped from 10.9 percent to 14.9 percent, at the expense of Golkar, and Megawati joined a group of PDI members of parliament who were calling on the party to nominate a presidential candidate to challenge Suharto.

Suryadi rejected this provocative move, but his electoral success worried the government. Preman directed by the home minister, General Yogie Memet, literally crashed a party convention in Medan the next year, driving a Jeep-type vehicle through the front door and taking over proceedings. Suryadi's position was ruled invalid by Yogie, and an extraordinary PDI congress ordered for later in the year.

At this meeting in Surabaya, an overwhelming majority of PDI branches backed Megawati over the home minister's preferred candidate. Yogie's acting board members tried to stave off a vote by disappearing from the podium until the permitted time for the meeting had expired. Megawati declared herself elected, and her position was reinforced when army commanders allowed a "national consultation" of PDI opinion, held later in Jakarta, to endorse her position.

Megawati had used her characteristic placidity to great effect. Her silences implied restrained anguish at what was going on. Ahead of the Surabaya meeting, the launch of a quickly compiled booklet of her thoughts drew an audience of old nationalist notables, human rights advocates, and family of the dumped military figure Benny Murdani. The booklet's most evocative image, as the political scientist Angus McIntyre has noted, was that of peasants displaced from their land to make way for golf courses and luxury housing estates.

In the tradition of other political daughters—Pakistan's Benazir Bhutto, India's Indira Gandhi, Bangladesh's Sheikh Hasina Rahman, Burma's Aung San Suu Kyi—Megawati symbolized a pure distillation of the father's legend, at least before attaining political power. Against a background of constant harassment of her party branches by Yogie and the armed forces commander Feisal Tanjung, which included frequent allegations of communist infiltration, she spoke out against a climate of "fear" and made clear she was planning to stand for president in 1997–8.

Under Suharto's orders, his generals began trying to stir a party revolt in favor of a new party congress. In June 1996 a staged congress in Medan voted out Megawati, bringing Suryadi back. She ignored this and continued to speak defiantly from the party headquarters in Jakarta. In July mobs of preman attacked the building, as the Jakarta garrison forces stood by. Among them were members of the army-supported Pemuda Pancasila, by then led nationally by Yapto Soerjosoemarno, the son of an army general friendly to the Suhartos. Between five and twenty people died in the attack and the subsequent protests, while dozens of arrested activists vanished, presumed killed in custody.

Megawati's strategy thereafter was to embarrass the government with a string of lawsuits against government and army figures, unlikely as they were to succeed. The same strategy had been pursued by the publisher and writer Goenawan Mohamad, after the respected weekly *Tempo* was shut down in 1994 for criticizing Habibie's purchase of the East German navy. In counterpoint, a section of the Pemuda Pancasila sued the new PDI chief, Suryadi, for underpayment of their agreed fee for storming the party office.

Meanwhile, the government had cracked the whip over its Muslim "intellectuals." The PPP parliamentarian Sri Bintang Pamungkas called Suharto a "dictator" while in Germany. He was expelled from the ICMI and the parliament and jailed under a surviving Dutch-era lese-majesty law and a Sukarno-era subversion law. Amien Rais, the head of the modernist Muhammadiyah movement, criticized the foreign ownership levels of Freeport and other mining ventures. He was also expelled from the ICMI.

Wahid decided that the survival of the NU was at stake and announced that the organization would support Suharto's reelection. Early in 1997, Wahid took Tutut on a tour of pesantren in Java, giving his backing to Golkar. With Megawati announcing a boycott of the election, the Suryadi-led PDI's vote dropped to a humiliating 3 percent. Golkar won a record vote of nearly 75 percent. It was soon meaningless.

Signs of the government losing control were appearing across the archipelago, with attacks on Christian churches in many towns and a headhunting sweep by Dayaks in Kalimantan against transmigrant settlers from Madura. Within two months, the bursting of financial bubbles across Asia, starting in Thailand, led to an accelerating fall in the Indonesian rupiah. An infusion of International Monetary Fund (IMF) funding in October added to the financial panic, especially when it was clear that Suharto was exempting family-connected banks and projects from austerity measures. His new budget, in January 1998, was based on transparently unrealistic assumptions about the rupiah's value and inflation. After sitting at 2,500 to the US dollar in May 1997, the currency dropped to 14,800 at the end of January 1998. Indonesian companies and state enterprises had no hope of servicing the estimated $40 billion in short-term loans set in dollars and yen. Share prices on the Jakarta stock exchange dropped to a fraction of their previous levels. Business shutdowns put millions in the formal sector of the economy out of work.

Suharto continued blithely to prepare for a seventh uncontested term as president. Trusted army figures were moved up: Wiranto to commander of the armed forces, and Prabowo to Kostrad chief. In March the MPR met and unanimously voted Suharto into a new term, with Habibie as vice president. Suharto then announced a new cabinet stacked with loyalists, including Tutut as social welfare minister and his busy crony Bob Hasan as trade and industry minister.

Protests intensified in mid-May 1998, as the government applied an IMF-mandated cut in fuel subsidies. Army snipers killed four students at Trisakti University in Jakarta, setting off a wave of demonstrations that was beyond control.

Suharto loyalists had already stirred up anti-Chinese sentiment. Tutut had blamed them for the failure of her "I Love the Rupiah" drive. Feisal Tanjung had called the Sino-Indonesian conglomerates "unpatriotic" for moving capital out of Indonesia. Another general had warned: "It's time to eradicate these rats." Now mobs attacked Chinese businesses in the Kota district, burning shops and homes, and gang-raping many women. The office of Salim's Bank Central Asia and the tycoon's home were gutted. Foreigners and ethnic Chinese were soon packing flights to Singapore.

Delegations of leading figures went to Suharto's residence to persuade him to step down. He tried to offer political reforms and fresh elections, suggesting that Habibie was not up to the job, should he resign. His former loyal information lieutenant Harmoko, now the parliament's speaker, joined the resignation calls and then threatened impeachment if Suharto did not. Another loyalist, the economic minister Ginanjar Kartasasmita, and thirteen other ministers said they would refuse to join a new cabinet. Having received assurances from General Wiranto that he and his family would be protected, Suharto made a national broadcast on May 21, 1998, announcing his immediate resignation.

THE DISASTROUS END to Suharto's thirty-two years in power overshadows all that was achieved in Indonesia during that period. He is widely portrayed now as an unalloyed kleptocrat, ruling entirely by armed force. But this is unbalanced. The record certainly shows nepotistic patrimonialism, which was starting to sprout in a third Suharto generation by the time of his fall. But for their ethnicity, the business empires of the former cukong would be seen as assets to any emerging economy. It has been argued that the Suharto children's ventures were the kind of indigenous business groups that arise in the hothouse of government favor anywhere in developing Asia. They at least broke through government monopolies in such areas as telecommunications, broadcasting, and civil aviation for others to follow.

From the time the PKI was eradicated in 1968 until the early 1990s, it could be argued that force was a last resort in political control—after persuasion, cooption, and bribery had failed. Suharto showed skill in attuning his development message and religious appeal to his changing society. Had he stepped down in, say, 1992, with the same sort of military protection afforded him in 1998, he could have claimed to have fulfilled his mission of basic development and stability. The economy had grown an average 7 percent per year since 1965, and continued at this rate until the sudden collapse in 1997. Self-sufficiency in rice production was attained in 1985, and the nation's nutritional intake had risen dramatically. The adult literacy rate was about 85 percent in 1997; the primary school attendance rate was 92 percent, with 60 to 70 percent of students going on to secondary school.

Others would have been left to steer Indonesia through an international environment that Suharto and his generals were now unable to handle. Anticommunist generals were no longer needed anyway. The end of the Cold War had diminished the strategic importance of Indonesia for the United States. Capital transfers were happening at the tap of a keyboard. The new economy and its institutional demands were beyond the command politics of the army. By the 1990s, a new cohort of Indonesians with higher education were ready to run it. Suharto had closed ranks at the very moment when his own success should have told him to open up and get out.

4

REFORMASI

BY THE END OF THE MORNING OF MAY 21, 1998, HABIBIE FELT LIKE THE MOST ISOLATED man in the world. Two months after being appointed as the latest in a long line of ceremonial vice presidents—a clear signal that Suharto had no intention of stepping down or anointing an heir apparent—Habibie found himself in charge. After Suharto announced his resignation on national television, he left for his private residence. Habibie was at the palace as head of state and head of government.

The state was in chaos. Despite the IMF rescue package (or because of it, in some eyes), the economy was in a state of collapse. Inflation was to reach 65 percent for the year, and gross domestic product was to shrink by 16.5 percent in a year. The rice harvest had been hit by drought the previous year, and millions in formal sector enterprises had been laid off. More than half the population was below the poverty line. The heart of Indonesia's commerce, the Kota district of Jakarta, was a smoldering ruin after the military-inspired anti-Chinese riots. Students and other activists were swarming over the parliament building in triumph at Suharto's removal and were demanding an immediate session in which root-and-branch reform could be initiated.

Habibie was an accidental president. Suharto had openly doubted his qualifications to take over during the days preceding his resignation, saying, "There is a question of whether he is capable." A few hours before resigning, Suharto had given the armed forces commander, General Wiranto, a letter authorizing him to restore order and political stability. It closely resembled the letter of March 11, 1966, the famous *Supersemar* that three of Suharto's generals had forced Sukarno to sign. Wiranto was thus the designated successor.

But a simple constitutional barrier stood in the way. As Habibie had conferred with Suharto on May 20 about the formation of a new cabinet, the president had informed him he would resign as soon as it was sworn in. Habibie later recalled that he then asked, "What is my position as vice president?" Suharto replied, "What happens, happens."

Although Suharto at no time spelled it out, it became clear later what was meant to happen: Habibie should have resigned too, clearing the way for the MPR to make a provisional appointment of a third figure to the presidency, just as it had done in 1967. The newspaper editor Endy Bayuni described the moment thus:

> In response to Soeharto's statement 'I am going to step down tomorrow', Habibie could have answered either A: 'So, I'm going to be the next president?' or B: 'I had better step down with you, Pak [Sir]'. He picked A. Had the German-trained aerospace engineer answered B, then he would have paved the way for a military takeover with Wiranto in charge, but with Soeharto no doubt continuing to pull the strings. Post-Soeharto Indonesia would have taken a greatly different historical path. Fortunately, or unfortunately, depending on where one stands, Habibie was not well-versed in Javanese tradition, where courtesans are expected to know, or at least guess, the correct response to a king's questions from his body language.[*]

Was it because, as a half-Makassarese who had spent much time out of Indonesia in Germany, Habibie had simply missed the message, in what commentator Wimar Witoelar has called a moment of "unbelievable naivety"? Was it because, as a research engineer, he

---

[*]Endy M. Bayuni, "How Soeharto Schemed and Habibie Botched It," *The Jakarta Post*, October 9, 2006.

was used to working logically from theory?[*] Or was it because his instincts were those of a "German liberal," as suggested by his long-time colleague in the ICMI and former minister, Adi Sasono? Was he irked by Suharto's disparagement? Whatever the mixture of reasons, Habibie chose to follow his constitutional duty, and his decision was a pivotal one for Indonesia. Fifteen years later, Indonesians were watching Egypt's failed transition to democracy and thinking: *That could have been us.*

Even so, Indonesia's was a fraught transition. In Singapore, the elder statesman Lee Kuan Yew gave Habibie's presidency a couple of months. His first big test—of the army's loyalty—came on his second day in the job.

Overnight, he had been putting together names for his new cabinet. One place remained to be decided: the combined post of armed forces commander and defense minister. The alternatives in the very senior ranks to the incumbent, General Wiranto, included officers with backgrounds in the tainted Kopassus Special Forces and one who'd been involved in violent suppressions of protest; all the rest were political unknowns. Habibie decided to stay with Wiranto and called him at 6 a.m. to tell him.

At 7:30 a.m. a military aide, Major General Sintong Panjaitan, came to see Habibie at his home. The Kopassus commander Major General Muchdi Purwopranjono, and a senior Kostrad officer, Major General Kivlan Zen, were outside with a letter signed by the Kostrad commander, Lieutenant General Prabowo Subianto, and the retired father of the army's "dual function" doctrine, General Abdul Haris Nasution. The aide suggested that Habibie receive the letter in person and read it, which he did at the door to his office. It advised that Prabowo be made chief of the army and that the incumbent, his close former Kopassus ally, Lieutenant General Subagyo Hadisiswoyo, be moved up to armed forces chief.

The two generals then asked for "instructions" from the president. Habibie said, "I have read the letter." They pressed him again. "I have read the letter," Habibie repeated.

---

*R. E. Elson, "Engineering from Within: Habibie the Man and Indonesia's Reformasi," SAIS paper, March 2007.

"Give us instructions," the two generals demanded.

Habibie gave the same answer and went into his office. The tactics of Supersemar had failed this time.

But the matter was not over. At 9 a.m., as Habibie drove to the palace on the north side of Merdeka Square, masses of troops and armored vehicles filled the streets and nearby parkland. His motorcade diverted to a side gate. Wiranto was waiting on the palace steps and took Habibie aside.

He reported that troops from outside Jakarta, under the command of Kostrad, had moved into the capital and taken up positions, concentrating on the presidential palace and Habibie's house. This had been done without the permission of the armed forces commander, Wiranto. Habibie ordered Wiranto to replace Prabowo as Kostrad chief and Muchdi as Kopassus commander "before sunset," and that they recall all their forces back to base.

Wiranto moved to carry out the orders, scheduling a formal replacement ceremony for 3:00 p.m. Shortly before that time, Prabowo arrived at the palace and asked to see Habibie. Apprehensively— Habibie knew Prabowo well from the Suharto and Islamic studies circles and was aware of his hot temper and schooling in applied violence—the president agreed.

With Habibie's military aides hovering on the sidelines, Prabowo walked in—without his customary sidearm, to Habibie's relief. "This is an insult to my family and my father-in-law's family," Habibie recalls Prabowo declaring, in English. "You have fired me as the *Kostrad* commander."

"You are not fired; you're being replaced," Habibie said, explaining the reason was the unauthorized deployment of Kostrad troops in Jakarta.

"I intended to ensure the president was safe," said Prabowo.

Habibie replied that that was the duty of the presidential guard, which came directly under the armed forces commander. "It is not your job," he said.

"What kind of president are you?" Prabowo retorted. "You are naive!" After attempting to bargain for an extension of his term, citing the reputation of the Sumitro Djojohadikusumo and Suharto families, and after trying to call Wiranto on his mobile phone, Prabowo was ushered from the room by Panjaitan, an old rival in the Kopassus hierarchy. Habibie says he hugged Prabowo in farewell and sent greetings to his father and father-in-law.*

The episode marked the beginning of a tacit partnership between Habibie and Wiranto. Suharto's decades of control had created a highly obedient military machine. Officers could make money, murder and torture activists who challenged the regime, terrorize civilians via murderous paramilitaries, and massacre perceived Islamic extremists at Tanjung Priok or Lampung, but they would defer to commanders up the line. The killers among the generals were balanced with "palace" officers, who were steeped in the nuances and balances of power in Jakarta.

Wiranto was one of these palace generals. To him, disobeying or overthrowing a constitutionally installed president was barely thinkable, although opportunities did present themselves in the first half of 1998. Prabowo denies intending to carry out a coup d'état that day, and that's probably true. The style of the Indonesian army, as pioneered by Suharto, was the "creeping" coup. The first stage was to overawe the sitting president, and the next was to steadily gather executive power from the footing of the army command.

With Habibie concentrating on political reform and economic rescue, Wiranto was left to manage a strategic retreat from the military's most egregious political involvement, though it was not without violent insubordination when it came to East Timor. Prabowo, Muchdi, and others were drummed out of the military later in 1998, and eleven Kopassus officers and soldiers faced a court-martial for their involvement in the *Tim Mawar* (Team Rose) abduction, torture, and disappearance of student activists over 1997–98, and some were given short jail terms.

Habibie's ties with Suharto were already cut, as he soon discovered. The new president made several attempts to reach out to his predecessor and repair their relationship by asking for his guidance, he told US ambassador Cameron Hume in 2007. Suharto declined the approaches. Finally, after nearly three weeks, on Suharto's birthday, June 8, Habibie called Wiranto while the defense chief was at

---

*B. J. Habibie, *Decisive Moments* (Jakarta: Ilthabi Rekatama, 2006); "Habibie's Book of Problems," *Tempo*, October 9, 2006.

Suharto's house and asked to be put through. When Suharto came to the telephone, Habibie wished him a happy birthday and asked to be allowed to come and see him to hear his advice. Suharto refused and said that, for the good of the country, the two should never meet again. Habibie should focus his energies on his job; Suharto would "remember Habibie in his prayers."

The two never spoke again. Even a decade later, when Suharto was dying, Habibie was turned away. It was another example of Suharto's cold, self-centered personality freezing out a trusted acolyte who showed independence and criticism. Habibie wrote that Suharto "treated me as though I never existed."

IN FACT, IT WAS FORTUNATE that the old general retreated into his shell, as Habibie was freer to follow both his instincts and the tide of sentiment outside parliament. A week after taking office, he appeared before the parliament, the DPR, and agreed that a special session of the MPR be convened by the end of 1998 to formulate new rules for free and fair parliamentary elections the following year, which would be followed by an MPR session to elect a new president. Habibie declared that the old rules about political parties were to go: "Anyone at all may form a political party."

New parties quickly formed outside the previously authorized trio of Golkar, the PPP, and the PDI—though until elections were held, they were outsiders to the halls of parliament, where Golkar members held a majority, with Habibie now the party chairman. The chairman of the modernist Islamic movement Muhammadiyah, Amin Rais, formed the Partai Amanat Nasional (PAN, National Mandate Party), which pushed a liberal agenda and opened its ranks to non-Muslims. Abdurrahman Wahid likewise decided against turning the NU into a political party again and formed the more widely inclusive Partai Kebangkitan Bangsa (PKB, National Awakening Party).

Habibie made no move to remove those leaders of the PDI who had been installed through the machinations and violence of the later Suharto years. Megawati Sukarnoputri thus remained distant, and in October she defiantly called a party convention in the Bali hotel built by her father with Japanese war reparations money. It took place after mass rallies outside, attended by thousands of mostly young supporters who waved red and black flags. Inside, the

thousand delegates gave Megawati full powers to appoint her own
council for what became the Partai Demokrasi Indonesia—Perjuan-
gan (PDI-P, Democratic Party of Indonesia—Struggle). Her style of
populism was relaunched. Motherly in her approach, she had none
of the oratorical flair of her father, but her speeches declared the
"Indonesian people" to be sovereign and implicitly asserted that she
was now their mouthpiece.

With these main parties in the van—Golkar, PDI-P, PAN, and
PKB—Indonesia moved toward the elections of 1999, its first free
elections since 1955, and their respective leaders—Habibie, Megawati, Amin Rais, and Wahid—emerged as leading candidates for
the presidency. Apart from Habibie, in the highly compartmental-
ized technology sector, none had any experience in government. The
latter three had spent their entire political careers testing the limits
of criticism and opposition under Suharto, sometimes in favor and
sometimes not, receiving at different times blandishments, threats,
and repression. Uncertainly, in alliances and rivalries that varied
from day to day, they pushed their ambitions in a political theater
where many of the screens and gags of the previous three decades
were suddenly removed.

In his first month, Habibie revoked the 1984 decree allowing the
Ministry of Information to cancel the publishing licenses of newspapers and magazines and lightened the obligation for private television networks to carry government news bulletins. He also revoked
the draconian 1963 antisubversion law that had been used by Suharto's government in its last years as a catch-all weapon against critics,
such as the trade unionist Muchtar Pakpahan and the Islamic liberal
member of parliament Sri Bintang Pamungkas. Although powers to
suspend publications and ban books remained, the changes removed
the threat of immediate censorship and closure, which freed up the
media's coverage of politics.

Habibie also ordered the release of many political figures. They
included Sukarno's former foreign minister Subandrio and the 1965
coup plotter Colonel Abdul Latief, and both elderly figures emerged
to fill in some details of those events for an avid media audience.
Three months into his presidency, Habibie also reached out to the
shattered and fearful ethnic Chinese minority, banning the use of
the distinction between *pribumi* (indigenous) and non-*pribumi*.
Later steps authorized the practice of Taoism, allowed the use of

Chinese writing, and eased the burdensome proof-of-citizenship requirements.

ALTHOUGH IN JAKARTA there was excitement and optimism among the educated elite, elsewhere on the archipelago long-suppressed ethnic and religious antagonisms were bursting out. In Kalimantan, the Dayak headhunters were again slaughtering hundreds of transmigrants from Madura. Across Java, local Islamic groups attacked and destroyed several Christian churches and places of allegedly sinful behavior. Mobs killed scores of individuals during a rumor-fed panic about black-clad ninja killers carrying out assassinations of *dukun* (mystical practitioners and faith healers). Crowds of supporters of Amien Rais and Wahid clashed at political meetings in East Java.

In Java and its cities, new groups of fundamentalist Muslims emerged, often dressed in Arabic-style garments. One was the Front Pembela Islam (FPI, Islamic Defenders Front), which had been set up by an Indonesian of Yemeni descent, Habib Muhammad Rizieq Syihab. It specialized in preman-style attacks on minority places of worship, on bars selling alcohol, and on demonstrations for religious tolerance. Another was the Laskar Jihad (Soldiers of Holy War), led by another from the Hadramaut community descended from migrants from that Yemeni region, Ja'far Umar Thalib, a former volunteer fighter in Afghanistan against the Soviet occupation. When clashes broke out in two places where Christian and Muslim numbers were closely balanced, Ambon and the central Sulawesi region of Poso, thousands of Laskar Jihad volunteers boarded interisland ferries to join the fight. By early 1999 both places were in a state of civil war, with thousands killed and tens of thousands displaced from their homes.

In Papua—still officially known as "Irian Jaya"—a crowd of indigenous people in Biak raised the "Morning Star" flag of the banned independence movement. After calling in reinforcements, the army and police attacked and killed scores of protesters. Dozens of survivors were taken out to sea by the navy and dumped overboard to drown.

East Timor had been slipping out of control since army troops had fired on a crowd commemorating the death of an independence activist at Dili's Santa Cruz cemetery in November 1991, with scores killed and dozens "disappeared." The capture the next year of the guerrilla leader José Xanana Gusmão, and his subsequent twenty-year jail sentence, installed him as a new symbol of resistance.

A new generation of youthful activists tested the limits of expression. The arrival of the Internet, mobile phones, and smuggled satellite telephones helped them get their stories out. The once-divided Timorese exiles formed a new political front and began more effectively putting the case against Indonesian rule. Prabowo and other officers from the Kopassus side of the military responded by recruiting and arming militias with fanciful patriotic names, which were then ordered to seek out and attack independence supporters. Ali Alatas, foreign minister for the last eleven years of the Suharto government, would later say that Santa Cruz was the "turning point" at which international support for Jakarta's rule in Timor started to wane.

Within the ICMI, the Islamic intellectuals' group founded by Habibie, the position of East Timor had been debated, says Adi Sasono, a member whom Habibie made his minister for cooperatives and small business. They concluded that East Timor was not an intrinsic part of Indonesia, having been outside the successor state to the Netherlands East Indies that was declared in 1945, and had only been incorporated as a result of Cold War pressures from the United States and Australia. It remained a "high-cost" burden for Jakarta, with the government constantly on the defensive over human rights abuses.

Through the remainder of 1998, this thinking seeped into the Habibie government's exchanges with foreign governments. Australia's government, under Prime Minister John Howard, became particularly alarmed at the possibility of Indonesia suddenly exiting East Timor, says Sasono. "They were saying: 'Please do not leave in a hurry. It will be an Australian burden.'"

In December 1998 Howard sent Habibie a letter, suggesting that Indonesia offer the Timorese a period of political autonomy for a decade or more, followed by a referendum on independence. This was based on the model used by France in its Pacific territory of New Caledonia. The proposal did not appeal: aside from the invidious comparison with a European colonial power, it offered Jakarta a long and expensive cultivation of the Timorese with the high probability of a slap in the face anyway.

Habibie decided to use Australia's switch away from outright support for Indonesian jurisdiction of East Timor as a reason to cut the territory loose. Indonesia had been in long and inconclusive talks with Portugal and the United Nations about an internationally recognized act of self-determination in Lisbon's former colony. Now Jakarta resolved to agree to such an act. Sasono recalls long and agonized discussions in the cabinet, with the military arguing that the sacrifice of 2,100 soldiers and police, plus 1,500 Timorese auxiliaries, should not be thought of as wasted. "Will we add more?" Sasono recalls Habibie responding. The decision to hold a referendum in 1999 was announced at the end of January that year by Habibie's information minister, Lieutenant General Yunus Yosfiah (who, coincidentally, was a former Kopassus soldier who had fought in Timor as a member of the original covert cross border attacks in late 1975).

The events of 1998–99 in Indonesia's regions of conflict showed the ambiguous nature of the military's bargain with Habibie, and Wiranto's ambivalence. On the one hand, the armed forces supported the constitutional rule of the Habibie presidency, notably by abstaining from a coup d'état and by suppressing direct attempts by military figures, such as Prabowo, to overawe the civilian leadership. On the other hand, army elements were arguing that they should continue applying forceful solutions to conflicts. Thus, Wiranto announced troop drawdowns in both Timor and Aceh in August 1998, only to have it revealed that the "withdrawn" units were secretly deployed elsewhere in the two regions. Likewise, the formation and dispatch of Laskar Jihad groups to Ambon and Poso received assistance from local military commands in Java, and certainly they were not impeded from boarding ships in Surabaya en masse to sail to the conflict zones.

In East Timor, preparations for the August 30, 1999 referendum under UN supervision proceeded, with the Indonesian army simultaneously "guaranteeing" security and yet standing back as militia groups brazenly carried out murderous attacks. It emerged that a network of mostly Kopassus officers, directed at the top by Lieutenant General Feisal Tanjung (from the normally weak position of coordinating minister for politics and security), was running this campaign of intimidation. In the end, it failed: 78.5 percent of the population of East Timor voted for independence.

In a final, disgraceful exercise, the military supervised the sacking and burning of Dili and other towns. With logistical assistance provided by the minister for transmigration, A. M. Hendropriyono (another ex-Kopassus lieutenant general), vast numbers of the local population were forced across the border into West Timor, in an effort to show that the Timorese were voting with their feet for Indonesia and that the UN-supervised ballot was therefore fraudulent. On September 12 Habibie agreed to let an Australian-led force take over security in East Timor under a UN mandate.

WHILE THIS MAYHEM CONTINUED, the form of a new and more democratic Indonesia was taking shape. Initially, Home Ministry officials proposed that the parliament (the DPR) have 495 elected members: 420 from single-member electorates and seventy-five chosen by proportional representation (with fifty-five of those appointed from the armed forces). A further eighty-one regional delegates and sixty-nine group delegates would join them to form the wider legislature that would appoint the president, the MPR. The single-member system had the advantage of connecting voters with their representatives, rather than letting parties choose their parliamentary numbers, often after murky payments.

Golkar was keenest on this system, having numerous governors, *bupati,* mayors, and other officials—people well known in their districts—to run as candidates. An outcry from the other parties and students at this possibility forced a reversion to a mostly proportional system of representation and a reduction in the military ranks to thirty-eight seats in a DPR of 500. The eligibility rules set stiff requirements for each party to have a nationwide organization, thereby to avoid a plethora of regional parties setting up. Elections were set for June 1999, and forty-eight parties fulfilled the criteria. With voters given a ballot paper containing only party symbols, not candidate names, electioneering became a matter of linking party leader with symbol.

But who was running against whom? It was clear that Megawati and her PDI-P were challenging the dominance of Habibie and Golkar, and that they expected to prevail. But who were her allies? Muslim parties wavered on whether Islam allowed a woman leader, especially one suspected of being a part-Balinese "Hindu." Wahid, or "Gus Dur," was proving especially hard for her to pin down.

Never in good health, he had been felled by a massive stroke early in 1998, which had left him nearly blind and with erratic judgment. He had been Suharto's wiliest critic and then had embraced his desperate last-minute plan to save his presidency. One moment he was Megawati's best friend, insisting her gender was no barrier, and the next he was casting doubt over whether she was acceptable to the majority.

The election was raucous, marked by large-scale motor cavalcades and mass rallies, but it was largely free of violence and fraud. In the result, Megawati indeed emerged with the largest vote, 33.8 percent, while her PDI rival virtually disappeared. Golkar came second with 22.3 percent, Wahid's PKB gained 12.6 percent, the Suharto-created Muslim party, PPP, won 10.7 percent, and the PAN of Amien Rais a disappointing 7.1 percent. Megawati's sense of entitlement to the presidency grew, but she neglected the reality that the system still required a president to win more than 50 percent of the votes in the MPR, where her party held only 185 of the 700 seats. Instead of cultivating the minor parties, she remained aloof.

Amien saw an opportunity for a third player and began pushing an alliance of Islamic-based parties called the "Central Axis," with Wahid as its presidential candidate. Wahid, meanwhile, kept professing that he supported Megawati for the presidency, and the leader of his PKB parliamentary block maintained that the Central Axis was "not serious" about proposing Wahid. When the MPR met, Wahid forced his own party to break a deal with the PDI-P about appointments to the powerful positions of speaker in both the MPR and the DPR. Amien Rais got the MPR chair, and Golkar's Akbar Tanjung the parliamentary speakership. With Amien and Tanjung out of the way, Wahid could now work on an alliance with Golkar, if Habibie was not running.

Even after the Central Axis and other parties nominated Wahid for the presidency, Megawati continued to believe that he would swing in behind her. Then the other shoe dropped. Habibie delivered his "accountability" speech (his formal report on his presidency) to the MPR, and it was rejected in a 355–322 vote. The establishment could not forgive him for "losing" East Timor. He then announced he would not be standing again. The same day, Wahid was elected president by 373 votes to Megawati's 313 votes. She accepted an invitation to run for the position of vice president,

winning a vote handsomely and immediately calling on her supporters to remain calm.

If Habibie's seventeen months as president had been tumultuous,
the twenty-one months of Gus Dur's presidency became increasingly
wild. He showed a contemptuous attitude to Megawati, frequently
making remarks to visitors about her mental capacities and several marriages. The same attitude extended to the parties that had
backed his candidacy. In early 2000 he dismissed two of their most
respected figures from his cabinet for alleged and unspecified "corruption," though the finger of suspicion about financial misdealings
had been pointed at Wahid himself by at least one of the ministers
concerned. This was over the allocation of $1.2 billion in loans from
a state bank to a struggling conglomerate whose owner had donated
heavily to NU.

In mid-2000 the DPR used its previously unexercised right of
"interpellation" to call Wahid before it to explain. He reluctantly
appeared, made a statement that explained little, and struck a bel-
ligerent stance, declaring that the government of Indonesia was "a
presidential system" in which the president was "not accountable
to the House." He later withdrew this remark, acknowledging the
DPR's right to question the president.

Wahid continued to travel frequently and to make startling suggestions. Some drew praise. He changed the name of Irian Jaya (in
western New Guinea) to Papua, and introduced special autonomy
laws. In Aceh he floated the idea of a referendum on autonomy but
then hastily withdrew it, instead offering Syari'ah law in the context
of wider autonomy. He proposed abolishing Suharto's 1966 ban on
the teaching of Marxism but then quickly backed away from that,
too, in the face of opposition from Islamist and military circles. General Wiranto was made coordinating security minister but sacked
after a report on the violence in East Timor gave him formal responsibility for it.

Two new scandals emerged. First, it was revealed that Wahid's
masseur had received a loan of Rp 35 billion ($3.5 million) from the
state logistics body, Bulog, which was charged with food price stabilization. And second, a donation of $2 million from the Sultan of
Brunei had gone into Wahid's personal funds. The cases consumed
the DPR. In February 2001 it voted to accept an investigation,
which concluded that Wahid had been involved in these untoward

transactions, and declared him to have violated his oath of office by failing to uphold laws and indulging in KKN (*korupsi, kolusi, nepotisme*—corruption, collusion, nepotism).

This was the first stage in a process that could end in a special session of the MPR and the dismissal of the president. Wahid attempted to forestall the vote by asking his senior military assistant, the coordinating security minister Lieutenant General Susilo Bambang Yudhoyono, to declare a state of emergency and thereby dissolve parliament. The military, or at least Yudhoyono, refused.

Wahid responded to the DPR's resolution in March 2000, declaring that he had no knowledge of or involvement in the Bulog loan, and that the Brunei money had been a personal gift and was therefore not state funds. This was plausible—the misuse of a superior's name is common enough in Indonesia—but the DPR was incensed by what it perceived as Wahid's wider failings of leadership and was increasingly drawn to Megawati's conservative approach to national security issues. It censured Wahid again.

Finding the president's response unsatisfactory, the DPR then summoned a special session of the MPR. Over June and July 2001, Wahid again and again suggested he would use his emergency powers, and he dismissed the reluctant Yudhoyono from the cabinet. The MPR brought forward its session, and Wahid issued his emergency decree, only to have it declared invalid by the Supreme Court. The MPR convened on July 23 and voted 591–0 to dismiss Wahid and elevate Megawati to the presidency.

While the short presidencies of Habibie and Wahid were marked by turmoil and reform, the three years of Megawati's presidency were characterized by inertness and complacency, although reforms already in train continued to be implemented. In her first National Day speech to the DPR, she said she had called her family together and made them give a "solemn pledge" not to give the smallest opportunity for KKN. Those in the audience might have glanced over at her husband, Taufik Kiemas, a PDI-P representative, whom the US embassy was describing in its secret cables as "notoriously corrupt."

Megawati also showed a fondness for the Indonesian military, despite having herself been a victim of its capacity for brutal political intervention. Back in March 1999 she had told a Singapore audience that she believed firmly in civilian supremacy, but also that "our archipelagic state, which takes the form of a unitary state, very much requires an effective and professional military." As vice president, she had shown a much less sympathetic attitude to the Papuans than Wahid. "It is sad that after all this pain and struggle to be part of Indonesia, then you emotionally declare your independence," she told a Papuan gathering in September 2000.

Four months after Megawati became president, the leader of Papua's main political movement, Theys Eluay, was ambushed and strangled to death after leaving a dinner at a Kopassus base. Six Kopassus soldiers were tried and given light jail sentences of twenty-four to forty-two months. Megawati's army chief, General Ryamizard Ryacudu, whom she was to promote to armed forces chief in the dying days of her presidency, commented, "For me, they are heroes because they murdered a man who was a rebel, the leader of rebels."

In September 2002 she reappointed the retired major general Sutiyoso, a former Kopassus officer, as governor of Jakarta, despite his having been the Jakarta garrison commander who had organized the 1996 attack on Megawati's own party headquarters, an incident in which five of her supporters had died and twenty-three others had been disappeared. Victims' families were given envelopes of money and told to be quiet. Amid bitter protests that were dispersed by water cannons, her delegates in the Jakarta assembly endorsed Sutiyoso. Megawati claimed, "It was not because of me."

Two former Kopassus-graduated generals with shadowy reputations from the later Suharto years and the 1997–9 transition, A. M. Hendropriyono and Muchdi Purwoprandjono, became director and deputy director of the Badan Inteligen Negara (BIN, State Intelligence Agency). Their organization would cap Megawati's term in office by orchestrating the assassination of the human rights activist Munir Said Thalib in September 2004.

As we will see, Megawati returned to an attempt at a massive military solution to Aceh's rebellion in May 2003. Within two years of her presidency, fourteen people had been sentenced to jail terms of up to three years under laws that made it an offense to show "deliberate disrespect" toward the president or vice president, laws adapted from the lèse-majesté codes of the Netherlands East Indies. By November 2006 she was bemoaning her endorsement of the 1999 political reforms, which she now said had fatally handicapped her presidency. Perhaps it was just as well. Her mental reversion to the populist rule of her father seemed complete.

THE INDONESIAN POLITICAL SYSTEM had indeed changed. Four sets of amendments to the 1945 constitution between 1999 and 2002 had greatly altered its balance of powers. The legislature had shown its teeth, using its interpellation powers to summon, question, rebuke, and dismiss the president. Two had fallen in the MPR in the space of just two years. The president now had to give an account of his or her policies virtually every year and was limited to a maximum of two terms, though the balance was tilted back with the commencement of direct presidential elections in 2004.

Also that year, the military's representation in the parliament was ceasing. The police had now been separated from the armed forces and put under civilian command. A constitutional court operated alongside the Supreme Court and showed a willingness to strike down legislation. A new judicial commission aimed to depoliticize the appointment of judges. The central bank, Bank Indonesia, had been given an institutional independence outside the cabinet. The national audit body was giving fearless reports on the bureaucratic misuse of funds.

Perhaps most dramatically, a decentralization law enacted under Habibie that took effect in 2001 saw substantial responsibilities and revenue flows devolved to the provinces (which now numbered thirty-three) and the *kabupaten* (regencies) and urban municipalities (which numbered 502). All now had direct elections for their executives and legislatures. Having been a state in which the public involvement in politics was no more than a ritual, within five years Indonesia was now almost constantly engaged in electoral contests at one level or another.

5

TSUNAMI

IT CAME WITHOUT WARNING, THOUGH IT HAD LONG BEEN BUILDING UP DEEP UNDER THE ocean floor, way out at sea—an earthquake measuring a mighty 9.0 to 9.2 on the moment magnitude scale, the third biggest ever measured on a seismograph, equivalent to the energy released in a nuclear war. In Banda Aceh, a city on the northern tip of Sumatra, it brought two massive shocks and collapsed many buildings. Survivors among the 400,000 residents rushed out into the open for safety, huddling on the rippling ground and dodging falling debris.

As some pulled bloodied bodies from the wreckage, a new panic gripped the confused people standing about. They accelerated away in cars and motorbikes or started to run. The undersea earthquake on December 26, 2004, set off by the pent-up pressure of the Indian Ocean tectonic plate against the Southeast Asian plate, sent shockwaves through the sea, causing tsunami waves on the surrounding shores. Thousands of villagers and tourists at resorts in Thailand and Sri Lanka were killed. The Indian air force station and most villages on the low-lying Nicobar Islands were swept away by the massive waves, as were cricketers on the long beach at Chennai and thatch-hut fishing villages along the Tamil coast. Moving at 800 kilometers an hour, the shockwaves took some time to reach these places.

Aceh was too close to be given much warning, even if an alert system had been in place. Twenty minutes after the earthquake, the sea near Banda Aceh pulled back two kilometers. Then waves de-scribed by many survivors as being as high as coconut trees—about ten meters—rolled into the city, a fast-moving flow of gray-black water sweeping along cars, trees, planks, barrels, and a few desper-ate people perched on top.

Banda Aceh and other populated areas along the northern and western coastlines of Indonesia's Aceh province turned out to have suffered the worst of the disastrous tsunami, with an estimated 200,000 lives lost in just half an hour. Residents still use the term "nuclear" to describe its apocalyptic effect. Yet the tragedy also brought an opportunity for Indonesia to break with an ugly past, one that, as we shall see, it did grasp. "It was a divine knock on the heads, telling us to stop," says Mohammed Nur Djuli, a key figure in a war that had raged for more than thirty years in Aceh.

As it was, it took days for the scope of the devastation to reach the outside world. The province had been closed to outside observ-ers for much of those thirty years, as the Indonesian armed forces tried to suppress a persistent separatist movement, the Gerakan Aceh Merdeka (GAM, Free Aceh Movement), to which Nur Djuli belonged.

The military effort had intensified the year before, in May 2003, when the central government in distant Jakarta called off a faltering cessation-of-hostilities agreement with the rebels, reapplied martial law, and sent in 50,000 to 60,000 soldiers. This was preceded by a show of force that was modelled, to the best of Indonesia's modest resources, on the George W. Bush administration's "shock and awe" overtures in Iraq (which the Americans had invaded two months ear-lier), with mass parachute jumps, amphibious landings by marines, naval bombardments, and supersonic booms from fighter jets.

Five years after the "contagion" of the Asian financial crisis had caused Suharto's apparently unassailable political system to break apart amid a debt crisis and street protests, Jakarta had regrouped under a president from the nationalist mainstream of Java, Megawati Sukarnoputri. The first of her three husbands had been a dashing air force officer killed in a plane crash in the Papuan territory wrested from Dutch control in the closing years of her father's presidency. She had a susceptibility to military glamour, and solutions.

For its part, the Indonesian military was still smarting from the loss of East Timor in 1998–99. Its hardliners were determined to stop the same thing from happening in Aceh, where half the population of 4 million people had turned out to demand a referendum on independence, like that given to the Timorese. By the military's own admission in 2001, only 30 percent of the province's villages were under government administration, with the rest run and taxed by GAM.

Aside from restoring military prestige and upholding the "unitary" nature of the Indonesian republic, which had become an article of faith for Jakarta officials, vital economic resources were at stake. Soon after Suharto's military had seized power from Sukarno in 1965–66, oil exploration leases had been sold to foreign developers in areas known since Dutch times to be sound prospects. An American company, later part of ExxonMobil, struck massive gas deposits around Lhokseumawe on the flat north coast of Aceh. As the new century opened, the highly protected petroleum enclave was still earning Jakarta about $4 billion a year.

By late 2004, after a government campaign that was supposed to take six months and eliminate GAM as a fighting force, the Acehnese still lived under a suffocating blanket of military posts, cordons, and checkpoints, and in daily fear of arbitrary arrest, interrogation, torture, rape, retaliatory mass executions, the burning of whole villages, and disappearance. Groups of preman freely roamed military-held areas, under the guise of youth groups with patriotic names, to help intimidate the population. So-called false flag rebel groups operated under the guidance of Kopassus. Jakarta's intelligence agency carried out bombings and killings to blacken the names of the actual separatists.

The rebels themselves were hard-pressed. GAM leader Nur Djuli was based in the Malaysian capital, Kuala Lumpur, where he acted as the intermediary between the network of fighters and supporters inside Aceh and the movement's top leadership, which was based in Sweden and grouped around Hasan di Tiro, a descendant of the most famous leader of the late nineteenth-century resistance to Dutch annexation, Cik di Tiro. With tolerance from the Malaysian police force's Special Branch, whose British-run antecedents had helped his older brother in the Aceh component of the Darul Islam rebellion against Sukarno's republic in the 1950s, Nur Djuli had been a low-profile point of contact, always careful not to break any Malaysian laws and, surprisingly, able to keep his Indonesian passport.

By 2004 the sheer weight of the Indonesian military and intelligence pressure was starting to tell. About a quarter of GAM's 5,000 armed fighters had been lost. "Not only were we no longer able to support from outside, but unit after unit of our people lost contact," Nur Djuli recalls. "For the unit in North Aceh to contact the unit in East Aceh, which is very near, it had to go through satellite communication with us, and eventually that was cut off. The provider in Medan was stopped. Usually we paid him, and that stopped. We were also collapsing: complete isolation. Then they sent these special troops that can stay and watch for a couple of days; when you go on an operation, you come back and relax and one by one you are stabbed from behind. This was a deep secret: we pretended we were very strong."

Shadia Mahaban had been balancing two of the most difficult and dangerous roles for anyone in the separatist movement. Educated in Jakarta and abroad, and accomplished in the English language, she had secured herself a job as a translator on the staff of the Indonesian general running the Aceh campaign, Bambang Dharmono, who was unaware of her Acehnese ethnicity. For eighteen months she had been a spy inside the military command, reporting to the GAM intelligence chief, Irwandi Jusuf. When Dharmono's troops had encircled a GAM stronghold at a place called Cot Trieng, near Lhokseumawe, in November 2002, she was feeding out tactical information to Irwandi. "It was a crazy game," Mahaban says. "I could have been killed."

By the time martial law had been imposed, she had left Dharmono's office and was working for foreign journalists as a local contributor. These included an American, Billy Nessen, whom she married. When Nessen went into the jungle to see GAM in operation (after a trial, Nur Djuli says, to see if he was a CIA or Mossad agent), Mahaban's position became more precarious.

Then, as the big army operation started, the Indonesians intercepted a satellite phone call between Irwandi and another GAM operative. Irwandi was pinpointed at Mahaban's house in Banda Aceh. A security raid found documents identifying her as the woman who had worked for General Dharmono, and a follow-up raid on her mother's house in Jakarta found incriminating material carelessly left there by another GAM member.

Mahaban decided to get out. But before that she tried to explain herself to Dharmono. "We'd been close—he'd told me all sorts of stories about his son, his family, his life," she recalls. "I thought, 'I can't betray this person just like that.' So I went to the military compound. It was insane; they could have killed me. But I felt I needed to see him for the last time. He refused to see me. He sent a note out saying he was busy. That's it. His adjutant asked for my identity card, the first time I had been asked for ID. I had three or four fake IDs at that time, so I gave one with my address in Jakarta. He photocopied it, and said to leave. My *becak* [pedicab] was waiting outside. But they didn't arrest me. Maybe they were not sure who I was working for, perhaps the US embassy."

She got on a flight to Bangkok with her two young children and from there obtained political asylum in the United States. Nessen came out of the jungle in a surrender supervised by the US embassy. He was put on trial for visa and other violations and sentenced to eleven years in jail but was deported after just forty-five days in custody.

In classic guerrilla war theory, setbacks do not necessarily mean a losing game. To hold out is often enough to deny the enemy victory or conclusion. The massive Indonesian military deployment in Aceh had no discernible "exit strategy." Already the strain was showing: there were firefights between army and police units, suicides of soldiers, and shooting rampages by troops on their way back from war duty. The vicious nature of the campaign was also swelling the rebel ranks, with some recruits being former soldiers or police who defected with their weapons. GAM simply had to hold out in the jungle-covered mountains of the Aceh hinterland and wait.

According to Nur Djuli and others, however, there was a realization that the settings in both Indonesian and world diplomacy had made the chances of support for independence as remote as victory in the field. Since 1977, when Hasan di Tiro had declared his rebellion to restore a successor state to the Aceh sultanate that had preceded Dutch conquest, his movement had attracted no foreign support, apart from the tacit sympathy of some elements in Malaysia (where some states had historical links to Aceh) and a period of military training for 300 cadres in Gaddhafi's Libya during the late 1980s.

"We in GAM understood very well that it was not possible to fight militarily to win," Nur Djuli says. "But we were waiting, although the term came later, for the 'Balkanisation' of Indonesia. A Singapore think-tank at that time thought Indonesia would break up into six components. So we had this war of attrition, a problem here and there and it would collapse. Indonesia was being described as a pariah state. It could not maintain the war anymore because investment was not coming and so on. We were waiting for that. Then something happened: Suharto fell, and then: decentralisation."

As we have seen, one of several reforms introduced by Suharto's successor, B. J. Habibie, was to devolve financial powers and government responsibility to provincial and third-tier district and municipal governments, whose leaders after 2005 were chosen by election rather than appointed by Jakarta. "It was decentralisation that killed our theory of Indonesia collapsing," Nur Djuli says.

The post-Suharto reformasi period also brought forward political figures from South Sulawesi, historically a region of independent-minded seafarers and traders of strong Islamic faith, where an Islamist rebellion under Kahar Muzzakar allied itself with Darul Islam in Aceh and West Java. Habibie was one of them; Jusuf Kalla, a Bugis businessman turned Golkar politician, was another. "The south Celebes [Sulawesi] people, the traditional ally of Acehnese people, the Kahar Muzzakar people, they are still there, but no longer interested, because they have enough for them," Nur Djuli says. "They can build up their economy, they have their Kalla, their Habibie, they are no longer interested. So Aceh is left alone to fight. With Papua, East Timor, Maluku, but there's no strength in that."

In addition, Jakarta had adroitly played the "religious card" to outflank the GAM on its home ground. Aceh had long had internal rivalry between its hierarchies of Islamic scholars, the ulema and the *uleëbalang*, a class of local rulers who controlled the coastal trading ports and other sources of wealth. After the Dutch's disastrous seizure of Banda Aceh in the 1870s, which cost them 30,000 deaths from fighting and disease, they had taken the advice of a savvy "native affairs" adviser, Christiaan Snoucke Hugronje, and suborned most of the uleëbalang aristocratic class, putting them on the payroll and ceding local administrative powers to them. In early 1942, as the Dutch East Indies surrendered to imperial Japan, the ulema mounted an uprising against the uleëbalang and welcomed the invaders. After the Japanese surrender in August 1945, the ulema repeated the bloodbath, achieving what the scholar Anthony Reid calls the "most profound social revolution anywhere in the Archipelago"—in contrast to the rise elsewhere of many elements of the aristocratic classes, such as Java's priyayi, to republican leadership and elite circles.

Aceh was the only region the Dutch did not attempt to reoccupy over the years 1945–49, remaining a bastion of support for the distant Indonesian leadership. It even bought two DC-3 aircraft, which became vital links to the outside world for independence leaders. Its nineteenth-century anti-Dutch heroes were appropriated by the new republic, being used in street names from city to city, despite their struggle having nothing to do with the future Indonesia.

In 2000–1, the government in Jakarta, under Abdurrahman Wahid, a hereditary ulema from East Java who headed Indonesia's biggest mass Islamic organization, borrowed the Snoucke Hugronje formula, but in reverse. He elevated the Aceh ulema's role by applying Syari'ah law in the province and conferring the traditional name of the old sultanate, Nanggroe Aceh Darussalaam (State of Aceh, Abode of Happiness). "GAM lost that game, and the national parties and the *ulama* won it, the campaign game of Islamisation in Aceh," Mahaban says.

When the tsunami hit, Nur Djuli watched in Kuala Lumpur the news of mounting casualties. He called Hasan di Tiro's office and got approval for a unilateral declaration of ceasefire. It was only on the third day after the disaster, however, that he made contact with the local commander in Banda Aceh.

"What am I doing here?" the man asked him. "The enemy was gone: 30,000 Indonesian troops sitting along the coast were all gone." (Indonesia has never confirmed the number of soldiers it lost, but it would be at least two-thirds of that figure.) The commander's own village was gone, and he was camped on a hill outside town.

Nur Djuli told him to wait while he talked with Red Cross representatives and the US military attaché in Malaysia, whom he knew well.

Three days later the commander reported an attack. The Indonesian army, or at least its surviving elements on the ground, was still operating to instructions that had been issued before the tsunami, in the apparent absence of new orders from above.

GAM came under heavy foreign pressure to enter into peace negotiations, with the Americans insisting it had to be based on acceptance of autonomy for Aceh within the Indonesian state, but otherwise unconditional.

The same pressure was being applied to the Indonesian government, which was urged to start negotiations and offer substantial concessions. By this time, the international community had a far more flexible and worldly president to deal with.

Susilo Bambang Yudhoyono came out of the army. In the 2004 direct elections for the presidency, however, he had worn a civilian suit and run at the head of his own newly formed party, the Partai Democrat (PD, Democratic Party), which appealed to voters in a liberal, secular way. In the first round of voting, he emerged as a frontrunner, second only to Megawati. In the runoff election, he pushed ahead with the support of the third-running Golkar, which was achieving some success in shaking off its image as the democratic prop of the Suharto regime. Crucially for Aceh, Yudhoyono's vice president was a Golkar politician from South Sulawesi, Jusuf Kalla.

Persuaded by the dimensions of the disaster in Aceh, by offers of massive foreign aid for the region's recovery, and by suggestions that it was an ideal time to put a savage chapter behind Indonesia, Yudhoyono appointed Kalla to supervise peace negotiations with GAM. That, at least, is the official account. Others have Kalla himself issuing a legally dubious "vice-presidential decree" for Aceh relief, which allowed international agencies to be involved on the ground. Later, Kalla seems to have made vital decisions in the peace talks without referring them to the president.

Even so, GAM negotiators, such as Nur Djuli and Mahaban, credit Yudhoyono with covering Kalla's back in Jakarta's prickly nationalist circles. "SBY without Jusuf Kalla: it would not have been possible," Nur Djuli says. "Kalla without SBY: not possible. SBY controlled the military. He blocked the Ministry of Foreign Affairs—there was no intervention from them at all."

According to an account by the Indonesian negotiator Hamid Awaluddin, who was reporting directly to Kalla, Yudhoyono covertly met with GAM leaders brought down from Aceh in mid-January 2005. Then, a week before talks (to be chaired by the former Finnish president Martti Ahtisaari) opened on February 25 in Helsinki, Yudhoyono abruptly replaced Riyamizard Ryucudu, the hawkish army chief installed by Megawati in the closing weeks of her presidency, who was still pushing for a military solution in Aceh. The new man was a moderate general, Djoko Santoso, who promised to keep the troops under control, in line with the peace initiative.

Nur Djuli says the talks opened with GAM hiding its weakness. "Previously we had our commander ready to reopen the attack if talks failed," he recalls. "It was very strong for a negotiator to have that, to know that you have tigers behind you. But this is different. This is really a poker game. Our troops were collapsed. No communications, no logistics."

The two sides closed the first round of talks, with GAM insisting on a ceasefire and Indonesia refusing until GAM explicitly abandoned its independence aim and its demand for a referendum. Ahtisaari got them back to the table the next month with a formula asserting that "nothing is agreed until everything is agreed."

When they returned, the Acehnese heard Ahtisaari talking on television about a solution involving "self-government" for Aceh. Although he first blustered that this was the same as the "special autonomy" the Indonesians were offering, he eventually agreed to switch to this broader notion, which didn't carry the baggage of East Timor's and Papua's experiences of Indonesian backtracking and cheating while offering "autonomy."

Despite wistful references by GAM negotiators to Aceh's past as a functioning, independent state—with diplomatic links to Europe, the United States, and Turkey for centuries before the 1873 Dutch annexation (and certainly decades before the idea of an Indonesian state covering the entire Netherlands East Indies began to stir in 1908)—the two sides moved toward an agreement in July 2005.

A last-minute hitch developed over the Acehnese insistence on being allowed to form locally organized and named political parties to contest elections for self-government. Awaluddin woke the vice president at 3 a.m. Jakarta time, after Ahtisaari opined that it was a deal breaker. Kalla and Awaluddin had a relationship of trust from their earlier negotiation of settlements for the Muslim-Christian civil wars that had broken out in Poso and Ambon soon after Suharto's fall, stirred by thousands of Arab-garbed Laskar Jihad (Soldiers of Holy War) who had been sent in by army black ops circles.

Speaking in their native Bugis dialect, Kalla quickly came back to Awaluddin with advice from a constitutional court judge that local parties would not necessarily be unconstitutional. Kalla ticked off the concession. The peace agreement was signed in Helsinki on August 15, 2005.

Banda Aceh became a monument to this switch from force to compromise, although Kalla and Awaluddin later fell out with Yudhoyono over who deserved primary credit in a team effort that might have otherwise earned a Nobel Peace Prize.

A casual look at Aceh now finds little evidence of the earthquake and tsunami damage, aside from some preserved incongruences kept as reminders, chiefly large boats stranded far inland. Two quiet parks, as large as football fields, cover mass graves for over 50,000 unidentified bodies. In small pavilions, there are people sitting quietly in prayer or meditation. Nearly everyone has missing relatives and friends.

The experience of self-government has brought the usual compromises and disappointments. Shadia Mahaban's former spymaster, Irwandi Yusuf, ran for election in 2006 and became the first locally elected governor of Nanggroe Aceh Darussalam in early 2007. This former veterinarian set out to run a "green" administration, freezing forestry concessions and introducing a carbon-trading system. By 2011, however, he was enveloped in controversy over a permit for clearing a tract of coastal peat swamp, the habitat of many Sumatran orangutans, for a palm-oil plantation. His good record in public health clinics and repairing roads did not outweigh allegations of cronyism in contracts, which he is contesting. In 2012 he was defeated by former GAM colleagues in their new Aceh Party and, into the bargain, was beaten up by their followers for "splitting" the struggle when he ran as an independent.

Hasan di Tiro returned to Aceh briefly in 2008, and permanently the next year, but did not take up the constitutional position of Wali Nanggroe, a formal guardianship of Acehnese tradition that had been created for him. He died in 2010, a day after his Indonesian citizenship was restored. An estimated 4 million people, equivalent to Aceh's entire population, watched his funeral procession to burial at Indrapuri, a place next to an extinct volcano rising out of the coastal plain near Banda Aceh. The grave, covered by smooth river boulders in a simple concrete enclosure, is scarcely visited.

The influx of foreign military personnel and aid workers after the tsunami ripped open the shroud of secrecy and propaganda around

Aceh. "When I studied in Jakarta, I cried many times because no one would believe what I was telling them about the situation," Shadia Mahaban says. "It was as if I am telling some kind of propaganda story."

When she returned in January 2006, after receiving an amnesty from Jakarta, it was different. The "nonorganic" soldiers and police from outside Aceh were being withdrawn, and civilian Indonesians were getting involved in the decommissioning of GAM's armory, so carefully built up over nearly four decades. The civilians were listening to stories of the conflict as well as of the tsunami.

Several years later, Aceh itself was starting to show some risks of slipping back into tension with Jakarta. The Helsinki agreement had not been followed up, or had been distorted, in the eyes of many Acehnese, in some key areas by its supposedly "enabling" legislation. For one thing, the promised truth-and-reconciliation commission to address human rights abuses had not been established, even eight years on. Jakarta was still hostile to the flying of the old crescent-and-star flag of GAM as the provincial colors, alongside the red-and-white national flag, despite having conceded in Helsinki the right to an Acehnese flag and emblem. For Jakarta, it remained a symbol of separatism, not local cultural identity.

To the visible anger of some Jakarta ministers, the flag was still flying defiantly in towns like Bireun in 2013, an act that would bring violent repression and jail terms for Papuans who tried the same with their Morning Star flag. But at least there was hesitation, and cooler heads were advising that a permissive approach would soon take away any emotional reward from raising the emblem.

It was another episode in which Yudhoyono stepped back from taking a firm line in either direction. Yet the opening of Aceh, the reconstruction, and the peace agreement had put a stamp of Western approval on Yudhoyono's presidency in his first year of office, one in which he was still basking as his permitted two terms of office drew toward their close in 2014.

6

BEYOND DWIFUNGSI

IN PRESIDENT SUSILO BAMBANG YUDHOYONO, THE INDONESIAN ARMY HAD ONE OF ITS own back in the Merdeka Palace, following a bewildering variety of civilian presidents: a mercurial scientist-engineer, a bold-thinking but erratic Islamic mullah, and a phlegmatic dynastic daughter. The five years of these presidencies had seen the military retreat from its octopus-like hold on political institutions and many elements of the economy. Would the retreat continue?

In that 1998–2004 reformasi period, the army had given up the most resented aspects of the Dwifungsi (Dual Function) doctrine formulated by General Nasution in 1958—a "middle way" in which the military did not take charge of government but was not simply a professional fighting force. This had been encouraged by the US Army's doctrine of "civic action" for the soldiery in weak states and then enormously distorted beyond reasonable balance under Suharto. Figures are hard to come by, but in the late 1980s about 16,000 commissioned and noncommissioned officers were in *kekaryaan* (civilian assignment) positions. At times these military personnel were more than half the senior executives in the civilian bureaucracy and three-quarters of the provincial governors and district bupati. Others sat in the national, provincial, and district legislatures.

Under General Wiranto, the military wisely decided not to defend Dwifungsi in the face of overwhelming public and elite support for democracy and the civilianization of politics. The army withdrew any remaining officers delegated to civilian ministries and state enterprises, and abolished the three-star position of assistant to the chief of staff for kekaryaan affairs. Around the same time, the military formally severed its ties with Golkar, telling its personnel that they now had to help secure elections in an entirely neutral way. As we have seen, the armed forces' representation in the DPR and the MPR also fell, and ended altogether in 2004. To emphasize the army's political neutrality, serving personnel were not even permitted individual votes, despite the removal of block representation on their behalf, a measure that continued through the 2014 elections.

Another notable strand of reform started in 2004 with the passing of a law requiring the armed forces to divest themselves of all business activities by the end of 2009. Under the New Order, side businesses had provided the forces with most of their operating funds, since the official budget at times covered only 30 percent of their needs. Companies owned by various military foundations gained lucrative contracts from state enterprises, such as the oil company Pertamina, often with help on the inside from kekaryaan officers or—as with the army's holding company, Tri Usaha Bhakti—control over state rights, such as forestry leases. Units leased out spare land for factories, hotels, and golf courses.

The army's more dubious corporate activities included the provision of security for individual businesspeople, factories, offices, and mines, which in many cases was no more than a protection racket; and then there were outright illegalities, such as gambling, prostitution, logging, smuggling, and drugs. Ostensibly, the businesses (at least the legal ones) were justified as topping up the miserable salaries and barracks of the 450,000 uniformed personnel. But it was all too evident that only droplets were trickling down after the very senior officers had taken their shares. Although the 2004 defense budget of $2.2 billion barely covered half the military's estimated expenditure for that year, Yudhoyono was tasked with ending the extrabudgetary support by the end of his first term.

The reform that most challenged the military, however, was one that sounded very simple when it was first proposed by Habibie in 1999: to detach the police from the armed forces command and the Ministry of Defense. The goal was to make it a standalone agency, renamed the Indonesian National Police, that would operate directly under the president.

Initially, nothing seemed different in practice. The police numbered only 170,000 for the vast nation. Their official budget was even more meager than that of the military. The police were generally despised: they collected small on-the-spot fines with a blow of the whistle, they ignored gambling joints and brothels, they stood back from thuggery committed against strikers and protesters, they assisted with land grabs, and they made themselves available for prosecution by the rich. *"Polisi tak mampu"* (or "The police aren't capable") was the general refrain from army personnel when they were reminded that the police now had legal responsibility for internal security.

Yet vast change started as foreign aid in the security sector switched from the army to the police. The national police began a steady expansion that was to increase numbers to 400,000 over the fifteen years after 1999. Resources were poured into training, high-tech equipment, and other areas. The police continued to be a major problem in the fight against corruption, but by the time the first major strike came from a new threat to the state—a jihadist group named Jemaah Islamiyah (Islamic Congregation), which operated from the myriad mosques and Koranic schools in crowded Java—the police were able to demonstrate their competence in handling it. Within a month of the first Bali bombing, in which 202 foreigners and Indonesians were killed at Kuta Beach nightspots in October 2002, the Indonesian police had tracked down and arrested one of the perpetrators. Although further bombings hit Bali, the Australian embassy, and several luxury hotels in Jakarta over the next five years, a new antiterrorism unit, named Detachment 88, steadily wound up the most dangerous Jemaah Islamiyah cells by the end of the decade.

That unit and the lead investigators, including police generals I Made Mangku Pastika and Tito Karnavian, attained a celebrity status once assigned to the military's fighting generals. Consequently, the stocks of the police have risen, and those of the armed forces are falling in career favor among the young.

"Compared to my era, where military cadets and young officers were favourites for mothers-in-law to be, now as in the general case, pragmatism is the word," says an influential retired army general,

Agus Widjojo, at the Jakarta think tank he now heads, the Centre for Policy Studies and Strategic Advocacy. "We are starting to feel we are trailing in the competition to attract the best and brightest of the young generation. We are late in trying to find a system to attract them. What shall we put in place as an incentive?" The police force is now more favored by young people than the army, navy, or air force, Widjojo says. "We see that police officers are better off compared to officers of the defence services, and they see no way for defence officers to have expectation to better their welfare. Because practically the defence forces are now cut off from their interaction with society. They only train, carry out tasks and missions."

The Indonesian army generals watched this development with some chagrin, but they were themselves partly to blame for it. The long string of human rights abuses—from the 1991 Santa Cruz massacre up to the abduction of students and the alleged promotion of anti-Chinese rioting over 1997–98, and the use of violent militias in East Timor's 1999 referendum—had made the Indonesian military a pariah in the West. Its officers were barred from attending staff colleges and other specialist courses, and sales of military equipment and spare parts were embargoed, grounding much of the air force.

The remedy would have been a thorough purge and the prosecution of personnel widely known to bear responsibility for the various atrocities. Instead, the response was partial and partisan in terms of internal army rivalries. The notable prosecutions were of eleven Kopassus junior officers and soldiers in the Tim Mawar case. But only some received (very light) jail terms, and they were released early. Their two commanding officers at the time—the Kostrad chief, Prabowo Subianto (who admitted "command responsibility"), and the Kopassus commander, Muchdi Purwopranjono—were dishonorably discharged and did not face court-martial. Their colonel was let off. As we shall see, the main case was the court-martial of other Kopassus members who took part in the November 1991 murder of the Papuan leader Theys Eluay, which also resulted in light sentences and pats on the back from the then army chief, Riyamizard Ryucudu.

Kopassus itself was reorganized in June 2001. Group 4, its component most notorious for the New Order's extrajudicial killings, and Group 5 were dissolved and replaced by a training command and a new antiterrorism force of two battalions, named Unit 81. But the 6,000 Kopassus personnel—a number that made it one of the world's largest Special Forces units—remained largely in place. Military chiefs insisted that the visible efforts, which included regular lectures on human rights by the International Red Cross and other bodies, satisfied all the necessary reforms.

Numerous international witnesses observed the military-sponsored campaign to intimidate the East Timorese against voting for independence in August 1999 and the deliberate killing, destruction, and forced population movement that followed. The permissive and complicit stance of the Indonesian army and police were all too apparent. Leaked intercepts showed a chain of command and control back to generals in Jakarta. Indonesia's own National Human Rights Commission identified many of those implicated. Yet at an ad hoc human rights tribunal, established in Jakarta, only six defendants were convicted: four of them Indonesian army and police officers, and two Timorese civilians. The convictions were all overturned on appeal, except for that of the hapless last provincial governor, a Timorese named Abilio Soares. Several other figures regarded as leaders in the state-sponsored terror campaign went on to higher positions; one of them, Mahidin Simbolon, became the military commander of the Papuan region.

The American-led "War on Terror" that began after the September 11 attacks by al-Qaeda in New York and Washington, and the subsequent invasions of Afghanistan and Iraq, began to break the isolation of the Indonesian military. Jakarta became a more important friend in the Islamic world. Australia and Britain took an early lead in resuming training with and support of Kopassus. The US military was prevented from following suit, however, by legislation known as the Leahy provisions. And all these governments maintained blacklists, against which defense attachés ran the names of personnel to be involved in training and visits. It was a constant source of Indonesian complaint and diplomatic démarche when high-level officers found themselves excluded.

The Aceh peace settlement in 2005 took the last big internal conflict out of the hands of the Indonesian military. The following year it was to hand over responsibility inside Papua to the police, along with lucrative assignments, such as protecting the Freeport mine, while its own combat soldiers there were tasked with protecting the very quiet borders. "The question now is: what does the defence force do?" asks the retired general, Agus Widjojo. "I don't see them out in the society. I don't see them being employed in counter-terrorism, or anything. So there is a challenge to inject the tradition and classical form of pride that [serving in] a defence force is an honour to defend the sovereignty and national integrity of the country."

THE PATHWAY TO THIS DILEMMA can be traced back to the very start of reformasi. In 1998 Yudhoyono, Widjojo, and another army general, Agus Wirahadikusumah, were invited to Canberra by the Australian defense department. The three had been classmates at the Indonesian armed forces academy in Magelang, Central Java, graduating in 1973. As the New Order began breaking open, they had all become known as critical and reformist thinkers who were advocating a more "professional" army that would fit into a more open society.

Apart from being too liberal, any one of the three would have met the widely perceived requirements to follow Suharto within the New Order: they were all Javanese, Muslim, and of the army, and all had formal higher education and international savvy. Wirahadikusumah had New Order lineage, being the son of one of Suharto's trusted generals who became a vice president, while Yudhoyono had married into an even more illustrious line. His wife, Kristiani Herawati, was a daughter of the Special Forces general Sarwo Edhie Wibowo, who had led the forerunners of Kopassus in the deadly campaign against the PKI in Java and Bali.

Wirahadikusumah was the boldest in advocating a complete and immediate return to the barracks. Widjojo supported a longer-term move in the same direction. Yudhoyono had had much more intellectual engagement with Western democracies than any of his peers. Two years after topping his class at the academy, he began the first of several postings overseas for military courses and a master's degree in business administration in the United States, alternating with service in East Timor (where no specific abuses were attached to him or his unit). Yet those who talked with the group found Yudhoyono to be the least comfortable with the idea that an Indonesian president should be open to free criticism by an uncontrolled media. "That has always been SBY," says Widjojo, speaking of his friend's notorious caution.

After returning from Canberra, Yudhoyono became the headquarters general in charge of social and political affairs, renamed as

the Territorial Command, which supervised all the many garrisons of
the army. He stood stoically at the shoulder of General Wiranto as reports streamed in of military-sponsored violence during the East Timorese referendum. Wahid made him minister of mines in late 1999
and then coordinating minister for politics and security from August
2000 but sacked him in July 2001 when he refused to back Wahid's
desperate plan for a state of emergency to prevent his impeachment.

As a cabinet minister under Wahid, Yudhoyono is not known
to have played any role, except passively, in what turned out to be
the career suicide of his classmate, friend, and coauthor, Agus Wirahadikusumah, who had been a strong internal critic of Wiranto
and had supported his sacking by Wahid in January 2000. Wirahadikusumah had also irked senior colleagues with his call for an
immediate end to the "territorial" role of the army, by which it stationed posts at the levels of province, the regions (or *kabupaten*), the
subdistricts (called *kecamatan*), and even the villages below them,
where noncommissioned officers, known as *babinsa,* kept an eye on
the very grass roots. In some ways this system was another aspect
of Dwifungsi, allowing the army to closely monitor and intervene in
civil affairs. It had been strengthened by Suharto, first in order to
eradicate the PKI and then to enforce tight political supervision. But
it had also become an excellent way to spot openings for moneymaking, legal or illegal.

The territorial role was one of the army's activities that the majority of senior generals were not willing to give up. It went to the
historic heart of their strategic doctrine. The military's change of
name in 1998—from the Angkatan Bersenjata Republik Indonesia
(ABRI, Armed Forces of the Republic of Indonesia) to the Tentara
Nasional Indonesia (TNI, Indonesian National Army)—was drawing a line in the sand. It connected the military directly to the nation
rather than to the state and harked back to the revolutionary days
of 1945–49. "The territorial function is a religion for the TNI," says
Agus Widjojo, quoting military historian Salim Said. "They perceive
the territorial function as the frontline for the oneness of the TNI
with the people, the frontline for social stability and intelligence
gathering, and TNI thought. As long as it is not used for political
purposes or business purposes, it's just normal."

Yet to its military critics, the territorial role was based on the
strategic premises of the 1940–70 period. The first of these was that

the Indonesian air and sea forces were not strong enough to prevent a foreign enemy from lodging in its territory, nor then to defeat that enemy with conventional power. Instead, Indonesian soldiers would have to be ready to sustain an indefinite people's war, in which the support and supplies of the civilian population would be critical. The second was that the TNI had to prepare for a war for hearts and minds against an enemy within domestic communities—ideological, religious, or separatist.

Wahid had Wirahadikusumah, the son of a general who had been one of Suharto's vice presidents, elevated to head the powerful Kostrad command in March 2000 and saw him as a future army chief. In this new role, Wirahadikusumah quickly began making waves, holding discussions on military reforms with a few like-minded officers and civilians. He also uncovered a large amount of embezzlement in Kostrad's welfare foundation. In June a mysterious document surfaced that claimed to be the record of a meeting held by Wirahadikusumah and another general, Saurip Kadi, at their military housing in Jakarta. It contained strong criticism of their senior officers and became the pretext for sidelining the two generals from important command roles. Wirahadikusumah died suddenly in August 2001, aged forty-nine, of a suspected heart attack.

It can only be said that Yudhoyono was one of the majority of generals who did not support the call for a radical retreat to "professionalism." On replacing Wahid, Megawati restored Yudhoyono as coordinating minister, and his time in that role included the return to conflict in Aceh in May 2003. Leaked cables from the US embassy in Jakarta show Yudhoyono equivocating about American suggestions to delay the withdrawal of foreign monitors, part of a diplomatic effort to keep the cessation-of-hostilities agreement alive.

When Yudhoyono became president in October 2004, many hoped he would push boldly ahead with deeper reforms in the area of political security, after the regressions under Megawati. The Aceh peace accord encouraged these hopes. His sweeping first-round victory in the 2009 presidential elections gave him an unprecedented, powerful mandate. When one looks back on his personality and record, however, it's clear that both Indonesians and outside observers should not have expected anything other than great caution from Yudhoyono in the area of military reform.

Early in his term, he showed some nervousness about possible intervention by disgruntled elements of the army. The WikiLeaks cables from the US embassy report that presidential aides sought urgent updates on the Thai military coup of September 2006, which overthrew the elected prime minister, Thaksin Shinawatra. Dadan Irawan, a member of *Golkar*'s central board who had good access to the palace, told the embassy that "the President was concerned that his enemies in the military, as well as the political elite, might find inspiration in the success of the bloodless coup."

Yudhoyono was also linking the Thai coup to another event. That June, an army officer visiting the house of a recently deceased general to collect his service pistol had been astonished to find a collection of 185 firearms, including assault rifles and ammunition. Yudhoyono's advisers were saying that the president took "extremely seriously" rumors of destabilization plans, based on the dead general's closeness to Riyamizard Ryacudu and other displaced generals. But this message could equally have been Yudhoyono's gambit to discredit his opponents.

But in general the military had a lot to thank Yudhoyono for. He dug in his heels against persistent American pressure to open up the records of Kopassus and remove individuals involved in abuses. Kopassus, backed by the airborne brigades of Kostrad, remained the spearhead of the Indonesian army's fighting force. Although, like Wellington's troops, it sometimes frightened its own commanders in chief, its mystique as the force that held the nation together at moments of extreme peril was something Yudhoyono and his family circle were evidently as keen to preserve as anyone else in the military.

The WikiLeaks cables reveal him saying that a resumption of ties with Kopassus was the key to the "strategic partnership" sought by George W. Bush's administration. With his brother-in-law Pramono Edhie Wibowo taking a turn as the force's commander, Yudhoyono felt able to give assurances of its transformed institutional culture. For one thing, all orders now had to be given in writing, which created an evidence trail of command responsibility. Things had been different in the past: the writer of a Kopassus history, author Ken Conboy, records Prabowo Subianto telling him in 1997: "Indonesia is the best country for conducting covert operations because there are no written orders."

The transition to American acceptance, however, was slowed when news got out in mid-2007 that the Kopassus Group 2, based near Yogyakarta, had feted Tommy Suharto, newly free after serving just five years of his fifteen-year sentence for the contract killing of the judge who had convicted him of fraud, at their anniversary party. "Officers interviewed by journalists after the event casually dismissed Suharto's checkered past as unimportant," the embassy reported.

As late as October 2009, when a visit by the new US president, Barack Obama, was being planned, the standoff between Indonesia and the United States was unresolved. "Yudhoyono takes the issue seriously to the extent that he wonders how he can proceed with a Comprehensive Partnership with the United States if the United States does not treat Indonesia as a true partner," presidential aide Dino Djalal (who later became his country's ambassador in Washington) was reported as telling the embassy. Joint activities with the Kopassus Unit 81 were eventually cleared during Obama's visit the next year.

Yudhoyono also stuck by his old academy classmate, Syafrie Syamsuddin, despite a UN investigation putting him near the top of its recommended list for war crimes prosecution over the 1999 violence in East Timor, over his presence in Dili at the time of the 1991 Santa Cruz massacre, over his command of the Jakarta garrison during the 1998 violence, and over his alleged role in the murky side of the Aceh conflict. Syafrie had remained the military chief of information while Yudhoyono was coordinating minister and then became the vice minister (or administrative head) of the defense ministry throughout Yudhoyono's presidency. He remained persona non grata in the United States, which was something of a handicap for Jakarta as it tried to develop a strategic partnership with the Americans. Ultimately, however, he was passed over by Yudhoyono in 2007 when he might have been made army chief.

A telling episode took place in August 2009, when an East Timorese man named Martenus Bere came across the border from Indonesia to attend a wedding in his hometown, Suai. Ten years earlier Bere had led a militia group that, along with Indonesian army and police, had massacred priests and civilians who had gathered for safety in the town's cathedral after the independence referendum. He was spotted, arrested, and taken to Dili. Timor's prime minister,

José Xanana Gusmão, came under heavy pressure from Yudhoyono to return Bere to Indonesia. He was duly handed over to the Indonesian embassy and allowed to leave.

In 2008 members of the DPR initiated a bill to put military personnel under the jurisdiction of civilian courts for offenses under civil law. Initially, Yudhoyono seemed to be in favor. Then the executive swung against it. Certainly, there were sound reasons to have misgivings. The law would have handed responsibility for investigating crimes by soldiers to the police. Ongoing interforce rivalries and suspected turf wars over protection rackets, which sparked frequent street brawls between soldiers and police, were one thing. But with the police still widely involved in case fixing with prosecutors and judges, the potential for soldiers to be drawn into corrupt settlements was very real.

The decision to stay with military justice did, however, create a need for the armed forces to demonstrate that they were serious about punishing abuses. In 2008 a court-martial gave jail terms to thirteen marines who had fired toward a crowd resisting eviction from their unit's land near Surabaya, killing four civilians. The military police opened cases against two generals for misappropriating state property. One of them, a retired officer who had become a film actor, saw the arresting party off with a firearm but then died before his case came to court-martial in 2010. In 2013 a military court gave a four-year jail sentence to a former Kostrad chief, Djaja Suparman, for selling military land in Surabaya to a toll-road company in 1998 and pocketing some of the proceeds; the case is now under appeal.

In March 2013 Kopassus again blotted its copybook. A sergeant attached to the Yogyakarta garrison in intelligence duties got into a late-night argument in a city nightclub with four toughs from the southeastern Nusatenggara islands. The four killed the soldier and were soon arrested by police. Three days later, eleven of the victim's Kopassus comrades, disguised in ski masks and armed with AK-47s, forced their way into the city's Cebongan prison. They threatened and beat twelve prison guards, two of whom required hospitalization, and then went to the cells and executed the four suspects. On the way out, they seized the prison's closed-circuit television recordings.

The case resulted in much stiffer punishments than those given in the Tim Mawar and Theys Eluay cases a decade or more earlier, with jail terms ranging from four to eleven years. Yet the sentences were widely seen as lighter than what could be expected for premeditated murder in civil law. In addition, the court-martial atmospherics caused much concern. The three judges were outranked by the defense officers. Several witnesses declined to testify. At no point was it explained why the Kopassus sergeant had been at the nightclub or what had sparked the fatal fight. Was he moonlighting as a security guard? Was he collecting intelligence of some sort? Or was he dealing drugs?

Inside and outside the court milled hundreds of former soldiers and other muscular civilians, dressed in camouflage, from a group called the Sekber Keistimewaan (roughly, the Secretariat of Special Autonomy), a coalition of Yogyakarta royalist and paramilitary groups. They disrupted hearings with shouts praising the accused as "heroes" and "warriors," locked the gates of the court compound, threatened civilian monitors, and shouted racist remarks at attendees from the home province of the victims. On being sentenced, the convicted ringleader vowed to serve his jail term and then resume the fight against *premanisme* (gangsterism). Clearly, training about human rights and the rule of law still had some way to go with Kopassus.

Progress on the divestment of military businesses lagged until March 2008, eighteen months out from the legally stipulated deadline. A Ministry of Defense team had identified 1,520 businesses, but only a dozen were of any size. Many of the others were bankrupt. The vast majority were small-scale cooperatives and charitable foundations aimed at helping out soldiers and their families with cut-price household supplies and education fees.

A respected accountant and stock market official previously on the board of the anticorruption commission, Erry Riyana Hardjapamekas, was brought in to sell off the larger concerns and to set rules for the smaller ones. He found twenty-three TNI-related foundations, with fifty-three associated enterprises, plus 1,098 cooperatives with a gross value of about $320 million at the end of 2007. About 40 percent of the 8,493 staff running the cooperatives were active-duty soldiers. In addition, about 25,000 hectares of military land was being farmed out for commercial use as mines, golf courses, markets and stores, factories, offices, storage facilities, animal keeping, meeting halls, gas stations, car showrooms, restaurants, hotels, television relay stations, mosques, public roads, hospitals and clinics, primary, secondary, and tertiary schools, and residential complexes.

Hardjapamekas recommended selling off the enterprises, putting the land under the control of the Ministry of Finance, and setting up a chain of civilian PX stores to provide goods for military families without active soldiers being employed. The divestment was reported to have been completed by the end of 2009, but few details were released. Anecdotally, it appeared that many prime military-owned assets, such as Jakarta's Borobudur Hotel, had already been sold to businessmen close to army leaders, such as the property, hotel, and entertainment industry tycoon Tomy Winata, as had some landholdings of the Suharto family.

The civilian defense minister during Yudhoyono's first term, a respected political science professor named Juwono Sudarsono, had been steadily working on the military budget to compensate for the loss of irregular income. The defense allocation rose steadily from $2.2 billion in 2004 and by 2014 was around $8 billion. Sudarsono pulled more civilian talent into his ministry and gradually assumed more influence over force structure and equipment procurement. His ministry developed a doctrine of the "minimum essential force" necessary for Indonesia's defense and gradually got it accepted by the uniformed services. The initial focuses were on improving airlift capability, so that forces and supplies could be quickly moved around the country, on reviving the navy's maritime security capability, and on building the army's ability to respond swiftly to the natural disasters that frequently hit the nation.

By 2007, resources were being found, somehow, for new strike capability. The air force gained spare parts to refurbish its largely grounded F-16 fighter squadron and ordered a squadron of newer models. On a trip to Moscow, Yudhoyono accepted credits worth about $1 billion to order a small number of the Sukhoi-30 fighters. Other orders were to follow over coming years; in August 2013 the defense vice minister, Syafrie Syamsuddin, announced a five-year weaponry modernization program costing $13.2 billion. The reported components included twelve of a version of a German-designed submarine to be built with South Korea, Dutch frigates, trainer jets, new-model Hercules and C-395 transport aircraft, and a fleet of eight Apache attack helicopters, declared to be for use against piracy in areas like the Malacca Strait.

Not to be outdone, the army spent $287 million to buy 104 used models of the German-made Leopard-2 main battle tank, as well as about fifty heavy armored cars, which Syamsuddin announced would be parked around Jakarta to "defend the capital," including some in a new underground car park under Merdeka Square. Military analysts were baffled by the deal, since the 62-ton tank was too big to put on any existing air force or navy transport to take to the Indonesian peripheries or to cross most of the country's bridges. Its most likely use would be to intimidate crowds in Jakarta, should riots on the scale of 1998 ever break out again. Prestige was also seen as a factor: Singapore had also bought the Leopard-2, and Malaysia, a similar tank from Poland.

The US diplomatic cables released by WikiLeaks show that the Indonesian air force was the most willing service to join supply-and-exercise arrangements with the United States; the "truculent" navy was the most wary. The diversity of sourcing reflected a lesson the Indonesian military had drawn from its experiences of the previous decades: it would try to minimize the risk of being immobilized by any further arms embargoes, particularly from the West.

BUT WHAT IS THE ARMY FOR? Agus Widjojo's question still haunts the 340,000-strong force. The legislated tasks "other than war" scarcely keep it busy, apart from after major natural disasters. Involvement in UN peacekeeping operations has been a valued activity, with about 1,000 personnel assigned to the UN force in Lebanon and contingents sent to the Congo and elsewhere. But rather than accepting a sharp cut in numbers, the army has turned back to its traditional doctrine of people's warfare, embodied in its "territorial" arm.

On being installed as the armed forces' chief in December 2006, army general Djoko Santoso pledged to work on "professionalizing" the military but added that *professionalism,* in the Indonesian context, meant not only tactics and control but also its identity as a "people's" and a national army. In November 2008 he declared that the territorial system, which had been undergoing dissolution, had been "reactivated" after the second Bali bombing, in order to help the police combat terrorism. Although the noncommissioned officers, or babinsa, at the lower levels of this system had only one role—intelligence collection—he claimed that they had proven effective in this role: in one case, they had tipped off the authorities to some non-Indonesian terrorists hiding in a mosque. Being permanently resident in local communities, these babinsa were able to detect in local residents' daily behavior evidence pointing to nonlocal elements. This program had been so successful that terrorists were no longer staying in the villages, Santoso claimed. (The general was wrong on the latter point, as the police continued to find Jemaah Islamiyah elements hiding in villages across Java in subsequent years.)

Widjojo sees little use for the *babinsa*. "If we go to the villages they are idle," he says. "What mission or task can you give them? Counter-terrorism—what can they do? They note down how many bearded people pass the Kodim headquarters? There's no legality of how a TNI soldier can act. And if we force them and give them expectations as though they can act, we will push them into problems. Just like we have pushed them in various instances before, including in East Timor."

But even the civilian defense minister at the time, Sudarsono, was sharing similar concerns with his uniformed counterpart, Santoso. He pointed out to American visitors the new threats from nonstate actors and the importance therefore of the Security Forces having the cooperation of the civilian population.

One corollary was that the army, if it wanted to win support across the whole diverse nation, had to reduce the historical dominance of the Javanese in its officer corps. In this, Sudarsono's efforts appear successful. In 1970 recruits to the armed forces academy comprised 58 percent Javanese (the Javanese proportion of the national population was then 51 percent) and 15 percent Sundanese (from West Java). A 2009 study by researcher Riefqi Muna found that 39 percent of the new recruits were Javanese (by then 42 percent of the population), while the Sundanese component had dropped back to 8 percent, even though they made up 15 percent of the population.

The usefulness of the army in fighting terrorism and unrest is now a constant refrain of successive armed forces chiefs, while the police continue to demonstrate that, at least with terrorism, they are coping quite well. In cases of serious civil unrest, the police have been less adroit. Particularly where religious or sectarian clashes are involved, police have hesitated to intervene, have sometimes ended up charging the victims of attack, or have been overwhelmed by the scale of rioting. Their ground commanders are reluctant to admit losing control. Any requests to call out the army would have to be passed to the police command, across to the president or his coordinating security minister, and back down the army's chain of command.

As the second decade of the century began, a series of attacks on the minority Ahmadiyah sect (regarded as heretical by many orthodox Muslims) and on Christian proselytizers for alleged blasphemy brought the issue to the fore. Colonels from both forces were sacked, and generals had their appointments to regional commands cut short, before Yudhoyono's government set down rules allowing provincial governors to call out the army whether or not requested by the police. But in a democracy, the use of armed soldiers must surely be the very last resort. A better answer is a well-trained police force, which should be able to use graduated methods of nonlethal crowd control, and whose local commanders should feel confident enough to call early for reinforcements if they are needed.

Still, the drumbeat behind the army's territorial role has grown louder. In 2000, the army announced a new scheme called TNI Manunggal Membangun Desa (Army Focus on Village Development), a name that recalled the ABRI Masuk Desa (Armed Forces in the Villages) program during the New Order, a version of the civic-action doctrine that became intensely resented for the intimidation that came with it. Army engineers were volunteered for new road building in Papua. New kodam (regional commands) have been created, one in Aceh and two in Kalimantan, each with its own hierarchy of "organic" posts stationed down to the villages.

The army has not eschewed the use of civilian militias to apply violence and collect intelligence at a remove. Of course, this is not unusual in counterinsurgency campaigns: it became a feature of American, Australian, and perhaps other allied forces in Iraq and Afghanistan. As Widjojo points out, it has spread to Indonesia's political parties, which all deploy various satgas (taskforce) or pemuda (youth) wings dressed in camouflage uniforms for their members' security.

In 2012, veterans of the first class to graduate from the Magelang defense force academy (in 1970) reflected ruefully on their careers, which were largely spent trying to quell resistance in Timor and to defend the New Order, only to end in retreat from both. Their book of reminiscences is bittersweet. "It's an irony that the involvement of East Timor in the history of Indonesia began and ended with a failure of intelligence," the authors wrote, referring to the assurances that their invasion of Timor in 1975 would meet no significant resistance and that the grateful Timorese would vote in 1999 to stay in Indonesia.

They also made a more general point: "The question that always crops up among us is that the 1945 Constitution never mandated the Dual Function, never mandated the integration of the police as a part of the armed forces, or the formation of civilian groups as part of the armed forces as well as the formation of armed civilian groups." The latter was the result of the "romanticism" that lingered from the last years of the 1940s in *wujud kelaskaran* (the formation of volunteer irregular soldiers).

Outside the military, the territorial doctrine also has many critics. Regarding the military business divestment, according to a leaked US embassy cable, the financial expert Erry Riyana Hardjapamekas privately expressed his belief that it was inevitably linked to the illegal side of moneymaking, including fishing, logging, the misuse of military assets, prostitution, and gambling. He rated these as more significant in their value and in their impact on morale than the legal activities and more widespread across the archipelago through the territorial commands. "Hardjapamekas sees the territorial administration as a legacy of the past which needs to disappear in order for a modern military to emerge," the embassy reported. "Curtailing the illegal lifeline would hasten the transition, he believes. This would go hand-in-hand with troop reductions to pare the TNI down to a leaner force commensurate with Indonesia's defence needs." Hardjapamekas saw extensive support within the TNI for such a move, as most of the illegal activities were in the hands of senior officers. The more junior officers and the rank-and-file soldiers either were not able to benefit or rejected the activity in principle, due to their exposure to democratic values. An order from the top could set this process in motion.

That order has not yet been given. The Indonesian army still has thousands of officers living and operating among the civilian population, carrying loaded sidearms. At their best, the territorial officers act as advocates and defenders of the powerless citizens, where the police are often more closely linked to local power groups and mafias. At their worst, they are oppressive and extortive. At the end of Yudhoyono's two terms, the armed forces remain in an awkward halfway position, stuck between being the pervasive political and social institution they were during the Suharto era, and developing as a modern fighting force that is capable of beating off external attacks.

7

SUPREME
COMMODITY

There is a fascination in coal, the supreme commodity of the age in which we are camped like bewildered travellers in a garish, unrestful hotel.

—Joseph Conrad, *Victory* (1915)

ON THE BANK OF A WIDE, DEEP RIVER LITTLE KNOWN TO THE OUTSIDE WORLD, THREE gantries deposit plumes of coal into huge square barges. Behind them, front loaders shuttle around piles of coal in a vast stockyard, loading it onto conveyor belts. Farther back, a straight dirt highway stretches thirty kilometers into the hinterland. On either side lie marshes, drainage canals, and rows of newly planted oil palms. Every hundred meters, a laden dump truck is heading toward the river port and then returning to unseen coal mines. A passing storm whips up clouds of black dust. The loading goes on. When each barge is heaped with 8,000 tons of coal, tugboats nudge it out into the current and guide it downstream to the sea.

The jetty at Sungai Puting, in the south of Kalimantan, as Indonesia calls its majority share of the vast island of Borneo, and many others like it tell part of the good luck story that arrived in Indonesia after the hard times and turmoil of the five years of reformasi.

If Yudhoyono and Kalla created political-strategic luck out of the Aceh calamity, their economic luck was a windfall, coming out of the commodity boom set off by runaway growth in China and India. The two rising Asian giants sucked in everything from gold and copper to timber, palm oil, and spices. In particular, their demand for thermal coal, used to generate electricity, seemed insatiable.

Indonesia was primed to take advantage. The main coal mines run by the Dutch, in Sumatra, had been taken over by a new state company in 1950. But since colonial times, coal had taken second place to petroleum, and there was little or no export trade. At the end of the 1970s, the Suharto government created a "master plan" for developing Kalimantan, and some of the big international mining and energy companies obtained leases.

As part of its acquisition of the American mining giant Utah, Australia's BHP gained an 80 percent share of a venture called Arutmin, with its 20 percent partner, the group owned by the rising business and political figure Aburizal Bakrie. The British-Australian firm Rio Tinto and oil giant BP found extensive coal reserves and got their Kaltim Prima Coal (KPC) mine into production in 1991. An Australian-born entrepreneur in Jakarta, Graeme Robertson, led a group of well-connected investors in a third very large thermal coal producer, Adaro. All these ownerships got a profound shake-up when the 1997–98 plunge in the rupiah raised the effective cost of debt financing, at a time when coal prices were in a long slump. The older foreign-owned ventures were also approaching the deadlines set in their contracts with the government for divestment of foreign ownership down to 49 percent. They wanted out.

By 2002, confidence had improved enough in Indonesia for Bakrie's Bumi Resources to buy out BHP's 80 percent stake in Arutmin and to acquire the KPC venture from Rio Tinto and BP. Control of the Adaro mine was snapped up by the Jakarta businessman Edwin Soeryadjaya, son of the ethnic Chinese founder of the Toyota distributor Astra, when a foreign bank gained a large block of shares as a result of a loan default. Robertson's group sold their remaining stake three years later, amid threats that forced him to move to Singapore for his safety. With this leg up from Australian and British investors, who opted out just as the coal market was about to turn around in the first years of the new century, Bakrie and Soeryadjaya had control of some of the world's biggest producers of high-calorie, low-sulfur, and low-ash thermal coal, which conveniently were located between China and India. The revaluation of the coal assets turned both men into billionaires. For Soeryadjaya, it restored the family fortune that had been shattered in the mid-1990s when a bank in his father's conglomerate had collapsed and he had lost control of Astra.

Meanwhile, the devolution of powers to Indonesia's kabupaten (regencies, or large subprovincial districts) took effect in 2001. The bupati (regents) now had the power to issue and regulate mining licenses. This set off a frenzied scramble for coal licenses across Kalimantan and parts of Sumatra. From the existing 850 or so mining leases issued in 2001, the bupati added another 11,000 over the next decade.

No previous experience was required for new small-scale miners. The level coal seams lay just under a moderate layer of overburden in the flatlands of southern and eastern Kalimantan; it only took bulldozer work to expose them. The wide rivers, such as the Puting, were natural infrastructure: no expensive railways were required, as in Australia or North America. Many local governments either failed to stipulate remediation of the land afterward or did not enforce any requirements. Parts of East Kalimantan now look like the aftermath of some nuclear exchange: they are dotted with vast excavations filled with water, which is too acidic for fish life.

The coal boom made millionaires of dozens of new entrepreneurs. Some were well connected, like the former Kopassus officer and general Luhut Panjaitan, who had been trade minister during Abdurrahman Wahid's presidency. At the other extreme were figures like the former truck and taxi drivers Aman Jagau, Abdurrahman Midi, and Andi Syamsudin Arsyad, who built up large coal mines from very small beginnings. All now wield significant clout: the last of the trio, known as Hajji Isan, owns a small airline connecting the provincial capital of South Kalimantan, Banjarmasin, to a town near his mines on the island of Pulau Laut. He became noted nationally for a feud with another new coal magnate, a former schoolteacher named Jahrian, over payment for a new access road to a loading jetty.

Another coal miner and part owner of the Sungai Puting jetty, Hajji Sulaiman, became the richest man in Banjarmasin. His father had been a small trader in timber and rattan. His son Hasnuryadi married the daughter of former vice president Jusuf Kalla and won a seat in the national parliament in 2014 as a Golkar candidate.

The yellow Golkar flag flies outside the palatial homes of wealthy hajji citizens in small towns like Binuang. In many cases, their pilgrimages to Mecca have not abated their propensity to spend on ostentatious luxury. Some build shopping malls and big hotels in their hometowns. Bentleys, Rolls-Royces, and Hummers trundle the streets of Kalimantan cities. One hajji is reputed to have lost $15 million on two occasions in the casinos of Singapore and has set up his own small (and illegal) casino on a leased island off the Kalimantan coastline. Hajji Sulaiman bought a football team, and he's planting huge palm-oil estates for when the coal runs out.

Getting a coal concession was the start. No further capital outlay was necessarily required. The operating rights could be hired out, and cash would roll in. Miners without any political clout or startup capital could dig a few hectares on the fringes of big concessions like Arutmin or Adaro to get some cash flow—not that anyone had much idea who had the rights to what. A review of five districts by one nongovernment organization found up to forty overlapping concessions on one piece of land. In another, successive bupati had issued coal leases that totaled three times the area of their kabupaten. Local elections became fights for the right to hand out mining licenses to cronies. The bupati became wealthy enough to bribe the judges in the inevitable appeals and to head off any move in the national parliament to curtail their powers.

The manager of one medium-sized mine has called the organization of coal loading at one river jetty as "organized crime." A "horror story" is how a cargo superintendent describes the same one. "The barges queue up, and you pay to jump the queue," he says. "The police and local authorities do everything they can to stop you loading. You pay $1 a tonne the first day, $1.50 the second day, or they might take your barge away. There's nothing you can do about it. It would take years to [get] settlement in court." At one jetty, thirteen officials in the customs office require payments, made through a colleague who issues receipts for all desks. Small miners demand cash from buyers: 50 percent down, 40 percent when the barge is loaded, and the final 10 percent with a certificate of analysis about the coal quality—the certificate being negotiable.

When the barges reach the coast, ships from China sometimes arrive without paperwork, load up, and sail off, relying on bribery if they're intercepted by the Indonesian navy. It's a similar story with those metal ores available by surface digging—notably nickel and manganese, which are found across the eastern islands of Indonesia. With or without licenses from local governments, small miners make direct cash sales and delivery, mostly to Chinese ships. Up to 3 million Indonesians are also active in informal sluicing for gold, from the hills of West Java, just outside Jakarta, to the inland jungles of Kalimantan (which are inhabited by the Dayak, former headhunters), to the waste dumps of the giant Freeport mine in Papua.

These exports are not always captured in official data, nor are royalties and other taxes paid on production and sales, but somehow it was calculated in 2011 that Indonesia had become the world's biggest coal exporter, shipping out 295 million tons, which pushed Australia into second place. Enough money flowed into the Indonesian economy to keep the trade balance in surplus through the 2000s and to drive 6.5 percent annual growth in gross national product. By 2008 Indonesia had moved out of the World Bank's category of poor nations into the "lower middle income" group, with a per capita income of $2,254.

The revenue flow and foreign reserve buildup allowed Yudhoyono in 2006 to make the grand gesture of repaying Indonesia's last debt to the IMF from the 1997–98 rescue package, a $7.8-billion reserve loan, three years ahead of schedule. He also dissolved the Consultative Group on Indonesia, the consortium of foreign aid donors who had met annually since the start of the New Order to coordinate their programs.

INDONESIA'S WEALTHY AND POWERFUL certainly did not feel their country was an aid case. The cities were awash with consumption. Land prices spiraled. The number of shopping malls in Jakarta reached 173 by 2013, outdoing one another in displays of luxury brands; one offered a $1.2-million Lamborghini as the prize in a lottery, which shoppers who spent a certain amount could enter. Similarly high-end cars lined the streets outside fashionable nightspots, like Tomy Winata's Bengkel (Repair Shop), where socialites thronged, wearing brand-name fashion and expensive jewels.

A much more modest economy prevailed in the village of Srihardjo, an hour's drive southeast of Yogyakarta, where the natural resources are just land and water. This was the site of a famous study of rural poverty in the early 1970s, by Masri Singarimbun and David Penny, which shattered complacency in Jakarta about Indonesia's happy peasantry. The researchers found that a typical household could get by if it had a hectare of land, 70 percent of it for rice growing and the rest for a vegetable garden and productive trees: this was *cukupan* (enough). But two-thirds of Srihardjo's people did not have enough.

The most important cash earner in the village was palm sugar, obtained by climbing a palm tree and cutting its flower so that the sweet sap flowed into a container over several hours. Four out of five villagers had never even been into Yogyakarta. No one had radios. These days, a sixty-two-year-old man, Sugarti, is the only one still engaged in the physically demanding work of tapping palm sugar. The village has developed some recognition across Java for a specialty snack known as *peyek,* a peanut-studded biscuit, made entirely from ingredients bought from outside. Farmers now use more machines in rice growing.

Few young people want to work on the land anymore, says village secretary Sunardi. Most go to high schools or vocational colleges before seeking work in cities. Family size has come down to two children on average, and several primary schools are close to being merged with others. Everyone has mobile phones, and there are 150 cars and many more motorbikes. The range of hills to the east, the Gunung Kidul, was once worn bare by poverty-stricken villagers grazing their animals. Now, the hills are covered by teak trees. The region is by no means prosperous, but it's resilient enough to have recovered from the big earthquake in 2006 that damaged most of the houses and killed eighty-nine of its 10,000 people.

Such progress had steadily reduced the proportion of Indonesians living in absolute poverty from about half the population when the Srihardjo study was made, to around 17 percent by 1996, just before the economic collapse of 1997–98. By the start of Yudhoyono's presidency in 2004, the poverty that had ballooned again during the crisis had been brought back to the same level. Then the rapid growth of the economy enabled further progress on poverty reduction, to just under 12 percent by 2011. This is based on a calculation of needs for bare existence: the number of food calories, shelter, and other necessities that are roughly attainable on $1.25 a day. Above that still hover about 40 percent of the population in a precarious, very low-income strata.

As Yudhoyono's presidency moved into its second term (2009–14), the top and bottom income earners diverged. The bottom 40 percent of the population saw their consumption grow by around 2 percent a year. But the top 10 percent enjoyed rises of 8 to 9 percent. The country's Gini coefficient (a widely used measure of income distribution, named after the Italian statistician who developed it) had been just 0.29 in 1959 in the meagre last period of the Sukarno era, which indicated a sharing of scarcity. Then it had fluctuated between 0.33 and 0.36 during the New Order, showing more divergence in wealth. Over the first decade or so of the new century, inequality jumped sharply, with the Gini measure going from 0.32 in 2001 to 0.41 in 2011. Although the income spread is nowhere as wide as in several other rising economies in Asia (China, Malaysia, and Singapore are in the range 0.46 to 0.48, and Thailand a sharper 0.54), "this is new territory for Indonesia," says Asep Suryahadi, the director of Jakarta's respected SMERU Research Institute.

The economic crisis of the late 1990s brought emergency measures to assist poor households, either with rations of subsidized rice or cash handouts. President Wahid started planning for a more concerted, long-term approach, and Megawati's government passed a law mandating a national social protection system, although it lacked practical detail. During Yudhoyono's presidency these efforts burgeoned into a more permanent set of social welfare programs aimed at direct support for the poor.

The most prominent of these was known as the Raskin program, which aimed to supply fifteen kilograms of subsidized rice each month to 17.5 million poor and near-poor households. Another program set aside fees at government public health clinics and hospitals for 18.2 million families, while another gave cash to nearly 5 million families to help with school fees (which were still levied above the eight years of compulsory primary and middle schooling) and other educational expenses. There were also periodic cash handouts at times of "macroeconomic shock," such as price increases caused by the lowering of subsidies on fuel.

But the impact of these on poverty was often dissipated. The Raskin rice handouts required the registration of households by village heads, who often found it hard to resist the clamor from less-deserving households to be included. In practice, the poor ended up with an average 3.8 kilograms of cheap rice. School fees continued to rise fast, encouraging a high dropout rate at the transition points between middle school and senior high school.

Provincial and district governments also started their own social welfare systems. In the Central Java city of Solo, the administration of Mayor Joko Widodo introduced free health treatment and other assistance for the very poor, though it had the effect of drawing in populations from surrounding areas, so the poverty measurement actually went up. Nevertheless, when he was elected to the governorship of Jakarta in 2012, Widodo brought the same measures to the capital.

At the start of 2014, these various health insurance measures were being enveloped in Yudhoyono's most ambitious social welfare scheme, which was to cap his presidency. A new social security agency was to start managing universal health insurance coverage, taking in the existing programs and some of the activities of the four state-owned insurance companies. It would initially cover 122 million people, about 96 million of whom were already included (at least in theory) in the previous health scheme for the poor and near poor; the remainder comprised civil servants and private-sector employees who were already in other state-sector insurance nets. A further 50 million would be covered by regional schemes, leaving about 74 million without cover. The World Bank has estimated it will take another five years, to 2019, to harmonize all the health schemes and extend coverage so that it becomes truly universal.

The government has undertaken to pay the premiums, set at about $1.50 a month, for 85 million poor and near-poor citizens, entitling them to treatment in a "third-class" room in public hospitals. The remainder will pay a basic 5 percent of their income as a premium (in many cases this is split with their employers); those who opt for a high level of coverage will get first- or second-class wards. The scheme is projected to raise and disburse about $20 billion a year, with the central government putting up about $5 billion of the premium income. A second state agency is due to start national schemes of accident and death insurance and age pensions in 2015.

These are highly ambitious goals for a country that is still in the lower-middle-income category, with a majority of its workforce not in formal-sector employment. Before they were launched, Indonesia's existing array of social welfare and free health-care programs were equivalent in total to 0.5 percent of the nation's gross domestic product, far below the average 2.6 percent in the region. Spending on health generally by government was also a modest 2.2 percent of GDP, against the 5 percent level that its own 2009 Law on National Health requires.

IF DOUBTS ARE RAISED about the government's ability to stick to its commitments, with the economic growth rate dropping below 6 percent in 2013 largely because of weaker commodity prices, the finger is usually pointed at the enormous burden of fuel subsidies, which crowd out other types of expenditure. From being an oil exporter up to the turn of the century, Indonesia has become a net oil importer. Oil production declined from 1.5 million barrels a day in 1999 to around 900,000 barrels a day in 2013, while oil consumption has climbed steadily to nearly 1.4 million barrels a day. The crossover from net exporter to net importer occurred around 2003, and the transition was marked in 2008 by Indonesia's withdrawal from the Organization of the Petroleum Exporting Countries (OPEC).

The shortfall has been filled by imports of refined products, since the state monopoly of refining under Pertamina is stuck at a capacity of about 1 million barrels a day. In 2013 these petroleum imports were costing $39 billion a year, running down Indonesia's foreign reserves and causing weakness in the rupiah, which fed domestic inflation. Subsidies of petrol, kerosene, and diesel were chewing up a larger and larger portion of government revenues. This was effectively a government system of reverse "welfare" that chiefly benefited those able to afford cars and motorbikes, who bought fuel more cheaply than motorists in any other net oil-importing nation (even the United States).

In 2005 and 2008, Yudhoyono faced political crises when his economic ministers forced him to go into battle with a parliament that was not ready to share the blame for petrol price increases but all too willing to make capital out of consumer protests. Then in 2009 Yudhoyono cut the administered oil product prices ahead of his reelection, while retaining the ad hoc welfare handout that compensated for the 2008 price rise. In 2012 he balked in the face of parliamentary opposition to another recommended price rise, even though his party was the biggest in the DPR and in theory led a majority coalition. This dragged out the problem, which returned in early 2013, when the subsidy threatened to blow out to $23 billion a year. With the electricity subsidy adding a further $9 billion, this comprised 20 percent of total revenues.

After months of hesitation, the government did increase fuel prices sharply. Even so, the remaining subsidy of about $18 billion still represented 13.3 percent of government revenue, and Indonesia's motorists continued to enjoy remarkably low prices (about 59 cents a liter for petrol, and 50 cents for diesel). The new finance minister, Chatib Basri, was the latest in a long line of economic technocrats who have fought—successfully, for the most part—to keep Indonesia's external balances, its budgets and monetary figures, in respectable shape. He argued for an automatic indexing of fuel prices that would eventually accustom Indonesian consumers to fluctuations and allow a gradual elimination of the subsidy altogether. Ahead of the 2014 election, he was finding no takers. As the economist Hadi Soesastro noted as early as 1979, Indonesia's fuel subsidies were a prison from which the inmates did not wish to escape.

Another way Jakarta could escape from its budgetary corner would be to raise its domestic oil production. Few in the oil business think Indonesia has fully explored its geology and located all its exploitable reserves. But much of the existing and prospective petroleum discoveries lie offshore, in places that require big capital investments and advanced technology. The multinational companies have held back their investments because of the tough bargains that Indonesia's oil and gas authorities won in previous times, and which they kept when more and more alternative locations for oil extraction had opened up around the world. One bright spot was an onshore field at Cepu in East Java, which ExxonMobil was due to bring into production in 2014 with a planned output of 165,000 barrels a day.

Many of the existing fields are running down, partly because of an investment freeze by their operators. About twenty-nine operating contracts will expire between now and 2021, but the government has delayed decisions on whether the existing operators will get extensions. The biggest is the giant Mahakam gas and oil field, developed and run off the coast of East Kalimantan by the French firm Total. With its contract due to expire in 2017, Total is holding back $6.6 billion in planned investments, which it has said are needed to keep up and expand production. The governor of East Kalimantan and the bupati of the nearby Kutai Kertanegara regency, along with nationalist politicians in Jakarta, have urged the state to resume ownership of the site, without suggesting where capital and expertise might be sourced.

While this shakedown was discouraging investment in oil exploration and investment, petroleum-sector ministers and officials were addressing one of the symptoms of the trade gap in oil and the subsidy burden by proposing an $8 billion investment in Pertamina's refining capacity. This would avoid the extra cost of importing refined products instead of crude oil. But given the worldwide overcapacity in refining that resulted from expansions in India and the Middle East, a removal of subsidies and liberalization of oil-sector policies seemed a better way to dampen domestic demand and encourage supplies. Government investment funds could then go to infrastructure that would underpin a broad range of enterprises.

But as well as spending on health, education, and welfare, the subsidy burden limited Indonesia's scope for capital spending. The nation's most conspicuous strides in infrastructure since reformasi have been in mobile telephony and civil aviation, resulting from the initial breaking of public-sector monopolies by the Suharto children and subsequent liberalizations, in which private-sector capital was the driving force.

Like their counterparts in China and India, Indonesians took to mobile telephones with great enthusiasm, buying cheap handsets and using prepaid subscriptions at some of the lowest call rates in the world. Throughout the first decade of the twenty-first century, subscriptions grew at more than 37 percent a year, with three big operators emerging: Telkomsel, Indosat, and XL Axiata. By contrast, the number of fixed-line connections has risen only slowly, to about 12 million, mostly for businesses and big hotels, which needed high-speed broadband.

Customers for fixed wireless connections in the more remote areas have diminished from 18.7 million to about 14 million as the coverage of mobile networks has increased. By 2013 Indonesians had 280 million connected mobile devices, far exceeding the population numbers. The number of individual customers was actually estimated at about 165 million, since many have two or more mobile phones, either to pick up the best reception or to juggle cheaper call prices. It became common to see Indonesian businesspeople laying out a couple of smartphones at a meeting or business lunch table. Indonesia became the third-biggest market for Blackberry by 2012; then the arrival of Android-based phones, which cost as little as $50, meant smartphones were soon used by about 15 percent of customers. This percentage was expected to rise to 40 percent—or 75 million smartphones—by 2015.

Indonesians were using these phones to connect to the Internet. They formed the largest national community on Facebook and accounted for 12 percent of all tweets on Twitter. About 63 million Indonesians were using the Internet one way or another by 2012, according to some estimates. The Internet and mobile messaging became channels for travel bookings and many other transactions, for advertising, and for organization, though the full potential for mobile banking, insurance, and other services was held back by the slowness of regulatory change. Indonesia also became the largest source of spamming and malicious software—at least by volume, if not produced with the same sophistication as that of Chinese or Russian hackers.

When it made use of Internet booking systems, the low-cost carrier model flourished in Indonesia's civil aviation. At first, new private carriers struggled with chartered and secondhand, older-model Boeing 737s. Brothers Rusdi and Kusnan Kirana, who ran a small Jakarta travel agency, started with a single jet in 2000 and gradually built up credibility with financiers and aircraft makers. In 2011 their Lion Air astonished the aviation world with an order for 230 Boeing aircraft, worth $22.4 billion, and then followed this in 2013 with an order for 234 Airbus passenger jets for $24 billion. Export credits from the United States, France, and the European Union financed this explosive growth.

The state airline suffered from the restrictions of state management and its work cultures. It too joined the rush into the low-cost carrier sector with a subsidiary called Citilink. By 2012 airports were overloaded: Jakarta's Soekarno-Hatta Airport, opened in the early 1980s, was at double its planned capacity of 24 million passengers. Big new terminals opened in cities like Medan, Makassar, and Padang, many with direct connections to other parts of Southeast

Asia. But ordinary middle- and lower-middle-class Indonesians now had the option of flights that were often cheaper than the long inter-city bus and interisland ferry trips that had been their main method of travel a decade earlier.

On the ground, it was not so easy to get around. The big cities became clogged with cars, while any gaps in the traffic were filled by motorcycles, which were imported or assembled at the rate of 7 million a year. The tollways around Jakarta from the Suharto era were extended, spreading congestion throughout West Java. At the end of the Muslim fasting month every year, the traffic jams reached from the capital into Central Java. It took until 2013 to double-track the railway between Jakarta and Surabaya, in order to take some of the heavy traffic off the roads. It was the economist J. K. Galbraith's "private affluence, public squalor." Jakarta's government had long dithered on starting a mass rapid-transit rail network: the first plan was drawn up in 1980, but the first contract was not signed until the end of 2013.

Another sign of modernity has been the visible spread of bank branches and their automatic teller machines. Behind this convenient front-office presence, however, Indonesia's banks still have quite a low penetration into the daily lives of its people. They have over 50 million accounts, but the deposit-to-GDP ratio has stayed down toward 20 percent, the lowest in Asia, while credit to GDP is also low, between 30 and 40 percent. Only in 2012 did investment loans exceed working capital loans. Those who could—notably, export-ers of commodities—put their savings and accumulated funds into places like Singapore. The rupiah remained a currency crippled by memories of 1997–98, which were kept fresh by its periodic falls in value. It remained a medium of exchange but not one of saving.

THE INDONESIAN GOVERNMENT'S WELFARE BURDEN could also have been relieved if formal-sector employment (or regular jobs) had been spread more widely by the fast growth of the century's first decade. Its foreign investment hawkers were advertising the "demographic dividend" of the nation's very young population structure. But it risked squander-ing this dividend.

Manufacturing as a contributor to GDP fell from 29.1 percent in 2001 to 24.7 percent in 2012. The big expansion rate of garment, shoe, and bag manufacturing in the later years of the New Order tapered off. The era of democracy loosened the repression of labor unions, allowing Indonesia to meet International Labour Organization requirements in 2005. Provincial and district governments took over the setting of minimum wages annually, based on surveys of cost of living.

Factory workers in the garment industry, mostly young women, were particularly squeezed, earning around $200 a month and paying up to $50 for *kost* (boarding) in shared rooms in shabby buildings. A legal requirement to give severance pay of two months for every year of service deterred many employers. The mostly South Korean owners of the garment factories avoided this impost by keeping their staff as casual employees, by squeezing more hours out of their workers, and by trying to keep union officials away—with the help of preman, who hung around factories helping with security and waste disposal.

Much of the cloth and other raw materials for garments came in "by submarine," as smuggling was called. The big sportswear brands tended to walk away from Indonesia. In the ruthless garment trade, the country's labor costs were closely measured against those in Bangladesh, Nepal, Cambodia, Vietnam, and Myanmar. By 2013, as the Jakarta administration gave another sizeable rise in the city's minimum wage, the exodus of garment and shoe manufacturing to cheaper locations in West Java continued, and Central Java cities with minimum wages half that of Jakarta, such as Semarang and Solo, became more popular. This was not a bad thing, as employment spread to areas, like Srihardjo, that had little to offer their young people, especially women. Back in Jakarta and nearby parts of West Java and Banten provinces, unions in sectors such as electronics, cars, and auto components, and other metal trades were able to extract much higher rates.

Overall, the problem was not that manufacturing was shrinking or had stopped growing but that Indonesia was not making the progress it needed in job creation. The rise in minimum wages was seen by economists Asep Suryahadi and Christopher Manning as effectively cutting off the traditional pathway into formal-sector employment, via migration to the cities and a spell in the informal sector. After declining steadily over decades, the proportion of workers in the informal sector—as peddlers, operators of street stalls, household servants, *ojek* (motorbike taxi) drivers, and the like—was rising again, reaching 71 percent of the workforce near the end of Yudhoyono's term.

"Now Indonesia is regressing," the eminent retired economics professor Satrio Budihardjo Joedono has said. "It is a commodity-exporting country again, as when we were a Dutch colony. The automobile makers are now exporting coal." There is some truth and some overstatement in this; the last remark is a reference to Edwin Soeryadjaya of Adaro Energy, even though in fact Astra International still makes Toyotas; it's just that Soeryadjaya's family no longer owns it.

While the finance ministry, the central bank, and Badan Perencanaan Pembangunan Nasional (Bappenas, the National Development Planning Agency) had the commanding heights of the economy, wielding the macroeconomic instruments, a band of cloud often obscured the ministries down the slope that were in charge of "enabling" regulations and discretionary powers. These ministries are the preserve of interventionists and economic nationalists. The government, guided by the Ministry of Finance, enacted an investment law in 2007 mandating "national treatment" for foreign investors, and published a narrow "negative list" that in theory opened all other sectors to investment. But "the seeming ease with which ministerial decrees ignore the list" was remarkable, according to the economist Vikram Nehru.

In 2012 the government was persuaded to issue a regulation requiring all mineral producers to stop shipping ores and to set up refineries for their production by 2014. At the end of 2013, the Ministry of Natural Resources and Mines was circulating drafts of a plan to nationalize all foreign-owned mineral producers over fifteen years, requiring them to offer shares first to the local regional governments and then to public-sector enterprises.

With the initial Freeport work contract coming to the end of its fifty years from 1971, when production started, it was unclear whether Jakarta officials had this big game in their sights, as well as the Newmont gold mine in Sumbawa. Freeport appeared confident of agreements on options of extension worked out with the Suharto government minister, Ginandjar Kartasasmita, in the 1990s and was planning a massive $14 billion investment in underground workings.

The feverish ambitions of nationalist officials could evaporate, as they had during previous interventions, but by early 2014 Jakarta had virtually stopped all new exploration and development of the harder-to-get minerals since the turn of the century. Likewise, the export of mineral ores, aside from the exempted cases of Freeport and Newmont, had come to a halt, robbing Indonesia of billions of dollars in export earnings and throwing thousands of miners out of work. The government had applied a ban on the export of ores and concentrates in the hope that this would enforce investment in metal refineries, thereby increasing the value of mineral exports. But most of the mining industry had held back, expecting the policy would be rescinded before it came into force. It was a classic case of industrial policy overreach. Even in the humble quarrying and processing industry of cement making, officials helped the local duopoly of Gresik and Indocement delay the entry of Bangkok Cement—from an ASEAN partner country that was theoretically in a free-trade arrangement with Indonesia—thereby keeping cement prices 40 percent higher than in neighboring countries.

The cost-of-living push on wages, too, could be eased by more deregulation of domestic markets. In the last years of the Yudhoyono presidency, the government's Ministry of Agriculture distinguished itself by creating the world's highest prices for beef, by then a staple source of protein for Indonesian households. A temporary cut in the shipment of live cattle from Australia to the country's abattoirs, after a television program showed video of cruel slaughtering practices, inspired ministers and officials to apply quotas on live cattle and beef imports, with the aim of achieving self-sufficiency.

Meanwhile, domestic supplies were constrained by the licensing of dealers for cattle raised inside Indonesia. The governor of Nusatenggara Timur authorized a Jakarta company as the sole buyer of cattle shipped out of the province, making the company the monopoly buyer. When politicians and officials were revealed to have been allocating beef quotas in return for large bribes, the face-saving exit from the predicament was to announce a plan to buy a million hectares of cattle ranch land in northern Australia as a way of achieving "self-sufficiency."

Since 2010, Jakarta also applied import quotas to rice, sugar, corn, and soybeans, with the aim of meeting all domestic demand. This was seen as being possible with rice, although urban sprawl was fast eating up a lot of rice paddies, and perhaps with corn as well. For soybeans and sugar, it would seem to depend on clearing or restoring land in the outer islands, a return to an old dream. Much of the new agricultural land was already earmarked for biofuel crops, to ease the petroleum supply gap. Cartels operated in numerous other food items and spices, helping keep market prices up and grower earnings down.

If the Indonesian army was still gearing itself to fight the Dutch military nearly sixty-five years after the Belanda (as the Dutch were known) gave up, Jakarta's civilian officials sometimes still seemed to be protecting the country against the ghost of the Netherlands East India Company. The protectionist attitude to domestic markets—that competition was unseemly and that private-sector profits were somehow only legitimate if conferred by official monopolies or licenses—is still holding the Indonesian economy and people back from their great dream of "emerging" in the twenty-first century.

8

CAPITAL

THE NEDERLANDSCHE HANDEL-MAATSCHAPPIJ (NHM, NETHERLANDS TRADING COMPANY) built its new branch in Batavia to last. Completed in 1933 and designed in a style related to art deco called "new objectivity," its white triple-fronted façade faced across a square to the terminus of a railway system that connected the main cities of Java. Just to the north, lines of ships from all over the Indies filled the old harbor, while a modern steamer port lay just along the coast. Incorporated under royal charter in 1824 to fill a gap left by the collapse of the Netherlands East India Company, the NHM had grown into a trading and banking giant.

Its grand new office in the main city of the Indies was a sign of the company's confidence that its role would continue throughout the twentieth century. Less than a decade after the office was built, however, the Dutch were swept aside by the Japanese, and the city was renamed Jakarta. Although the NHM and other Dutch firms regained control of their trading houses and plantations after the end of the Second World War and continued to operate them into the first decade of the Indonesian republic, they were all nationalized by 1960 in Sukarno's initial response to the Netherlands' refusal to transfer sovereignty in western New Guinea. The NHM's assets, including the building, passed into the hands of a succession of state-owned banks, the latest being Bank Mandiri, formed out of the wreckage of the 1997–98 financial crisis.

The building's interior is much as it was when the Dutch left in 1942. It has a shadowy central banking chamber cooled by fans, which is furnished with solid wooden counters and steel grills to protect the cashiers. Heavy safes are visible in back rooms. With a sentiment not always associated with banking, its new owners have kept it as a museum, equipped with cumbersome electromechanical calculators and a phantom staff of mannequins dressed in early-twentieth-century clothes, including a European "manager" in a white cotton drill suit, who sits behind a vast desk.

Bank Mandiri's museum, often overlooked by tourists on their way to buildings from the earlier centuries of imperialism in Jakarta's old Kota district, is a quirky and unintended reminder of the lessons in commerce given to the Indonesians by their former rulers. The core elements of the modern economy started with a push from the state. This intangible legacy of the NHM remains, even if the company itself does not. A second layer of activity formed out of numerous medium and small enterprises that were linked by networks of mostly Chinese family businesses, plus some of Arab or Indian origin. A third layer was an even more "informal" stratum of petty trading among the various indigenous peoples of the Indies.

This heritage has been hard for the Indonesian state to throw off, perhaps because many of its leaders and officials are not conscious of it. Most of the enterprises inherited from the Dutch administration—what became the national airline, Garuda, the shipping company, Pelni, the railways, and so on—or nationalized in the late 1950s remain under state control, if partially privatized in some cases. The idea of the state as a pioneer of industrialization and technological advancement is dearly held. It overlays an older heritage of tax, opium, and other "farms" allocated by rulers to favored merchants. Where it does not run the activity directly, the state regulates competition to avoid "waste" and other adverse effects.

Indonesia's first leader was less aware of private-sector entrepreneurialism as a driver of economic growth and innovation. But Sukarno's better educated colleagues would have known that Joseph Schumpeter's ideas about the "wild spirits" of capitalism apply in the archipelago as much as anywhere else. The political dilemma, as noted by the development economist Gustav Papanek and others, was that Schumpeter didn't address what happens when the wild spirits of innovation emerge first and most visibly among an ethnic minority.

Across Southeast Asia, these local innovators have tended to be the Chinese settlers and their descendants, or southern Indians in the case of Burma. In some countries (Thailand and the Philippines) these communities have been sufficiently assimilated to lessen envy. In others (Indonesia, Malaysia, Vietnam, and Burma) the rise or return of indigenous political dominance brought responses ranging from discrimination in economic policies to outright expulsion.

Chinese migrants had been in the Indies for centuries, some as semiprivileged "compradors" and intermediaries for the Dutch, many others as laborers or small traders. These older families became partially assimilated into the Indonesian societies around them, speaking the local language more fluently than their ancestral Chinese dialects, their knowledge of Chinese written characters slipping away over the generations. Sometimes men took local wives, and most still held to Buddhism or Taoism if they did not convert, as many did, to Christianity. These were the *peranakan* Chinese, a name suggesting intermarriage.

As their new generations took advantage of education in government and church schools, the peranakan moved into bureaucratic, commercial, and academic roles. Then in the 1920s and 1930s came a new wave of Chinese settlers, many from the coastal province of Fujian, which doubled Indonesia's ethnic Chinese population to about 1.2 million. Escaping civil war and poverty, they were a brash lot, desperate to make their fortunes. The name for these Chinese immigrants was *totok,* meaning "full-blooded and newly arrived." They moved out into provincial cities and towns, setting up shops, trading houses, and restaurants. Some of these entrepreneurs helped the Indonesian republicans evade the Dutch embargoes during the independence struggle, smuggling commodities out to earn hard currency and bringing arms back in. Some of the peranakan, too, became revolutionaries. Generally, however, Indonesians regarded the Chinese, along with the part-European or "Indo" minority, as political fence-sitters.

In April 1950, only four months after the formal transfer of sovereignty from the Dutch, Sukarno applied what was known as the *benteng* (fortress) policy, to give preference in import licenses and the allocation of foreign exchange to companies that were at least 70 percent owned by pribumi (literally, "sons of the soil," or indigenous) Indonesians. The policy did help the formation or growth of several pribumi enterprises, notably that of Sudarpo Sastrosatomo (who ran the Samudra shipping line and distributed Remington and Univac business machines), and also those of Achmad Bakrie (trading and rubber processing) and Hajji Kalla (trading). It was also widely subverted through the use of so-called Ali Baba companies or by simply selling import licenses to Chinese traders, the pribumi thus acting as a broker or seller of privilege rather than an entrepreneur. Another policy promoted the formation of cooperative societies, particularly in agriculture. It was part of the dream of a harmonious village society. Tens of thousands of cooperatives formed and were later promoted by the army as an alternative to communism. Many still operate, though they amount to only a tiny percentage of the gross national product.

By the late 1950s, the benteng policy was dropped as Sukarno's attention turned to nationalization of Dutch assets, and his leftist senior ministers threatened Caltex and other foreign oil producers. The question of whether the Chinese belonged in Indonesia simmered. Their citizenship was left in doubt. Then, in 1959, Sukarno issued a decree banning foreign-owned shops and businesses in rural areas. Some provinces ordered ethnic Chinese to move into the cities. In 1960 about 130,000 took up an offer of repatriation by the communist Chinese government in Beijing.

The links formed between army commanders and Chinese merchants in the independence war had not ended in 1949, however. Regional military commanders allied with local traders to raise cash to pay their troops and to finance operations, giving protection to smuggled exports of sugar and other commodities out to Singapore, Malaya, and the Philippines, and imports of goods in short supply. Suharto was among them, as a colonel and then commanding general in the Diponegoro (Central Java) division, which was based in the port city of Semarang, for most of the 1950s. Diponegoro's chief financial and supply officer, Sujono Humardani, combined the foraging talents of a Milo Minderbinder with deep insight into Javanese spiritualism, meaning that he got on very well with his superior.

As we saw in chapter 3, Liem Sioe Liong (Sudono Salim) was one of the region's totok merchants, initially in Kudus, a manufacturing center for the kretek (clove-scented) cigarettes that are the poor man's luxury in Indonesia. When war and Dutch embargoes disrupted the supply of cloves for the kretek factories, Liem found ways to bring them in from the other islands. In the late 1950s, with a new disruption to the domestic clove supply caused by the Permesta rebellion in Sulawesi and the Moluccas, Liem tapped a new external source with imports from Madagascar and Zanzibar, via Singapore and Hong Kong, with protection from the Diponegoro officers. Another rising business talent in Semarang was Mohamad "Bob" Hasan (born The Kian Seng), who was initially known to the officers as a foster child of the division's first commander, Gatot Subroto, and later became close to his successor Suharto. In the 1960s Liem moved his operations to Jakarta, setting up two new banks in the old Kota commercial district, Bank Central Asia and Bank Windu Kencana. Bob Hasan also followed the political sunlight to the capital on Suharto's rise to power.

As president, Suharto took a two-level approach to the position of the ethnic Chinese. Although the Chinese embassy was sacked after the September 30, 1965, "affair," the Indonesian communists had already decided to keep ethnic Chinese figures out of leadership positions. The anti-PKI massacres did not spread to the Chinese community in Java and Bali, though a pogrom did occur in West Kalimantan for distinct reasons; indeed, several peranakan Chinese, such as the legal scholar Liem Bian Kie (later Jusuf Wanandi), became leaders in the student movements against Sukarno and the leftists.

Under pressure from his more chauvinist regional commanders, Suharto applied a new policy that was intended to assimilate the Chinese rather than expel them. The public display of Chinese script and religious practices was banned, and the adoption of Indonesian-style names was encouraged. Some simply merged their names into one, like the historian Onghokham or the banker Jusuf Panglaykim. Others took the kind of grandiose Sanskrit names favored by the Javanese aristocracy.

Liem took advantage of the second level of Suharto's policy. In 1968 he and Suharto's younger half-brother Probosutedjo received the exclusive rights to import cloves directly from the Indian Ocean islands, with part of the profits going to "charitable" foundations set up by the president. The following year, Salim (as we will now call him) gained one of two import licenses for wheat and flour milling. (A Singaporean rival was confined to the less-populated eastern islands.) His Bogasari Flour Mills received its imported wheat via the state food-price stabilization agency known as Bulog, getting a hefty subsidy on the way. Then it sold the flour back to Bulog with another high profit margin. Suharto also gave Salim licenses for cement making, and his firm Indocement steadily overtook the state-owned Semen Gresik, becoming the largest producer by the mid-1980s.

A constellation of other totok businessmen started as Salim's lieutenants and partners, and many later formed separate but friendly business empires. Mochtar Riady worked with Salim in banking before consolidating his Bank Lippo group; Ciputra in property; Eka Cipta Wijaya in palm-oil plantations and processing, later separating as the Sinar Mas group; Djuhar Sutanto in cement; the Malaysian tycoon Robert Kuok in flour milling. Salim was also careful to cut in Probosutedjo and Suharto's cousin Sudwikatmono as minority shareholders, or as beneficiaries of profit shares. Later, this "first family" homage extended to the Suharto children, two of whom owned 32 percent of the shares in Bank Central Asia, which became the largest private-sector bank.

Suharto's favors carried other obligations. Salim dutifully helped bail out a loss-making sheet mill that the government had attached to the state-owned Krakatau Steel at Cilegon in West Java, another money sink under the Pertamina umbrella. He also helped open new land for rice and sugar at Suharto's behest. Further introductions by Suharto's financial adviser and spiritual guru, Sujono Humardhani, linked up Willem Soeryadjaya with Toyota and Thajeb Gobel with Matsushita as local manufacturing and distribution partners.

The rise of this clutch of mostly totok tycoons—many of whom, like Salim, spoke only rough Indonesian—to domination of the modern private sector did not go unnoticed by the Indonesian public. The term *cukong,* roughly meaning "boss," came to refer to ethnic Chinese businessmen who had thrived under military patronage. The link became highly contentious for Suharto. He ordered investigations of corrupt linkages, but little or no action followed. By 1973–74, criticism from newspapers and students, and internal regime rivalries, led to the so-called Malari riots in Jakarta, which targeted businesses seen as being symbolic of the favoring of ethnic

Chinese and foreign capital, such as Astra's showrooms for Toyota cars. As well as political repression, Suharto's response was a new suite of policies aimed at favoring pribumi-owned businesses. The issue was revisited in the 1980s, and in 1990 he gave his cukong a public dressing down, calling them to his cattle farm in the hills outside Jakarta and ordering them to transfer 25 percent of their listed-company shares to Indonesian cooperatives; this demand was later watered down to a token 1 percent.

Complaints continued from pribumi businessmen that they had missed out on the head start given to Suharto's favored cukong, which they blamed for their absence from the top corporate rankings. Yet many had a natural advantage as indigenous champions and were not without their own preferential policies. They suffered from a perception that pribumi tended to onsell licenses rather than steadily develop businesses themselves and to regard loans, particularly those from state banks, as gifts not needing to be repaid. Nonetheless, several pribumi businesses grew strongly in the latter years of the New Order, notably the Bakrie group and the Kalla group. Both of these cultivated political support through active membership in the New Order's favored political machine, Golkar. Chinese and pribumi enterprises alike became active listers in the Jakarta Stock Exchange, revived in 1977 after being two decades dormant, which lessened the overwhelming reliance on banking finance.

From the mid-1980s, the Chinese were eclipsed somewhat as targets of resentment by the burgeoning business groups of the Suharto children. Still, the ethnic Chinese tycoons kept their heads down as much as possible. Where they were noticed intervening in politics, it was outside Indonesia. Mochtar Riady got into controversy in 1977 by offering to buy US president Jimmy Carter's budget secretary, Bert Lance, out of some embarrassing bank shares. His son James Riady pursued connections in the United States, befriending then Arkansas governor Bill Clinton and getting embroiled in campaign-donation and money-laundering scandals in the mid-1990s—to the point that he was persona non grata in the United States until Hillary Clinton became secretary of state fifteen years later.

But if licenses and monopolies were part of the explanation for the success of some Chinese immigrants, many displayed deep business acumen. Salim's Bank Central Asia became regarded as a comparatively well-managed institution. His flour-milling franchise led to the development of the best-known international brand to come out of Indonesia, the instant noodles known as Indomie.

IN COMMON WITH THE REGION'S other emerging economies, Indonesia avidly took up the loans offered to its entrepreneurs by international investment banks during the 1990s. When Thailand ran out of money to prop up its banks in mid-1997 and unpegged its currency from the US dollar, the contagion spread. Indonesia's rupiah began a slide from 2,500 to the dollar to 14,800 in January 1998. With some $80 billion in borrowings denominated in foreign currencies, it soon became apparent that the Indonesian corporate sector was beyond rescuing by the central bank, which had only $20 billion in foreign reserves.

Suharto agreed to a $43 billion bailout from the IMF in October 1997, which was offered on the condition that he ended monopolies given to cronies and family—Bob Hasan's plywood, Salim's flour, Tommy Suharto's cloves—and also ceased giving subsidies to Tommy's national car scheme and B. J. Habibie's aircraft venture. The IMF also demanded that sixteen insolvent banks be closed. It was not until two months later that Suharto signed on the dotted line, having dragged his heels on these "conditionalities." Meanwhile, thousands of small and medium businesses collapsed, bank customers rushed to withdraw their savings, and the economy went into a 16.5 percent contraction within a year.

The well connected managed to save themselves, at least from total ruin. Salim sold 40 percent of his Indofood Sukses Makmur (the maker of Indomie) to his majority-owned Hong Kong investment house, First Pacific. Even before the crisis, Salim had diversified some 40 percent of his total turnover outside Indonesia, pulled by the rising economy of his homeland and pushed by the end-of-regime feeling in Jakarta.

Alongside his deal with the IMF, Suharto had quietly ordered Bank Indonesia to ramp up its "liquidity support" program to help out private banks. Eventually Rp 145 trillion was pumped in. But only Rp 50 trillion was disbursed to account holders. The rest is presumed to have been used by bank owners and related companies to buy foreign exchange and evacuate their capital, mostly to Singapore. One of Suharto's favored business allies, Marimutu Sinivasan, of the textile group Texmaco, alone managed to secure $900 million.

The bank liquidity loans were part of an overall domestic bailout of the banking sector that came to total Rp 644 trillion (roughly $77 billion, at an average exchange rate from 1997 to 2003). The funds were to be repaid by equity in the rescued banks and companies, held by a specially re-created Indonesian Bank Restructuring Agency (IBRA), which was to recover funds by selling shares when stability returned.

By 2004 the crisis was over, and Indonesia's gross domestic product had regained its lost size. The corporate landscape had changed. The old Hong Kong trading firm Jardine Matheson had gained control of Astra, the leading industrial company. The IBRA had taken over thirteen private-sector banks. Others were left to sink or swim, with some protection for deposit holders. In 2001–2 the IBRA began selling off equity in one of the larger private banks, Bank Danamon, with the Singapore state investment fund Temasek gaining what became a 67 percent stake. In other cases, the previous owners were allowed to continue managing their banks. Suspicions were voiced that this enabled them to take actions that lowered the attractiveness of shares when they were floated or put to auction, which permitted the original owners or their allies to recapture control at bargain prices—possibly with funds derived from the central bank's bank liquidity program and spirited out of Indonesia. In the end, the IBRA recovered just $2 billion of the $77 billion it had shelled out.

With Indonesia's biggest private-sector group, Salim's family had lost control of Bank Central Asia in the crisis. This was not, its executives still insist (though others would disagree), because of poor-quality assets, but because of a run on savings in which 50 percent of its deposits were withdrawn in two weeks. The bank and the Salims were too closely identified with Suharto: rioters were to wreck many of the bank's offices, as well as the Salims' home in Kota. The Salims handed control to the central bank, and their equity and that of the Suharto children went down from 100 percent to 5.4 percent.

The IBRA relisted the bank in 2000 and sold 20 percent of shares to the public. Then in 2002 it auctioned a 52 percent stake. Two bidders emerged: the British-Asian bank Standard Chartered, and a consortium of a Mauritius investment firm named Farindo and the ethnic-Chinese Hartono brothers, owners of the Kudus-based kretek cigarette manufacturer Djarum. The local team won with a $525-million bid, giving rise to recurring speculation that the Hartono brothers had benefited with some kind of blessing from the Salims, who of course had got their start in trading cloves at Kudus. Yet the founding family has only a symbolic 1.4 percent shareholding—held by Anthony Salim, son of Sudono Salim, who died in Singapore in 2012—and no seat on the board.

Like many other New Order tycoons, the Salims took heavy blows during the crisis, selling off numerous companies and assets to pay back loans and retain control of their best businesses. Yet surveys of Indonesia's corporate activity show that these tycoons still sit in the top strata in both size and market share of key sectors, though in a vastly more diverse group of business peers. A corporate "rich list" published annually since 2007 by the magazine *Globe Asia* (owned by the Riady family's Lippo group) reveals miracles of commercial escapology.

The most dramatic has been that of Eka Tjipta Widjaya (formerly Oei Ek Tjhong), a former partner of Salim who spun off his palm-oil and paper group, Sinar Mas, during the New Order. During the crisis, his Asia Pulp & Paper was discovered to have issued corporate bonds totaling $13.9 billion. In 2001 it announced it could no longer service these borrowings. Mysteriously, it was unable to collect $1 billion in cash owed by trading firms registered in the British Virgin Islands or $220 million from a bank deposit in the Cook Islands or indeed $220 million lost in foreign exchange dealings. Bondholders were further deterred when a Jakarta court declared that one $500 million issue had been illegal and therefore need not be repaid.

It was found that while Asia Pulp & Paper owned various timber and pulp mills, the forestry concessions that supplied their raw material were held personally by the company owners. Appeals by the governments of the United States, Japan, Canada, and major European countries for the Indonesian government to intervene got nowhere. While looking after his investors and lenders in China, Widjaya steadily wore his other creditors down. After four years, most bondholders agreed to a deal that returned 18 percent of their money. In 2013 Widjaya was ranked number two on the Indonesian rich list, with his assets in palm oil, pulp and paper, property, finance, and mining estimated to be worth $13.1 billion.

The Hartono brothers, Robert and Michael, were at the top of the list with $15.5 billion in assets, thanks to the combination of their Djarum cash cow with Bank Central Asia, by then one of the five large banks that together account for about half the financial sector, and further ventures such as the vast Grand Indonesia shopping mall in Jakarta and palm-oil plantations in Kalimantan. Anthony Salim's group, by now operating under the name First Pacific, was at number three, with $10.1 billion in food and investment assets.

Other names from the New Order cukong era and still in the top fifty in 2013 included the Riady family's Lippo group (property, investment, education, and media), Sjamsul Nursalim's Gajah Tunggal (tires, retail, and property), The Nin King's Manunggal group (property, textiles, and other manufacturing), Ciputra (property), Edwin Soeryadjaya (not from his father's Astra group but with his own coal-based conglomerate), Prajogo Barito's Pacific group (petrochemicals), and the late Suharto-era figures close to the Indonesian military, Tomy Winata and his patron Sugianto Kusuma (A Guan), whose Artha Graha group includes hotels, entertainment spots, and a bank.

Five of the Suharto family remain on the *Globe Asia* rich list: son Tommy (Hutomo Mandala Putra), with his Humpuss investment and shipping interests put at $550 million; in-law Sukamdani, with hotels and other businesses worth $367 million; son Bambang Triatmodjo, with Asriland property worth $220 million; daughter Tutut (Siti Hardijanti Rukmana), with her toll roads and other investments worth $150 million; and Agus Sudwikatmono, son of Suharto's cousin, with his Indika coal and oil venture that has an estimated value of $665 million. In March 2014 Tutut won a legal case that regained her control of the Media Nusantara Citra television network, in theory ousting the tycoon-politician Hary Tanoesoedibyo, running mate of the former general Wiranto in the presidential race, though the ruling was not immediately enforced. Other scions of powerful figures in the New Order include Pontjo Sutowo, son of the late Pertamina chief Ibnu Sutowo, whose Nugra Sentana group is active in hotels and property, and former president Habibie's sons Ilham and Thareq, whose Ilthabi Rekatama group is invested in plantations and technology.

IT WAS A WARY RETURN to wealth and power for the ethnic Chinese. In the last throes of the New Order, they had been the scapegoats for the plummeting currency. Military and police commanders had stood back as preman led rioters on an orgy of pillage and rape through Jakarta's main district of Chinese businesses and homes. It even looked like a deliberately instigated riot to blacken the prodemocracy uprising: calls for an investigation into the matter are still stonewalled (and, as Prabowo Subianto earlier remarked to author Ken Conboy, the Indonesian military didn't leave written orders).

Estimates of the funds held in Singapore by ethnic Chinese and other Indonesians go as high as $200 billion, more than double Indonesia's foreign exchange reserves at the height of the first resources boom. Perhaps $30 billion of that came from capital flight around the collapse of the New Order. For the middle-class Chinese-Indonesians who decided to get out, to Australia and elsewhere, the move was often permanent. Much of the capital held by the big tycoons has flowed back, being used to reinvest in old businesses or to acquire new ones. They kept their feet in the game in Indonesia, but their children and primary homes remain in Singapore and Taiwan.

In 2006 President Yudhoyono tackled the long-unsettled issue of the place of the Chinese in Indonesian society. A new citizenship law revised the definition of indigenous Indonesians to include all citizens who had never assumed foreign citizenship. This eliminated—in theory, at least—the need for ethnic Chinese to show a "citizenship certificate" whenever they needed government services. These certificates were often withheld arbitrarily by officials. Several discriminatory laws and regulations have remained on the books, including a 1967 decree that bars ethnic Chinese from the armed forces, and identity cards still carry a number that identifies race. But combined with the freedoms already granted by President Wahid— to practice Chinese religions, study Chinese at schools, celebrate the lunar new year, and publish in Chinese—the new law promised to lift decades of discrimination.

The profile of the ethnic Chinese was blurred also by the survival of some of the leading pribumi entrepreneurs from the Suharto era. In Hashim Djojohadikusumo's case, it was a return from the corporate dead. The son of the economist, rebel figure, and minister Sumitro Djojohadikusumo, Hashim had built up the Tirtamas group (turnover of $7 billion a year), centered on a large cement maker, Semen Cibinong. When the 1997 crisis hit, building stopped, no one bought cement, and his company was left with $1.2 billion in mostly foreign debt. In addition, Hashim had a problem recovering money from remote tax havens: $250 million had disappeared from Semen

Cibinong into small banks in Vanuatu and the Cook Islands. The Tirtamas group collapsed, but fortuitously Hashim had just bought into an oilfield in Kazakhstan for about $200 million, a stake in what was called Nations Energy, which he was able to sell for $1.2 billion in 2006. He returned to the corporate scene and built up his new Arsari group, with assets put at $1.05 billion.

Aburizal Bakrie had a narrow escape from bankruptcy in 1997. His group had been built up largely on the engineering and construction contracts awarded by government agencies under the various pribumi preference schemes. The crash left him with share prices at rock bottom and $1.7 billion in debt. It was not entirely his fault. Bakrie had attempted to corner the Indonesian market for the seamless pipes and casing used in the oil industry, through a partnership with Krakatau Steel and the Asian Development Bank called Seamless Pipe Indonesia Jaya, while the state oil firm announced that all piping would have to be locally sourced. But as his venture's brand-new and debt-financed plant neared completion—with a capacity greater than the then Indonesian demand and perhaps some inflation of the costs—Suharto's daughter Tutut set up a rival plant on Batam Island with secondhand machinery from the United States.

After a year of default, Bakrie managed to square off with 300 creditors in a debt-forgiveness deal. As we have seen, he pursued a dual career in the reformasi era, deftly gathering up plum coal resources in Kalimantan as demand from China and India boomed and becoming minister for social welfare in Yudhoyono's first term. In October 2008 Bakrie & Brothers was back in the same precarious position, thanks to the global financial crisis and the drop in coal and other commodity prices and a high level of debt. Investors rushed out of his three listed vehicles, causing the Jakarta Stock Exchange to shut down for a month. The finance minister, Sri Mulyani Indrawati, was giving Bakrie's companies no extra time to pay their large tax backlog.

In East Java, hot volcanic mud had erupted in May 2006 alongside a gas exploration well bored by Bakrie's majority-owned company Lapindo Brantas at Sidoarjo, just south of Surabaya. The mud cut the main toll road and railway south from Surabaya, and at one point ruptured the main natural gas pipeline into the city, causing an explosion and a flood of hot mud that killed fourteen people and caused blackouts and industrial shutdowns. The mud "volcano" flowed and flowed, eventually displacing 20,000 villagers and by 2013 nearly filling a ten-meter-high containment dam. American contractors brought in to stem the blowout complained of resistance by Lapindo to solutions that might have diverted and capped the flow, on the grounds of expense. After a while, the well was so enlarged that capping it became impossible.

Within two years, the Bakries achieved a triple act of escapology. Lapindo was sold off to a shell company in a tax haven. More expensive loans were secured to keep creditors at bay. In September 2009 Beijing's sovereign wealth fund, the China Investment Corp, announced a $1.9 billion loan for Bumi Resources, the Bakrie coal-mining flagship. The same year, police declared they could find no criminal liability on Lapindo's part. The company argued that the large earthquake south of Yogyakarta before the mud eruption had fractured the geology under Sidoarjo and caused the disaster; its own well drilling alongside was incidental. Though the weight of geological expertise concluded it was drilling without the protection of casing pipe that was to blame, a parliamentary commission chaired by a member of Bakrie's own Golkar party declared the mudflow a natural disaster, getting the company largely off the hook. In the parliament, Golkar was out of government after Yudhoyono's reelection; it joined the claque attacking Sri Mulyani, the finance minister, over the bailout of a badly run private bank in 2008 to avoid a domino effect during the 2008 global financial crisis. In 2010 Yudhoyono eased her out to a senior position at the World Bank in Washington.

Bakrie has never been short of new investors ready to be dazzled by his local knowledge and connections and by the promise of Indonesia's natural resources. In 2010 he teamed up with Nathaniel Rothschild, a scion of the old European banking house. Rothschild floated an investment company in London, raised $1 billion, and then engineered a reverse takeover with two Bakrie-linked companies in a share and equity swap that resulted in the London-listed investment company, renamed Bumi PLC, owning 29 percent of Bumi Resources and 85 percent of another large thermal coal producer, Berau. The deal created a company valued at $3 billion, while the Bakrie group's $3.8-billion debt load was temporarily relieved. While Rothschild became cochairman due to his 15 percent equity, he allowed Bakrie to nominate the chief executive and chief financial officer.

Just over a year later, Rothschild was raising the alarm about large sums that were disappearing from the books of Bumi Resources and Berau. One of the Bakrie-linked vehicles used in creating Bumi PLC, an investment fund called Recapital, had just previously borrowed $231 million from Bumi Resources and was not repaying it. In late 2013 Recapital's chief was buying a share of the Italian football club Inter Milan. Around the same time, Berau placed $75 million in a trust known as the Chateau Asean Fund 1. Two years later it was declared unrecoverable. Another $115 million went missing from a share-market float of a Bumi Resources subsidiary called Bumi Resources Minerals, while a $363-million stake in two Yemeni oilfields, possibly nonexistent, was written down to zero. Further questions hovered over the sale of two coal infrastructure companies in 2012, despite them having been announced as sold to other buyers two years earlier, and over a sale of 30 percent of Bumi Resources to a subsidiary of India's Tata Power for $1. Every month, $2 million was being taken out of Berau as a fee, which was put at the personal disposal of the Bakries.

The Bakries began their exit, taking with them as much of their money as possible. In early 2012 Samir Tan, of Borneo Lumbung Energy and Metal, bought half of the Bakrie stake in Bumi PLC, 23 percent, for $1 billion and gained control over the other half. This put him in control of the company. The leakage continued. The board later admitted that during Tan's tenure as chairman in 2012, a further $152 million was spent "with no clear business purpose" from subsidiary Berau. In early 2013 Rothschild was openly alleging "malfeasance" on a grand scale, accusing the Bakries and allied parties of having "looted" Bumi Resources and Berau. Trading in shares of Bumi PLC was suspended.

In July 2013 the London company announced a two-stage deal to sell its 29 percent of Bumi Resources back to the Bakries and to acquire the remaining Bakrie shares in Bumi PLC. Rothschild bitterly denounced the proposed deal and launched a court action to unseat Tan. It was unclear whether, with this separation, the Bakrie group was avoiding another debt crunch. Refinancing at a massive 11 percent margin on the London interbank interest rate meant a payment of $150 million due in August 2013. Then another subsidiary owed $350 million in September. In 2014 all pretax cash earnings would be consumed by interest payments, unless coal prices sharply increased.

In addition, the Jakarta holding company PT Bumi faced $750 million in loan paybacks to the China Development Bank and also had a $375 million convertible bond issue maturing. Some analysts, including the ratings agency Standard & Poor's, concluded that the Bakries' finances were unsustainable without major asset sales. Aburizal Bakrie was, meanwhile, still gearing up as leader of Golkar in the money-chewing parliamentary and presidential election campaigns of 2014.

IF BAKRIE CUT A SORRY FIGURE as a standard-bearer of Indonesian (and pribumi) corporate governance, and if the Bumi PLC saga was a lesson in naivety and failure of due diligence at the London end, many other new figures—both pribumi and Chinese—in the top business ranks have more inspiring stories. William Katari's Wings Group challenged Proctor & Gamble and Unilever in the soaps and toothpaste market; Chairul Tanjung rose in the media and retailing sectors; Djoko Susanto built a chain of 7,000 Alfamart convenience stores; Rusdi Kirana built his Lion Air into the largest rival to state carrier Garuda in a decade; Purnomo Prawiro expanded his Blue Bird taxis to a nationwide fleet of 22,000 vehicles and set new standards of service and safety.

Media groups flexed new muscle in the liberal era. The Kompas print group, led by Jakob Oetama, and the Surabaya-based Jawa Pos group of Dahlan Iskan now dominate the newspaper scene, as does the Tempo group in magazines. In the absence of cable television, the six free-to-air television groups remain the big moneymakers, particularly as the issuing of new broadcast licenses is frozen. In addition, the networks are helpful to the political careers of owners such as Chairul Tanjung, Surya Dharma Paloh, Dahlan Iskan, and Aburizal Bakrie; the latter three emerged as presidential hopefuls in 2014 (though unsuccessfully).

Despite many continuities in the corporate lineup from the New Order, the return of stability in the demokrasi era has not quite meant business as usual. Closeness to the president is no longer a guarantee of getting the best contracts from government. The media and the anticorruption commission are ferocious watchdogs for any corrupt deals. Although police and prosecutors can still be employed to harass complaining customers and inconvenient business partners, defamation is no longer a criminal offense, meaning that critics can no longer be threatened with jail.

Of course, good relations with political players are still a help, but decision makers are dispersed across the decentralized political system. For some pribumi entrepreneurs, government relations have been tackled in person—by getting elected or being appointed to cabinet, or by forming their own political parties if they are unsatisfied with their reception. Indeed, Aburizal Bakrie and Jusuf Kalla have become leading figures in Golkar's parliamentary ranks. The Acehnese former street trader Surya Dharma Paloh did not take his lack of promotion in Golkar lying down, forming his own Partai Nasional Demokrat (PND, National Democrat Party) in 2011. During Yudhoyono's second term, Dahlan Iskan of *Jawa Pos* (the *Java Post* newspaper) accepted an appointment as minister for state-owned enterprises.

Founding families still mostly own and run the big business houses, including the former cukong conglomerates, but they have surrounded themselves with professional managers and now operate under somewhat stricter reporting and auditing requirements. With second-generation owners taking over, many of whom have been raised in Indonesia and educated at Western universities, the era of the robber barons is fading in Jakarta, if not in the coalfields and plantations of Kalimantan and other outer islands.

9

BETWEEN
MECCA AND
THE SOUTH SEA

IN A LITTLE SHRINE IN WEST JAVA, TWO YOUNG MEN SIT CROSS-LEGGED, HEADS BOWED in pious absorption over open copies of the Koran. An example of orthodox Islam? Not exactly. Behind one worshipper is a large oil painting of a young woman, her shoulders bare, wearing a green gown that shows off the curves of her body. She is set against a background of blue ocean waves. The other man sits beside a bed that is draped in green silk, with a multitiered ceremonial parasol and a green chandelier above it. The shrine sits on a little outcrop of volcanic rock, jutting into the surf of the Indian Ocean shoreline.

The province of West Java, modern successor to the ancient kingdom of Sunda, is known as one of the most devoutly Islamic regions of Indonesia. In recent years it has voted in a governor from a new Islamist party, the Partai Keadilan Sejahtera (PKS, Prosperous Justice Party), which some say draws inspiration from the Muslim Brotherhood of Egypt and the like-minded Islamist party that has ruled Turkey since 2002. As the PKS gathered in electoral strength over the first decade of this century, many Indonesians worried that it had a hidden agenda, one it would reveal only on gaining power: to convert the country into a state ruled by Islamic law, instead of the multifaith model enshrined by Sukarno in his Pancasila compromise of 1945.

Yet here, close to a fishing and tourism town called Pelabuhan Ratu, an older and indigenous form of worship is still peeping through this wave of purist Islam. While reading the words of Muhammad, two devout young men are seeking to draw strength from Nyai Loro Kidul, a female deity or spirit said to reside in the ocean south of Java; her name is sometimes translated as "Queen (*Ratu*) of the South Sea." She is a wrathful spirit, needing to be appeased with annual offerings. Her color is green, though a richer aqua green than that of Islamic banners, and one not to be worn by seafarers or bathers along this treacherous shore.

Sukarno had a modern tourist hotel built here, one of the four financed by Japan's war reparations. Guests in one room soon started complaining of disturbed sleep, of visions in the night. Room 308 remains set aside for Nyai Loro Kidul. No one else can stay there, though visitors can enter to commune with the goddess. Over centuries, she has been the mythical consort of successive kings and sultans in the Javanese dynasties. The late Sultan Hamengkubuwono IX of Yogyakarta, highly educated in the Netherlands, wrote of how she appeared to him while he meditated. When he lay dying in 1988, royal servants in the kraton reported sightings of her bidding farewell the much loved and respected ruler, independence leader, and vice president.

Java could be mapped intensively according to concentrations of geomantic forces, which draw seekers of spiritual strength on *ziarah* (pilgrimage) on auspicious days in the Javanese calendar or on Muslim feast days. The place might be the graveyard of the Yogyakarta and Solo royal houses at Imogiri, built by Sultan Agung of Mataram in the 1640s. Or it might be the mythical haunt of gods in the great Hindu narratives, the *Ramayana* and the *Mahabharata*. These dramas might have been located originally in the landscape of India, but in Javanese tradition their characters—Rama and Sita, the warring Pandawa and Kurawa, plus local inserts like the clown-god Semar and his three doltish sidekicks—lived and fought in Java "before there were people." It might be the Sendang Semanggi, a spring near Yogyakarta, or the Gua Sirandil, a sea cave near Cilicap, or the Gua

Semar, a cave on the misty Dieng Plateau, inland from the Borobudur monument.

The mythical heroes and great historical characters are believed to leave some of their power at their dwelling places, graves, or sites of great achievement. With patient meditation and fasting, and by sprinkling flower petals and lighting incense, ordinary people can soak up some of this power. Some take it further, into a deep mysticism known as Kebatinan, in which meditation, self-denial, and ascetic practices, such as sitting under waterfalls, take the practitioner to a higher plane of consciousness. In the early part of his career, Suharto used to meditate in the Gua Semar, since he identified with this native wise fool of the *wayang* theater. In 2002 the police chief I Made Mangku Pastika, seeking a breakthrough in the Bali bombing case, went to a mountain to clarify his mind: the vital clue soon arrived to identify the vehicle used in the car bombing of a nightclub.

Pastika is a Hindu, like nearly all the 4 million Balinese. But most of those following such practices in Java will have "Muslim" on their identity cards and, if asked, would declare themselves as such. This ambivalence infuriates scholars and preachers of Islamic orthodoxy. In Islam, worship at the graves of saints or great men, even that of the Prophet Muhammad himself in Medina, has been contentious down the ages. The purists of the Sunni tradition see it as superstition: the dead leave nothing of their being, and graves are simply a reminder of mortality, but better an unmarked burial place in the desert anyway. The great split of Islam started soon after Muhammad's death, with his descendants venerated as caliphs. In Java, installing a human intermediary between a formless Allah and the individual of the *ummat* (Islamic community) can signify more than superstition and folk impulse. It can point to the stubborn survival of the pre-Islamic faith, both the Hinduism of the premodern era and even earlier forms of animism.

Even late in the twentieth century in Indonesia, it seemed that this was a social reality that simply had to be accepted—perhaps reluctantly by strongly devout Muslims, but with relief by those who saw this syncretism as a sturdy foundation for a pluralist nation that encompassed many non-Muslim religions. If large segments of the population of Java, two-thirds of the Indonesian nation, could adhere to an accommodating mixture of tradition and theology, then Indonesia would be predisposed to religious tolerance.

The American anthropologist Clifford Geertz's book *The Religion of Java* (1960) became for decades the dominant paradigm in the West with which to explain the "moderate Islamic" character of Indonesia. He saw the Javanese as falling into three *aliran* (streams). One was the *santri* (devout), comprised of those who were highly observant of the rituals and demands of the Muslim faith: prayer five times a day, the halal diet, observance of the fasting month of Ramadan, the pilgrimage to Mecca. Around them was the mass of villagers whom Geertz categorized as *abangan* (roughly meaning "vernacular"), who might attend the mosque on Fridays and observe Ramadan but who might also make offerings to spirits, seek magical help from faith-healers, and take moral lessons from the Hindu epics. The third category comprised the Javanese aristocracy and gentry, the priyayi, who could be quite overtly Hindu in style—by using Sanskrit names, for example, and in some cases by pursuing highly developed forms of Kebatinan.

Historians suggest that this divergence resulted from the pathways by which Islam came to the archipelago and from the political structures of that time. The religion came along with the trade in textiles and precious commodities that ran through the sea routes along the southern edge of the Asian landmass, from China and Japan around to the Persian Gulf and the Red Sea. Muslim communities were observed by Marco Polo in Sumatra at the end of the thirteenth century. The adoption of Islam by the ruler of the new trading city-state of Malacca in the fifteenth century helped it spread to the trading seaports around the Java Sea. It was a religion suited to the commercial classes, supporting the notion of parties dealing on a footing of equality and trust in the marketplace.

Then came a new example of the good Muslim in the shape of Sufi missionaries, who showed a pathway to transcendental religious experience not unlike that pursued in Hinduism. Indeed, many of the Sufis would have come from India or Central Asia, where mystical elements would have been absorbed into their practices, making them already attuned to the attitudes of the Javanese in the agricultural inland. The earliest of the legendary *Wali Songo* (nine saints) said to have brought Islam into inland Java in the fifteenth century, Maulana Malik Ibrahim from Samarkand, seems to have been such a missionary.

At the end of the sixteenth century, the kingdom of Mataram arose in central Java, the last to have independence before the tightening of Dutch rule. Its rulers adopted Islam and the title of "sultan." But this was an expedient strategy to help them face the rising power of coastal states, so the conversion was a surface one. Rulers and the priyayi continued their existing practices of building power and legitimacy from their perceived closeness to great spirits and deities. By the time Islam penetrated through inland Java, many compromises had been made.

Yet conversion has been and remains an ongoing process. Dutch rule helped make Islam a self-identifier for the subjects of the Indies and helped rally support behind rebellions in Java, West Sumatra, and Aceh during the nineteenth century. The cooption of many elements of the priyayi class and the outer-island rajahs into the colonial administration tended to discredit the holders of traditional power and customary belief.

The greater interconnection of the world through the steamship and the telegraph brought Indonesia's Muslims into closer contact with schools of thought arising in the Middle East. More were able to make the hajj to Mecca and learned of the Wahhabis, who were seeking to return Islam to its austere and simple origins. Some young people went to study in Cairo and became immersed in the reformist school, which not only sought to strip away the compromises with pre-Islamic beliefs but also looked at ways of combining Islam with the modern world.

In 1912, two significant movements began that showed a stirring within Indonesia's ummat. The Sarekat Islam was an early nationalist organization, formed largely among santri elements in trading ports and market towns. The apolitical Muhammadiyah organization set out to reeducate Muslims through a network of schools and local branches in the spirit of the reformists of Cairo.

Clifford Geertz described how Muhammadiyah's followers took the santri in new directions. They emphasized the importance of individual effort, of engaging in secular activity, of keeping faith pure, and of observing proper behavior, and advocated the use of logic and pragmatism. The more traditional Javanese Muslims tended to be fatalistic, to weave religion into all aspects of life, to accept other beliefs and practices, to take a more literal approach to texts, and to value inward religious experience over outward activity. They tended to gravitate to the NU, formed in 1926 partly in reaction to the rise of Muhammadiyah.

The two organizations grew in strength through the twentieth century, until each could claim 30 to 40 million members, making them the largest Muslim bodies in the world. The NU was more inclined to jump into politics, contesting the elections in 1955 and 1971 under its own name (and later, in the reformasi era, through the PKB). The Muhammadiyah held back as an organization, though many of its members entered politics through the various Islamist parties. Labels are difficult: "orthodox" does not necessarily mean conservative; "progressive" or "modernist" can also look orthodox and revivalist.

AS WE HAVE SEEN, Sukarno came from the priyayi stream on his father's side, while his mother was a Hindu from Bali. Although he adopted the forms and practices of Islam, he was a careful balancer of the three forces of his precarious Nasakom coalition. At the very beginning of the Indonesian republic, he turned aside demands for a *Negara Islam Indonesia* (Islamic Indonesian State) by producing the Pancasila doctrine, and he later also resisted the fallback position of the Islamic party: the Jakarta Charter, which would have obliged all those who identified as Muslims to follow the requirements of the faith.

Suharto arrived in power by smashing the communist component of Nasakom and then turned his attention to taming the other two. The gradual eclipse of Sukarno between 1965 and 1970 was accompanied by machinations within the PNI to promote New Order sympathizers. On the religious front, Suharto started his long presidency as very much a product of his upbringing and experience. Like many of his fellow army officers, he was "small town Java" (to use Harold Crouch's words), distinctly abangan in upbringing, and had been exposed to Kebatinan through an apprenticeship with a well-known dukun (faith-healer). His early postindependence experience in the field had come when he had quelled a rebellious Islamic militia in Java, and he'd then fought the Islamist rebellion in South Sulawesi.

In the early years of his national leadership, Suharto's immersion in Javanese mystical practices was scarcely a secret, and he made much use of names from the wayang theater as political symbols. His political operatives under Ali Murtopo, who included priyayi and Catholic figures, tackled political Islam through several initiatives. A friendly figure, John Naro, was installed as head of the main Muslim political party, *Parmusi,* which from 1977 was dragooned with all the others into the blandly named PPP. At the same time, Murtopo's Opsus group kept contact with surviving members of the Darul Islam and Negara Islam Indonesia insurgencies in West Java, always handy for black operations to discredit mainstream Muslim groups. The regime also fostered Kebatinan, to the point that, in the early 1970s, it seemed the practices would be recognized as an official religion. This, too, was not without its political dangers, however: the messianic Mbah Suro cult in East Java caused the army to crack down in 1967 out of a fear that remnants of the PKI might use mysticism as a cover to regroup; the elite-level Kebatinan circle, led by the minor bureaucrat Sawito Kartowibowo, in 1976 suggested that Suharto had lost the wahyu that made his rule legitimate.

However, Suharto was careful to appoint widely respected Muslim figures as his ministers of religious affairs, who were responsible for dispersing official support for mosques and schools and administering the hajj. As years of high economic growth began to lift living standards, it became apparent that greater relative prosperity was being accompanied by a general rise in piety and religious observance. (This is not a phenomenon unique to Indonesia: witness the rise of Christian evangelism in nineteenth-century Britain, for example.) Observing Islam enhanced the people's feelings of respectability and provided them with a framework for living in a confusing modern world—this was especially true for people newly moved from villages to cities. In an environment where the young, in particular, were beset by temptation, Islam provided a moral compass and plenty of people and places to go to for guidance and help.

With pathways into political change blocked, the newly devout channeled their energies into *dakwah,* the proselytizing of the faith. Funds poured into the building of mosques and madrassas and *pesantren* (Islamic schools), with some of the money coming from the oil-rich Arabian countries. More Javanese women and girls started wearing versions of the *jilbab* (headscarf). Charter flights made it cheaper and easier to make the hajj. Hundreds of students went off each year to study in the Islamic centers of Egypt and Saudi

Arabia. A few joined the mujahideen fighting the Soviet forces in Afghanistan. Five times daily, in villages and urban neighborhoods alike, came the amplified call to prayer, often overlaid from several mosques. Like the calls of a watchman, this became a comforting soundtrack to daily life.

As we saw in chapter 4, all this did not go unnoticed by Suharto, who steadily adopted more of an Islamic identity himself. Through the Muslim intellectuals' association, the ICMI, he cultivated a range of young academics and professionals. The army, too, felt uncomfortable at the perception of it as the enforcer of Westernized ways, especially after armed clashes with Muslim communities in incidents at Tanjung Priok in 1984 and Lampung in 1989, and many of its senior officers took on a "green" identity as devout Muslims.

On Suharto's resignation in 1998, the patron of the ICMI, B. J. Habibie, stepped up to the presidency and brought several of the group's leading figures into his government as ministers or advisers. As we saw in chapter 4, it was a short-lived presidency, as was that of his successor, Abdurrahman Wahid. Neither the NU nor the Muhammadiyah camp gained enough traction through their respective political parties to capitalize on the religious identity of 87 percent of Indonesians. Wahid, as the head of the PKB, finessed a relatively minor 12.6 percent vote in the 1999 election result to emerge as a consensus president, based on his personality as much as or more than on his religious standing. The PAN, led by Amien Rais, the Yogyakarta political science professor and former Muhammadiyah head (and ICMI member), gained a disappointing 7.1 percent, less than the PPP's 10.7 percent.

With the impeachment of Wahid, the presidency returned to the secular nationalist figures Megawati and Yudhoyono. In the following elections, in 2004, the main Islamic parties all slipped backward: the PKB to 10.6 percent, the PAN to 6.4 percent, and the PPP to 8.2 percent. Incumbency—with Wahid as president and Amien Rais as chairman of the MPR—had not helped at all (not that it had helped Megawati either—her PDI-P's vote dropped drastically from 33.7 to 18.5 percent). Muslim leaders, once they entered the snake pit of Jakarta political power, turned out to be politicians just like all the others.

Yet the combined vote of all Muslim-identity parties held up at around 33 percent, just as the secular nationalist total stayed about the same, and Golkar, increasingly the party of business and the outer islands, held at about 21 percent. In the nationalist camp, the newcomer was Yudhoyono and his Partai Demokrat: he went on to defeat his old boss Megawati in the first direct presidential election held that year. In the Muslim camp, the new force was the PKS, which was formed out of an earlier group that had won only 1.7 percent of the vote in 1999: it gained 7.3 percent of the vote, and its leader, Nur Hidayat Wahid, became chairman of the MPR, replacing Amien Rais (who was to trail behind Yudhoyono and Megawati in the presidential election). Significantly, the new PKS and PD emerged as the first and second parties in Jakarta, the urban melting pot that pointed to future trends. In 2008 the PKS went on to displace Golkar from the governorship of West Java, the most populous province in Indonesia, which partly rings the national capital.

For the following five years, the PKS seemed to be the party that would ride the wave of Islamic piety into power. It explained itself as a party that had grown out of the *dakwah* (outreach) and *tarbiyah* (education) movements during the Suharto era, making its biggest impact among both local students and those returning from overseas. Several of its leaders had been to Egypt and become familiar with the (then underground) Muslim Brotherhood, but the party has long been ambivalent about whether this organization is its model. Taking *"Bersih dan Perduli"* ("Clean and Caring") as their slogan, the party's elected representatives made a point of ostentatiously refusing "envelopes" when money was being offered around.

By 2008 PKS claimed to have half a million cadres active in its branches, all chosen and trained to be walking examples of principled and pragmatic politics, ready to pitch in and help when natural disasters or other problems arrived. It made good use of the Internet and other modern technologies, yet preached a conservative social agenda. While espousing the equality of women at one level, its religious council was talking of the "natural division of labor," in which women were suited to supporting and domestic roles; the council also enjoined women to follow demure ways of dressing and behaving.

Those suspicious of a hidden agenda noted the inclusion of several descendants of Darul Islam figures. Over 2006 and 2007, the central board of Muhammadiyah was concerned enough to issue a warning about PKS infiltration and moved to expel members who had dual loyalty. It saw a sharp division between itself and the rising party. Muhammadiyah accepted the Indonesian state as it was, governed by the multifaith Pancasila. The PKS, on the other hand, had as its goal the steady Islamization of the nation, so that an Islamic state would eventuate by universal consent. Around the same time, the NU became more vigilant against PKS cadres entering its pesantren and warned against the influence of "transnational" Islamic movements, such as Wahhabism, Hizb ut-Tahrir (the Party of Liberation, a transnational movement working for a borderless Islamic caliphate), and Ikhwanul Muslimin (the Muslim Brotherhood, meaning the PKS). Women activists, meanwhile, claimed to have traced a movement in Yogyakarta to separate boys and girls at schools to a PKS initiative.

For its part, the PKS denied having any strategy to infiltrate other organizations. As for its long-term goal, it was not interested in the Jakarta Charter of legally obliged Islamic behavior, but what it called the "Medina Charter," which it said was based on Muhammad's rule in the Arabian city, and under which all religious minorities had freedom of worship.

Yet the PKS was soon to hit a ceiling. In the 2009 election, its vote rose only slightly, to 7.8 percent, compared to the widely mooted goal of 20 percent, which would have put Nur Hidayat Wahid in a good position to contest the presidency. It did much better than the other Muslim parties. The PKB's vote dropped to 5 percent amid squabbling over the succession to Wahid, who died at the end of that year; the PPP's vote dropped to 6 percent, as did that of Amien Rais's PAN, while some smaller Islamic parties dropped out of parliament altogether. Still, the PKS's small share was a sign of lost momentum, despite its vastly increased national profile and flow of funding.

One reason was the old phenomenon of political contamination. As a minority group, the PKS politicians could not change anything, and not all the party's cadres could maintain their "Clean and Caring" stance. With the party deciding to join Yudhoyono's grand coalition for his second term, the contamination became more pronounced. The PKS gained three cabinet positions: Agriculture, Social Services, and Communication. In 2013, as we shall see, a massive scandal enveloped the party over manipulation of beef import quotas in the Ministry of Agriculture.

Another factor may have been a backlash among women voters. The PKS had been one of the strongest supporters of a new antipornography law, passed in 2008. In its application at the local level, it soon became an excuse for vigilantism against women seen as dressing immodestly or moving about on their own. A woman coming home in the early evening in one West Java town, for example, was stopped and searched: the lipstick in her handbag was seized upon as evidence of "prostitution." Several of the top PKS leaders practiced polygamy; one middle-aged man took a teenage bride. The example of the wildly popular Muslim televangelist Abdullah Gymnastiar, known as Aa ("Big Brother") Gym, showed the force of a female backlash: in 2006 he took a second, much younger wife, and his ratings plummeted.

But the more important factor in the stalling popularity of the Islamic parties was that everyone to some extent started playing "the Islamic card" in politics, not least Yudhoyono. Although he was educated in the United States, his openness to the West was balanced by the careful modesty he showed in his personal life, by his undertaking of the hajj, and by his adherence to foreign policies supporting the Palestinian cause and opposing the Western interventions in Iraq and Afghanistan. At home, he included Muslim parties in his ruling coalition even after the 2009 election gave him and his PD an unprecedentedly strong mandate. Members of Habibie's Muslim intellectuals' group moved into his and other secular parties. "We have taken the leadership from the radicals and the simplistic people in Islam who push a black and white solution," says Adi Sasono, an ICMI member who was a minister in Habibie's government and who now heads the Indonesian cooperative movement's main body.

BENEATH THE GOVERNMENT, there is now a creeping orthodoxy. From the start of his presidency, Yudhoyono gave enhanced space and semi-government status to the Majelis Ulama Indonesia (MUI, Indonesian Ulamas' Council) and its fatwas, or rulings on matters of theology, and appointed a highly conservative figure from the PPP, Suryadharma Ali, as his minister of religious affairs. One result was passage of the antipornography law. Another was increasing pressure on the minority branches of Islam regarded as heretical by the orthodox Sunni.

The half million members of the Ahmadiyah sect, who recognize a prophet who came after Muhammad (to most Muslims, the last and greatest messenger of God), escaped an outright ban by Yudhoyono's government. But an edict warned them against making their own interpretations of Islam or trying to spread their beliefs. Across several regions Ahmadiyah mosques were shut down by local authorities. In 2011 a 1,500-people-strong mob attacked an Ahmadiyah group in Cikeusik, Banten province, and killed three, while police stood by. The twelve rioters brought to trial received sentences of three to six months in jail, while an injured Ahmadi was charged with provoking the attack and given seven months.

Over 2011 and 2012, Sunni groups attacked and evicted communities of Shia on the big island of Madura, adjacent to East Java, and a court gave one of the local Shia clerics four years' jail for heresy. In both cases the response of Yudhoyono's religious affairs minister was to advise the minority to convert to mainstream Sunni practices or to agree to be declared non-Muslim. Yet both the religious affairs and home ministries have dug their heels in against any more registration of religions beyond the six allowed on official identity cards—Islam, Catholicism, Protestantism, Hinduism, Buddhism, and Confucianism—even though the constitutional court has ruled that the state may not limit the number of religions. Even supporters of Yudhoyono were mystified that the religious affairs minister was not replaced.

The larger Christian minority also felt nervous under Yudhoyono. They, too, had been swept up in the wave of piety that accompanied fast economic growth and political turmoil. The decadal census shows their place in the Indonesian population remaining much the same, about 7 percent of Indonesians being Protestant and 3 percent Catholic, with the largest concentrations in North Sumatra, West Kalimantan, Manado, Maluku, and Papua.

Yet many Christian observers feel that the official figures somehow understate the reality, as indicated by a highly visible wave of church building across cities and rural areas. Many new believers flock to evangelical churches in the Java countryside. In the Temanggung regency, Central Java, where about forty churches have sprung up in recent years, angry Muslims ransacked a courthouse after a judge gave a Christian evangelizer a five-year jail term for distributing leaflets critical of Islam, instead of the death sentence they were demanding. The same fervor grips large sections of the ethnic Chinese minority, especially in Jakarta, where there are now "megachurches," such as preacher Stephen Tong's $27-million Reformed Millennium Centre, which holds up to 4,500 worshippers. The second-generation scion of the Lippo Group, James Riady, is one such born-again.

A backlash against this Christian expansion has taken several forms. One is the application of building consent rules that require the agreement of surrounding communities; these are not usually bothered with in the case of mosques. A notorious case is a large church project in the West Java city of Bogor that has stalled for years, despite a court ruling that it must go ahead. A smaller church for people of the Batak ethnic group in Bekasi was demolished by local authorities in early 2013.

All these minorities feel threatened by Muslim vigilantism, chiefly from the Front Pembela Islam, a preman-style organization of white-clad thugs who take it on themselves to put down Christian churches and Islamic minorities and to disrupt places of entertainment that they see as locations of prostitution and alcohol consumption. Founded in 1998 by military and police officers for use against student protests, the FPI has been tolerated long after another violent, military-sponsored Islamic group, Laskar Jihad, was shut down following the first Bali bombing in 2002.

In 2006 a US embassy cable said an official of the BIN, or State Intelligence Agency, had mentioned that the then national police chief, General Sutanto (who would later head the BIN), had been funding the FPI right up to the time it attacked the embassy that year. Sutanto had described it as a useful "attack dog" that could spare the security forces from accusations of human rights violations. Another cable reported that former Jakarta police chief Nugroho Djayusman admitted contact with the FPI, though he claimed it was to monitor its activities.

In mid-2008 a mass of FPI members attacked a multifaith crowd that had gathered at the foot of the National Monument in Jakarta to protest against the then imminent antipornography law. The police stood by as dozens of demonstrators were injured by the FPI. Following a public outcry, police reviewed video recordings and arrested several FPI members, including the group's head, Habib Rizieq, who received an eighteen-month jail sentence some months later. The group continues its violent attacks across Java and, in

2013, celebrated its fifteenth anniversary with a large-scale motor-cycle parade through Jakarta.

When pressed, government officials claim the FPI is now "out of control" and functioning as muscle for hire. Yet the wilting of Laskar Jihad, once the support of the security apparatus was removed, suggests that Yudhoyono's government has not really tried to keep the FPI's activities within the law. On the other hand, the army's continually professed willingness to help out the police against terrorism and interreligious violence offers a cure that would be worse than the disease.

An example of what could be done came in February 2012, when masses of the local Dayak people in Palangkaraya, Central Kalimantan, occupied their airport to prevent the disembarkation of four FPI leaders who had arrived to set up a provincial branch. The FPI delegation was kept on the aircraft and sent back to Java by security officials. When Yudhoyono went to New York to collect an award for religious tolerance from an American private foundation, media coverage had an almost derisive tone and highlighted protests by members of the demolished church in Bekasi and by Shia and Ahmadiyah representatives outside the presidential palace.

BELOW THE SURFACE, a much more sinister form of Islamist violence has stirred, and the government and the police deserve much more credit for their response to it. The jihad in Afghanistan during the 1980s attracted a small number of volunteers from Indonesia, Malaysia, and the Philippines. On their return in the 1990s, these people were drawn to the purist teachings of figures like Abu Bakar Ba'asyir, an ulema of Yemeni descent who founded the Al-Mukmin pesantren at the village of Ngruki near Solo, Central Java.

Ba'asyir had fled to Malaysia for seventeen years during the New Order, after frequent arrests for advocating the adoption of Syari'ah law and ultimately for his involvement in a bombing at the Borobudur monument. By the time he returned to Indonesia in 1999, the country was awash with jihadist literature and teaching. The new Internet and video technologies brought texts into immediate, vivid life, promoting the school of thought known as Salafism (similar to Wahhabism and also originating from Saudi Arabia), which envisions a transnational caliphate of Muslims who follow a social and religious life modeled on the era of the Prophet.

When the first bombing of tourist targets in Bali in October 2002 shattered some of the general complacency about Indonesia's "moderate" Islam, the manhunt for the plotters led Indonesian police and their foreign advisers to a circle of younger jihadists linked to Ba'asyir and the Ngruki pesantren. They operated under the name Jemaah Islamiyah (Islamic Congregation), the police believed, with Ba'asyir as their spiritual leader. For his part, Ba'asyir denied any connection with terrorism or that Jemaah Islamiyah even existed outside the constructions of the police and Western intelligence agencies.

Already suspecting Ba'asyir over church bombings in Java, the authorities looked for evidence that linked him with the Bali bombing. They obtained convictions for conspiracy and immigration offenses, but on his release after twenty-five months in jail, the Supreme Court overturned his conspiracy conviction. He returned to making ambivalent messages about martyrdom in the cause of jihad and in at least one sermon called foreign tourists "worms, snakes and maggots." In 2011 a court sentenced him to fifteen years in jail for organizing a secret terrorism training camp.

Cells of Jemaah Islamiyah continued to mount roughly annual major bombings against targets linked to Western influence, including the Australian embassy and the Marriott Hotel. An allied group called Kompak (Komite Aksi Penanggulangan Akibat Krisis, Crisis Management/Prevention Committee) in Poso, Central Sulawesi, kept up terrorist attacks after a short-lived but fierce religious war between local Muslim and Christian communities was ended via the mediation of Jusuf Kalla while a minister in Megawati's government. But after coordinated suicide bombings against two big hotels in 2009, a steady manhunt by the new Detachment 88 unit from the Indonesian police produced results, with some 400 adherents of Jemaah Islamiyah arrested and 250 convicted. The unrepentant perpetrators of the first Bali bombing had been executed by firing squad at the end of 2008. Scores of others were serving prison sentences. Still, authorities and the police resisted calls from foreign governments for the banning of Jemaah Islamiyah. Better to keep it on the surface, they argued, where they could track its activities.

The Detachment 88 police also took a soft approach to those Jemaah Islamiyah members under arrest. Aware that prisons could be schools that only hardened extreme ideologies, they attempted to "deradicalize" about 200 of the convicts, starting by trying to learn about their motives. This involved senior police eating meals with them, taking them out for limited excursions, and even encouraging marriages for some. "It's a sign they are coming back from *al-hijrah* [a mental state of readiness to sacrifice one's life] to the real world," one Densus leader said in 2008. Detainees who seemed less committed were separated from hardline mentors. By overcoming suspicion of the *thagut,* or evil police, investigators aimed to turn detainees from what they called the "lesser jihad"—or a narrow focus on violent methods—to a "greater jihad" of nonviolent or spiritual struggle.

By 2013 the police had arrested about 900 people in their antiterrorism campaign and killed about ninety suspects during raids. Jemaah Islamiyah and its splinter group Jemaah Ansharut Tauhid were disrupted, broken into small cells, largely cut off from sources of funds and technologies, and their bomb-making experts removed. The surviving militant jihadists turned to drive-by assassinations of isolated police officers.

While the threat of terrorism has abated, it has not disappeared. About three-quarters of the terrorists in jail are due for release over the coming decade, many of them still comparatively young. Police think that perhaps 40 percent will have become even more motivated while in prison. In addition, between 150 and 200 Indonesian jihadists are thought to have joined the so-called Islamic State of Iraq and Syria which carved out a "caliphate" across the border of these two countries. Foreign counterpart agencies worry at the lack of a clear "proactive" strategy by Indonesian security agencies to identify and diffuse violent jihadism. The signs are there, they say, in literature, Internet postings, and sermons: what is needed is early intervention with a "counternarrative." The obstacles to this have been the turf wars between the various police, military, and intelligence agencies; lack of capacity to track student movements to jihadist centers in the Middle East and South Asia; and a protective reaction by the ministries of religious affairs and education when, say, a radical pesantren is identified.

The vagueness of Indonesian law about conspiracy to plan terrorist acts also discourages early intervention. Instead, police feel they must wait until the plotters are ready to strike, hence the high incidence of shootouts and deaths of suspects during arrests. In 2010 Yudhoyono set up the Badan Nasional Penanggulangan Terrorisme (BNPT, National Counter-Terrorism Agency), headed by a retired police general with a retired Kopassus officer as his deputy.

It organized meetings known as *Klinik Pancasila* to educate young Muslims about the national ideology and distributed a pamphlet titled *Buku Cinta NKRI* (Book of Devotion to the Unitary State of the Republic of Indonesia).

WHILE THE VIOLENT ATTACK on Indonesia's status quo appeared quiescent at the end of Yudhoyono's presidency, the general picture was one of a nation undergoing an intensification of its conversion to Islam, which started centuries ago but was speeding up in the digital age. The explicitly Islamic parties might have been in decline, but all parties and leaders in a position to take power were taking on an increasingly Islamic character, sought out running mates among respected Muslim figures, and organized Islamic affiliates. The division between santri and abangan was blurring in Java. Alumni of Habibie's association of Muslim intellectuals were now ministers and potential presidential candidates in ostensibly secular parties.

The issue of the nation's "Arabization" became a running topic. Devout Muslims were fixated with the Middle East as the center of Islam. New media were transforming the culture of learning, as observers like the sociologist Yudi Latif noted. "The *ulama* had been the cultural broker or interpreter who adjusted the signal from the Middle East in a harmonious way [that was] within the capacity of local culture to absorb," Latif says. "The new media have bypassed the local *ulama*. There is a transnational Islamic movement. The new-age Muslims tend to be cut off from the roots of Indonesian historical tradition and attach themselves to Middle Eastern epistemology." To many worried minorities and more secular Muslims, it seemed that the goal of the "greater jihad," a process of deepening faith that would eventually lead to a voluntary embrace of Islamic law and governance, was possibly underway among a large majority of Indonesians.

Yet the example of the PKS showed that a great moderation of the Islamist signal follows when an Islamic grouping shifts into the formal power structure from the outside. The move toward Syari'ah law by Indonesia's empowered regional governments was also running out of steam in the later years of the century's first decade, no more so than in Aceh, where it had been applied as a concession to mollify the GAM rebels during Wahid's presidency. Like other senior GAM figures who had always seen their struggle as primarily

a nationalist one, Shadia Mahaban is appalled at the religious zeal-
otry this unfettered. Local newspapers continue to report groups
of ulema burning stacks of jeans, which religious police seize from
passing women and replace with skirts, or proselytizing on the sin-
fulness of women straddling motor scooters as drivers (rather than
riding sidesaddle as pillion passengers), and generally urging women
to retreat from public office.

Such purification campaigns bemuse those who know Acehnese
history. The old sultanate had a string of female rulers. Houses
were always passed to daughters, along with nearby rice paddies, so
their husbands were virtual guests. Acehnese women—notably, the
heroine Cut Nha Dhien—fought alongside their menfolk in wars,
to the consternation of the more sensitive Dutch soldiers. Uniquely
among women of the Malay archipelago, the Acehnese female dress
included loose pantaloons, not the tight and hobbling sarongs worn
elsewhere. As Mahaban declares, trousers and jeans were thus more
authentically Acehnese than the loose skirts handed out by the ulema
like prudish nineteenth-century Christian missionaries. Mohammed
Nur Djuli says he was branded a "Westernised orientalist" when he
wrote about this in the main local newspaper.

Mahaban sees the promotion of Syari'ah as part of a wider struggle for cultural dominance and power that has ramifications across
Indonesia. "They are trying to tell the whole of Indonesia, 'We're
doing this, we're still powerful,'" she says. "I hate to say it, but it
was Gus Dur's fault. It was his biggest fault, allowing this to happen
here, without thinking about Indonesia as a whole. If you look at it
culturally, anthropologically, in Aceh it was never like that. This is
something very new. It's like a born-again Islam or something."

Without the Aceh precedent, the enforcement of Syari'ah by local
administrations in parts of West Java and Kalimantan might not have
progressed. "It's not working here, so what makes you think it will
work in West Java?" Mahaban asks. "There's no such thing like this
in South-East Asia. It's something very new. Some kind of identity
you want to show, something that we lost during the Suharto era, the
Dutch period: the only identity is by showing how religious you are."

Perhaps this suggests that Indonesia's long contest between cus-
tom and religion is as much a struggle with its feminine side as with
anything else. It may be too early to write off the influence of the
beautiful Queen of the South Sea, Nyai Loro Kidul.

10

KORUPSI

Geckos versus Crocodiles

AS INDONESIA BEGAN ITS ERA OF DIRECT ELECTIONS AT CENTRAL AND REGIONAL LEV-els, it soon became apparent that funding democracy would be an expensive exercise. Soon after Yudhoyono's installation as president, his coalition member party, Golkar, held a congress in December 2004 at which the vice president, Jusuf Kalla, wrestled the party leadership from the incumbent, Akbar Tanjung. Though a veteran from the Suharto era, Tanjung was widely respected as someone who had adjusted happily enough to the new era. But he was hopelessly outgunned by the money Kalla threw at the party election.

The vote was taken from the 484 provincial and district del-egations, each with equal weight. Kalla's team, according to cred-ible reporting by American embassy officials on the scene, offered each district delegate Rp 200 million (then about $22,000) and each provincial board Rp 500 million or more. There was a cash down payment, with the balance to be delivered after the vote for Kalla came in. The DPR speaker, Agung Laksono, had Rp 50 billion ($5.5 million) to spend, and the wealthy businessman-politician Aburizal Bakrie, who was the economic coordinating minister in Yudhoyono's cabinet, splashed out Rp 70 billion ($8 million) to secure Kalla's win.

It was a happy event. As well as collecting their cash and enjoying a good time in the capital's top hotels at someone else's expense, the delegates who had backed Kalla could look forward to being closely tied to the government and to receiving support for their own political careers as gubernatorial and bupati candidates. And this was just an internal party election, although admittedly it was in the party traditionally closest to the business plutocracy, which included in its top council some big tycoons, like Bakrie and the Acehnese media entrepreneur Surya Paloh, as well as smaller ones, like Kalla.

As the Yudhoyono decade progressed, it became apparent that politicians and their party machines had an almost insatiable appetite for funding. The new Komisi Pemberantasan Korupsi (KPK, Corruption Eradication Commission), which had been set up by law in 2002 and had begun operations in 2004, soon found some of its most egregious suspects among ministers and legislators. As scams and fraud were brought to light, and successful prosecutions launched in a special corruption court, public opinion surveys showed that the parliament was regarded as the most corrupt institution in the country. Positions in the DPR "commissions" (or committees) that oversaw the various ministries became ever more highly coveted. Membership meant having a say in whether an allocation for a particular program or purchase should be passed or adjusted upward, and in whether a particular contractor or supplier should be approved. The DPR member involved stood to gain kickbacks both from the ministry that proposed the budgetary allocation and from the supplier who benefited.

The new generation of democratic politicians (who, in many cases, were simply recycled authoritarian spear-carriers) found many willing partners in the bureaucracy and a flexible culture of fiscal probity. Many, if not most, civil servants did not think it unethical, if their department's outside requirements could be supplied at a cost below the budgeted amount, to keep the difference themselves by arrangement with the contractor. From there, it was but a short step to inflating the budget estimates so that there would definitely be such a margin. This applied to everything from purchases of stationery to high-tech items, such as aircraft and power plants. Kickbacks of 10 to 15 percent were routine in government procurement, the World Bank reported, and contributed about 40 percent of official corruption. In late 2013, as Yudhoyono's ten years in office neared their end, an even more alarming claim was made by his own former party treasurer, Muhammad Nazaruddin, a former member of the DPR budget committee who was now serving a jail term for rigging a tender. Nazaruddin alleged that an allocation of Rp 5.8 trillion ($523 million) for a new electronic identity card system included a markup of 45 percent, resulting in $500,000 bribes all round for the politicians who approved it.

Satrio Budihardjo Joedono, an economist who served as trade minister and ambassador to Paris in the last years of the Suharto government, was made head of the National Audit Agency by President Habibie in 1999, with a mission to pinpoint financial irregularities in the government apparatus. "You were surprised when anything is not corrupt," Joedono recalls of his five years in the position. "It was very unusual if you did not find anything." What he found was a pervasive blurring of the distinction between state property and private property, an attitude carried over from premodern political systems and intensified by the "traditional feudal system" that Suharto had built. "Activities which in a modern legal system would be corrupt, here were not," Joedono says. All his predecessors since 1945 had signed off on these practices.

The cases rolled on. A former minister of fisheries in the Megawati government was charged over a 32 billion rupiah ($3.5 million) "off-budget" fund derived from funds siphoned out of his ministry budget, plus contributions from fishing industry figures. A former minister for religious affairs, Said Agil Hussein Al Munawar, and his former director general for Islamic guidance and hajj affairs, Taufiq Kamil, were convicted of embezzling nearly $71 million in funds earmarked for Indonesians performing the hajj. Former Investment Coordinating Board chairman Theo F. Toemion was sentenced to six years' imprisonment for misappropriating $2.5 million from the budget for promoting foreign investment. A former election commissioner, Daan Dimara, was given four years for rigging procurement contracts in the 2004 elections.

In the middle of the 2006–7 avian influenza epidemic, which killed 159 Indonesians (out of a worldwide total of 359 deaths), the then director general of medical services at the health ministry, Ratna Dewi Umar, marked up the price of the oxygen ventilators that were urgently required to save patients. The contract went to a company owned by Bambang Rudijanto Tanoesoedibjo, brother of the media mogul and politician Hary Tanoesoedibjo. The illegal margin was estimated to have cost the state Rp 12 billion ($1.2 million). The official, who eventually got a five-year jail term, said she'd followed orders from her boss, the then health minister, who continues to be under investigation for allegedly receiving 10 percent of the markup.

Egged on by a public that was accusing it of ignoring the "big fish," and having been granted more investigative resources, the anticorruption commission took on suspect parliamentarians. In 2008 it made a 2:00 a.m. raid on a luxury hotel, arresting, among others, a DPR member from the PPP. He was nabbed in his car while in possession of Rp 71 million ($8,000) in cash, which he had just been given by another suspect from Riau province who was involved in a plan to rezone a large swathe of national forest for development (for which the developer had allocated $300,000 to pay off politicians). One colleague in the DPR expressed skepticism about the charge because it was "impossible anyone would offer a lawmaker an amount of money that small."

Another DPR member, from Golkar, was arrested for marking up the price of fire trucks bought while he was previously governor of Riau. Under Megawati, the home ministry had issued an instruction making a single company the only authorized distributor of fire trucks to provincial governments. A member of Yudhoyono's PD was forced out by the DPR's own ethics committee for trying to squeeze commissions out of the hajj program.

In August 2007 Nurdin Halid, long a controversial Golkar politician and commodity dealer, became the first sitting DPR member to be jailed (although his two-year jail term was in fact for milking $18 million from a palm-oil fund while he was running the national food-price stabilization body, Bulog, in the late 1990s). That Halid was a longtime associate of the vice president, Jusuf Kalla, made his conviction more significant, as it signaled that the anticorruption drive was showing less fear and favor. But as well as discomfiting high-level party patrons, the KPK was pushing into dangerous ground.

INDONESIANS GENERALLY DO NOT TRUST the people who are supposed to look after their safety and punish wrongdoers: police, prosecutors, and judges. Few go to them for help. Out of the 5 million cases that go through Indonesia's courts each year, about 4.8 million relate to traffic offenses. Almost all the rest are criminal cases. In other words, these are not cases in which citizens are actively applying for remediation via the judiciary. Trust in the legal system, say many experts, is about the same as it was under colonial rule.

During a closed-door session of the American Chamber of Commerce in 2007, an attorney who advised foreign companies in Jakarta described the local legal system as "harrowing" to a visiting senior official from Washington. "He advises clients in commercial disputes that they cannot afford the corrupt court system and will lose because they cannot play the game the Indonesian way," noted the US embassy. "Western company executives are sometimes jailed in the case of a dispute with a local partner."

In commercial and other civil cases, taking a dispute to the police or the courts can be an invitation to extortion. In 2013 a large foreign enterprise in Jakarta with an online payments system found that its network had been hacked and that $2 million in credits had been transferred to a domestic bank account. The company's IT specialists and accountants identified the account and its owners. But the firm's legal advisers, one of Jakarta's top law partnerships, recommended against taking this evident fraud case to the police: doing so would put the company in a bidding war with the fraudsters to get a partisan performance from investigators, prosecutors, and judges. Meanwhile, police detectives would browse through the company's books, looking for unrelated matters that could be blown up into criminal cases, thereby creating further opportunities for extortion. The company and its foreign owner decided to let the $2 million go.

Also in 2013, a foreign investor in another business, a mine that had failed to produce enough of the high-grade coal promised by its geologist, found himself called to the Jakarta police headquarters (known as Polda) for questioning over a personal guarantee for part of the mine's financing. The lender had not even initiated civil proceedings for recovery of the loan, and the loan agreement had an arbitration clause anyway. The investor found himself immediately taken away to the police cells on suspicion of fraud, where he spent two months while his staff and family worked for his release. When he finally won a court order declaring the case a civil matter and ordering his immediate release, the police rearrested him outside the court. Stepping up the pressure, they transferred him to the capital's

Cipinang prison, where he spent a week sleeping on the floor of a mass holding area with common criminal suspects. Becoming seriously ill, he was transferred to a hospital. Some weeks later he was allowed home, with the police case still pending.

Conversely, the system is highly useful to rich vested interests who are trying to protect themselves against efforts by the state or other parties to investigate or retrieve ill-gotten gains, and to lighten or evade punishment.

The desultory pursuit of the Suharto family and its wealth after 1998 is the prime case in point. As we have seen, Suharto's resignation was followed immediately by a public pledge by the defense forces chief, General Wiranto, to protect the ex-president and his family. Leaked conversations showed that his successor, Habibie, was similarly inclined. The law enforcement agencies reacted to calls for his prosecution timidly. They put Suharto under "city arrest" in early 2000 and announced that he would be prosecuted for embezzling some $571 million in government donations to charitable foundations under his control. But the courts repeatedly excused him from attending hearings on the grounds of ill health, certified by his own doctors, despite his frequently being photographed receiving visitors and making public appearances.

When Suharto did enter a final decline in May 2007, prosecutors decided to close the case, with Yudhoyono and his senior ministers saying it would be improper to order otherwise. In August that year, the Supreme Court gave another warning to his critics. In 1999 the US magazine *Time* had published a cover story alleging the Suhartos had accumulated about $15 billion worth of land and other wealth, and that a single transfer of $9 billion at the time of his fall had caused a tremor in European financial markets. Suharto sued. Two lower courts dismissed his case, even though *Time* was unable to prove its figures, notably about the alleged transfer of secret overseas funds. (Though the figure may have been questionable, that Suharto kept money hidden overseas was not. In 2007 the US ambassador Lynn Pascoe reported an executive of the Swiss-based UBS-Warburg as saying that Suharto had been "one of the biggest Indonesian customers" of its private banking arm for many years.) After a six-year delay, the Supreme Court suddenly upheld the defamation action, awarding Suharto Rp 1 trillion (then $106 million) in damages. The magazine would have the judgment overturned in a review, but for a while the decision had a chilling effect on the media. It was widely seen as a case of "judges for hire."

The former president's family members had a harder time but were not without help from corruption in the legal system. In 2000 his least popular child, Tommy Suharto, got an eighteen-month jail sentence from a Supreme Court judge over an $11 million land swindle. Tommy went underground but remained in contact with friends, who presumed him to be somewhere in the network of houses on Jakarta's Cendana Street, owned by the Suharto family and hallowed ground that was still guarded by the military, and which the civilian police hesitated to search rigorously.

While Tommy was on the lam, the courageous judge Syafiuddin Kartasasmita died in a gangland-style hit. The assassination was traced back to Tommy, who was found in 2002 and sentenced to fifteen years in jail. Tommy served his sentence in a suite of eight air-conditioned cells in a luxury wing of Cipinang prison, one cell fitted as a billiard room. He had access to a special badminton court and once a week was seen at an exclusive golf course on "medical" parole. In a mysterious decision under Yudhoyono's government, authorities released Tommy in 2006, only five years into his jail term.

In 2003 Suharto's half-brother Probosutedjo also faced court on corruption charges. His jail term was four years, which was then reduced to two years. When he later complained that the reduction had cost some $600,000 in payments to the judges via his lawyers, without him knowing how much was really needed, his full sentence was reinstated. Probosutedjo was pulled out of a hospital and sent back to jail.

After Suharto died in January 2008, efforts turned to a civil action started in mid-2007 to recover some $1.6 billion ($440 million in state funds and over $1.1 billion in damages) from the seven *yayasan* (charitable foundations) that had been controlled by the former president. The money donated by or extorted from businesses— in the case of one foundation, a 5 percent levy on the profits of state-owned banks since 1976—had gone to many worthy causes, including thousands of scholarships, in displays of Suharto's patronage. In the latter years of his presidency, it had also been shelled out to the president's cronies, such as Bob Hasan, in unsecured, unrepaid "loans," as well as to family interests. In March 2008 a Jakarta court ruled that one of the foundations, the Yayasan Supersemar, had to repay a quarter of the funds from state levies, $110 million, but declared the Suharto family itself not liable. Delivery of a single rupiah was still being awaited several years later.

Tommy continued to have friends in some courts. Prosecutors launched civil suits to recover assets and profits from his various land scams and initiated actions to seize $50 million deposited in the tax haven of Guernsey. Mysteriously, $10 million of this hidden money came back to him via an account held by the Ministry of Justice. When the state logistics agency Bulog sued Tommy for Rp 250 billion (then $28 million), which it claimed to have lost in a 1995 land deal, the judges at the South Jakarta District Court threw out the suit and instead awarded damages of $550,000 to Tommy for "defamation of character," declaring him to be a businessman with "an international reputation." The then finance minister, Sri Mulyani Indrawati, had a better run with Supreme Court decisions, enabling her department to seize back $134 million in state funds from Tommy's defunct Timor car project.

IN INDONESIAN CIRCLES, the terms "legal mafia," "case broker," and "account owner" are frequently used to describe coteries within the law enforcement and judicial communities. In these, there is little loyalty to the law, the government, or the judicial hierarchy, but a strong sense of entitlement to moneymaking opportunities.

On the founding of the republic, the Indonesian police inherited a tradition of military-style security enforcement from the colonial *Feldpolitie*. In 1966 Suharto put them under the Ministry of Defense as the fourth arm of the military. The attorney general's office and the prosecutors beneath it were also put under tight military control, with top positions filled with army legal officers.

In the New Order, the highest priority was loyalty to the government and fulfillment of its objectives. Otherwise, resources allocated to the police and judiciary were tight, and agencies were left to raise their own funds. They became extortion rackets. The idea of prosecutors and defense lawyers being "officers of the court" went out the window. Police and prosecutors negotiated with the courts as equals, taking search-and-seizure orders as "requests" that had to be agreed to at top level. The law was a business, and all but a courageous few were part of it.

After 1998, reform measures tried to change this. The police were separated from the armed forces in 1999–2000. The court system and its administrative staff were placed under a Supreme Court that was given more independence, and judges were monitored and trained by a new judicial commission. But corrupt practices persist, with cases surfacing of large payments to court officials, and defense lawyers telling their clients of direct demands for payoffs from judges. Even in middle-level courts, these payments can amount to $50,000, in repeat doses, to stave off arrest. Whether defense lawyers are telling their clients the truth is another matter. As one academic legal expert puts it: "If the judgement is known in advance, they can play with that, and get someone to think they are paying for it." The Indonesian legal community has numerous professional associations, for the simple reason that as soon as a lawyers' body tries to exert any discipline on its members, it splits.

The Indonesian National Police were ill-prepared to take over their role as the country's principal enforcers of law and public security, either in total manpower (150,000 in 1999), technical resources, or accountability. Its staff augment their low official salaries with distributions from blatant and illegal fundraising systems. Unofficial traffic fines collected in on-the-spot settlements by police are pooled at headquarters by designated "quartermasters" and then distributed down the ranks in regular extra pay envelopes. Ambitious police officers develop protective relationships with businesspeople, in many cases from the vulnerable ethnic Chinese community. The businessperson gets protection from violence and ad hoc extortion; the police officer gets money with which he or she can fund promotions or transfers. Less scrupulous protection rackets involve illegal drugs, prostitution, and gambling, and often are centered in sleazy nightclubs and short-stay hotels run by retired police.

One full-time focus for a number of officers is to look for opportunities for police to insert themselves into civil disputes and turn them into criminal cases, as in the failed coal mine case. Usually this involves debt disputes. Anecdotally, the practice is spreading wider. A housewife who borrows from a moneylender, a business unable to service its debts—all become prey.

Even the biggest multinational companies are not immune, despite being vital to the Indonesian economy. In 2013 local prosecutors in the attorney general's office in Riau province persuaded the corruption court to jail two midranking employees of the biggest oil producer, Chevron, for allegedly defrauding the state of funds from an environmental cleanup that had never happened. Yet evidence showed that Chevron had not claimed any tax offset or other benefit, while soil testing made it clear that no problem existed. Another case launched by the attorney general's office involved the alleged misuse of a wireless-spectrum license by Indosat, one of the largest telecom companies and controlled by Qatar Telecom. Its former chief executive got a four-year jail term.

Both cases are under appeal. To legal experts, they demonstrate two things. First, judges who had effectively been unexposed to commercial cases throughout their earlier legal careers were ill equipped to spot even blatant misapplications of the law and were often biased against big business. Second, the cases were a signal that prosecutors were willing to go after even the biggest oil and telecom companies.

In March 2008 the anticorruption commission fired what turned out to be the opening shot in a war with senior elements of the police and the attorney general's office, a struggle that ultimately would threaten the KPK's credibility. The agency arrested one of the top prosecutors in the attorney general's office, Urip Tri Gunawan, while he was in possession of $600,000 in cash. Urip had been one of the leading figures in a drive launched by a new attorney general, Hendarman Supandji, appointed by Yudhoyono in 2007, to show that his department was in fact a credible anticorruption force, not part of the problem.

Along with the civil actions against the Suharto foundations, Supandji had decided to target one of the biggest elephants in the room. During his five-year stint at the National Audit Agency, the economist Joedono had discovered that the largest leak of government money had occurred in an institution that was meant to be a pillar of fiscal reform, the central bank.

Bank Indonesia had addressed the collapsing banking system in the 1997–98 Asian financial crisis by setting up a special liquidity fund to support commercial banks hit by runs on their deposits. One of the biggest private banks, Bank Central Asia, then controlled by longtime Suharto business associate Sudono Salim (Liem Sioe Liong) and two of Suharto's sons, lost 50 percent of its deposits over two weeks. "The central bank would send truckloads of rupiah to the back door, and the employees would rush them to the tellers at the front," recalls one banker. In all, Joedono says, some $64 billion in the rupiah value of the time was pumped into the system (by other calculations, the bank bailout amounted to $77 billion). In many cases, it went everywhere except to the bank customers, such as out to companies in Hong Kong, which were immediately folded up. Bank Central Asia was one that behaved "decently," says Joedono, paying its account holders and quietly transferring equity to the government. But overall, only a small fraction was ever repaid or properly accounted for.

Joedono found the missing billions listed in Bank Indonesia's books under "accounts receivable" as "perpetual interest-free loans." The amount was big enough to throw the central bank into negative equity, if properly disclosed. "It was difficult for me to remain polite," Joedono says. He refused to sign off on Bank Indonesia's accounts and instead wrote a "no opinion" finding.

The then president, Abdurrahman Wahid, called him in urgently. "Whatever you do, don't issue a no-opinion on the bank," Joedono recalls Wahid saying. "That would be catastrophic. Confidence in the whole of Indonesia will vanish and the rupiah will have no value. We will be bankrupt!"

Joedono mentioned that Bank Indonesia had given him two different lists of its assets. "How can you have an opinion if you have two lists?" he asked Wahid.

In the end, Joedono stuck to his guns and issued the no-opinion report. The Ministry of Finance immediately recapitalized the central bank, and a crisis was averted. Joedono wrote a sixty-five-volume report, one volume on each of the banks refinanced by the liquidity fund, detailing what had happened to the money. He sent copies to the police, the attorney general, and the speaker of the parliament. Nothing happened for years, until Supandji decided to take the liquidity fund case up in 2007.

When Supandji's investigator decided in March 2008 to close the investigation into two of the bailed-out banks, Bank Dagang Negara Indonesia and Bank Central Asia, for "lack of evidence," the anticorruption commission was alerted. Some days later, it arrested Urip in the act of taking a $600,000 payment from a Jakarta socialite and business deal fixer, Artalyta Suryani, who happened to be a friend and neighbor of Bank Dagang Negara Indonesia's former owner, the Sino-Indonesian tycoon Sjamsul Nursalim, who had moved his office to Singapore. Other senior prosecutors were called in for questioning. Six months later Urip received a twenty-year jail sentence in the corruption court, and Artalyta later got five years. No link to Nursalim was found. Soon after her release from her spell in jail—which included a cell with luxuries like air-conditioning, a widescreen television, and a sprung bed—Artalyta was questioned in Singapore over the case of a palm-oil plantation in Sulawesi that eventually saw the local bupati jailed.

After securing these convictions, the anticorruption commission took over the liquidity fund investigations from the shaken attorney general's office. More embarrassing arrests followed. They included the central bank's senior deputy governor, Miranda Goeltom, who up till then had been regarded as a path breaker for women into the top ranks of public service. It turned out that the approval of her appointment in 2004 had been eased by payments of $54,900 in traveler's checks to forty-one of the fifty-six members of the parliament's financial affairs commission. Further inquiries fingered other top Bank Indonesia officials whose appointments were also won by payments to parliamentarians. They included the father-in-law of one of Yudhoyono's sons, who went to jail for five years. Government was bribing government.

In 2009, however, confidence in the anticorruption commission was badly shaken. In May that year, police arrested its chief commissioner, a former star prosecutor named Antasari Azhar. He was charged with ordering the execution of a Jakarta businessman, who had been found in his car with bullets in his head. The businessman was killed, police alleged, because he was blackmailing Antasari over an affair with his wife, a twenty-two-year-old golf caddy. Antasari was immediately fired by Yudhoyono and the following year was given an eighteen-year jail term. He continues to explore avenues of appeal, putting forward technical evidence showing that a threatening message to the victim could not have come from his mobile phone, as police alleged. His case that he was victim of a frame-up continues to have some credibility among the Indonesian public.

In September 2009 the police declared two other KPK commissioners, Chandra M. Hamzah and Bibit Samad Riyanto, as suspects in a case involving bribes from a businessman, Anggodo Widjojo, who was allegedly involved in a corrupt deal to supply communications equipment to the forestry ministry. The president suspended both commissioners from duty, and the KPK operated under a skeleton leadership. Then, in a sensational twist, transcripts of secret recordings surfaced that implicated Widjojo in a conspiracy to frame the two commissioners: the plot involved senior officials, notably a former deputy attorney general, Abdul Hakim Ritonga, an assistant attorney general for intelligence, Wisnu Subroto, and the national chief of detectives in the police, Inspector General Susno Duadji. The police proceeded with the case, arresting the two commissioners, and Yudhoyono ordered an inquiry from an independent team led by the prominent human rights lawyer Adnan Buyung Nasution.

A Facebook campaign in support of the KPK and its embattled commissioners gained more than a million supporters. Several thousand demonstrators took to the streets of Jakarta. When the recordings were verified in the constitutional court, open to a fascinated and disturbed public, the police released the two men. Nasution's "Team of Eight" found the original bribery case against the two commissioners to be weak and recommended that it be dropped. They urged action against the officials pushing it, as well as reinforcement of the KPK's status and wholesale reform of the police and prosecution branch.

In a virtual challenge to the president, a senior attorney general's department official declared that prosecutors were ready to proceed with a case of extortion against the commissioners, while the police restored their chief detective, General Susno, to duty.

In December 2009 the attorney general's office announced it was dropping all charges against the two commissioners, whom Yudhoyono then reinstated. Over the next year, the KPK moved against participants in the frame-up conspiracy, including the three-star police general, Susno. The police were reluctant to sack their third-ranking officer. When they did, he negotiated to be replaced by a close ally who was known to have a dubious record of protecting illegal gambling and logging.

It took over three years to put Susno in jail. After exhausting his appeals against his forty-two-month jail sentence for corruption and abuse of power, he took to the hills, broadcasting on YouTube that he was only upholding the law because his detention order had not been delivered properly. He was found in the West Java capital, Bandung, after several days on the run and in the protection of police colleagues, including at the provincial police headquarters, from where he was eventually extracted and taken to prison.

In custody, Susno cooperated with KPK investigators by blowing open many of the rackets involving the police and legal mafias, networks so serious that the anticorruption commission was like "a gecko tackling a crocodile," he claimed. "Suharto was the smiling general," he told interviewers, a reference to the title of a hagiographic book about the previous regime head. "I'm the singing general."

Whether or not Susno's information actually helped, the KPK did move against corrupt elements in the police and judicial system. The agency gained the conviction of a former Indonesian diplomat who was known as a leading "case broker" in the law courts, a man said to be working with a retired police general. He had offered Susno a big bribe to turn a civil case into a criminal one.

In September 2013 Djoko Susilo became the first serving police general to be convicted for corruption, for which he got ten years in jail. The former head of the Indonesian National Police's traffic division had gained Rp 32 billion ($2.6 million) from the winner of a tender for providing driving simulators, in a contract inflated by Rp 145 billion ($12 million). The anticorruption agency presented the court with evidence that Djoko had amassed over Rp 100 billion ($8.3 million) in assets over the previous ten years, despite having a salary of only Rp 28 million ($2,300) a month. The ownership of luxury houses across Java and Bali, tour buses, petrol stations, and other properties was put in the names of his three wives and other relatives. On receiving a copy of Djoko's autobiography during a tear-filled defense plea, the judges were astonished to find a $100 bill slipped between the pages.

BY THE END OF Yudhoyono's second term, the anticorruption commission was one of the more successful additions to the armory of the newly democratic Indonesian state. Its headquarters and leaders were known to all and sundry. Tens of thousands of tip-offs flowed in each year. Swarms of reporters camped at its front door every day, waiting for fresh news. The anticorruption drive was supported by many of the biggest civil society groups, including NU and Muhammadiyah.

But the KPK had its weaknesses, which are only gradually being addressed. Many of its operational difficulties stemmed from the reluctance of Indonesia's ministries and agencies to cooperate and share information with other arms of government or even with different branches of their own agency. This continues despite the formation in 2005 of the Interagency Team to Eradicate Corruption. Inaccessible reporting by the two government audit agencies, especially since some 30 percent of government spending is devolved to provinces and regencies, removes a vital support for the anticorruption effort. Speedy access to bank records has been another problem area, as searches require high-level formal requests to the central bank for permission. A new witness protection agency can be employed to keep the anonymity of whistleblowers and informers, but the KPK lacks the power to give immunity from prosecution, lessening the chances of low-level participants in corruption squealing on those higher up. Judges are slowly getting used to new forms of evidence, such as secret recordings, financial data, and retrievals from computer hard drives.

An anti-money-laundering law was passed in 2010, but it is still not used. Indonesian law enforcement agencies remain weak when it comes to following money trails, except when large amounts of cash are hand delivered. Even then, golf instructors, security guards, and even parking attendants are employed to maintain a cutout in the chain of responsibility and to take the rap if necessary. Not having the power to terminate an investigation can make the KPK hesitate to start one. Poor definitions of a "loss to the state" lead courts to conclude that corruption cannot exist without such a proven loss. Conversely, judges and prosecutors often conclude that "losses to the state" must result from corruption rather than from mistaken decisions, such as with loans from state banks that become nonperforming. An extradition treaty was signed in 2007 with Singapore, the bolt-hole where 18,000 Indonesian millionaires resided with total estimated assets at the time of $87 billion. It remains unratified by the Indonesian parliament.

The integration of the corruption court into the general court system under the aegis of the Supreme Court, resulting from a constitutional challenge to a "separate" judicial system, led other agencies to file cases with the corruption court. The Chevron and Indosat prosecutions were two examples in which regular state prosecutors made criminal cases out of what looked to every expert in those fields to be just routine and perfectly legal technical matters. While the KPK continued to have a 100 percent success rate with its cases in the court, the attorney general's office started recording some acquittals, raising suspicions that some cases had been doctored to fail.

The parliament, whose members were so often in the sights of the KPK, also jumped into the corruption hunt for evident political purposes, notably in the long-running Bank Century case. The medium-sized bank was showing signs of failure as the global financial crisis unfolded after the collapse of Lehman Brothers in September 2008. Fearing contagion in the Indonesian banking system should Century also fold, Yudhoyono's coordinating economic minister, Sri Mulyani, and the Bank Indonesia governor, Boediono, decided in November 2008 on emergency capital injections amounting to $677 million. After Yudhoyono's sweeping election win the following year, during which he replaced Jusuf Kalla with Boediono as vice president, the bailout became a weapon used against Yudhoyono.

Kalla led criticisms that the rescue money had been diverted for nefarious purposes, including the financing of Yudhoyono's election campaign. Indeed, well-connected big corporations and state enterprises had gotten their money out quickly, and the bank's two owners, Rafat Ali Rizvi and Hesham Al-Warraq, disappeared; both were later given fifteen-year jail terms for embezzlement.

Another target of the parliamentary claque was Sri Mulyani, who had reverted to finance minister in the second-term government. As we have seen, she was pursuing the leading figure Aburizal Bakrie's business group for large unpaid taxes, was refusing to put government money into his financially troubled coal mine, and would not certify the Lapindo "mud volcano" in East Java as a natural disaster rather than an accident. The parliamentary uproar did not dislodge Yudhoyono or Boediono, but it did claim the scalp of Sri Mulyani for Bakrie. The news that she was moving to the World Bank in May 2010 shattered confidence that Yudhoyono's second term would see him move ahead with serious reform and stamped him as a weak, consensual leader. Five years later, the parliament, the KPK, and the state auditors were still looking for any evidence that Sri Mulyani and Boediono acted out of any motive other than preventing a general bank run, or that they might have known about fraud in Bank Century at the time, and were not finding it.

A decade on from the start of Indonesia's era of direct elections and political devolution, big corruption cases kept coming. Perhaps the most stunning fall from grace was the involvement of top figures in the PKS, a party of pragmatic work and faith that was based on the Muslim Brotherhood model in Egypt and Turkey. Campaigning on personal ethics and zero tolerance of corruption, it had won the fourth-biggest block of seats in the 2009 parliamentary election. In January 2013, KPK investigators raided a Jakarta hotel room to find one Ahmad Fathanah, a naked female student, and a suitcase containing Rp 1 billion. Ahmad turned out to be a secretary to Luthfi Hasan Ishaaq, chairman of the PKS. The case developed into a corruption scandal that reached up into the PKS and the agriculture ministry, one of the appointments allotted to the party in Yudhoyono's ruling coalition. Money was coming via Ahmad from a company given a larger quota to import beef, a foodstuff in short supply. Millions were being raised with an eye to funding the approaching elections in 2014, less sizeable amounts siphoned off in passing by individuals for cars and gifts to female models.

Yudhoyono himself managed to get to the end of his decade in office without a financial scandal hanging over him personally, which was no mean achievement. But by then his own PD had taken a big blow. In 2012 his youth and sports minister, Andi Mallarangeng, had been forced to resign over alleged kickbacks from a contract to build a sports complex at Hambalang, in West Java. In early 2013 the anticorruption commission had also listed as a suspect Anas Urbaningrum, the party's chairman in the parliament and a rising star who was being mentioned as a possible successor to Yudhoyono as presidential candidate.

From one point of view, the parade of big corruption cases rising higher and higher in the political world was a good sign for Indonesia. From another and more depressing angle, it seemed to show that years of active anticorruption detection and punishment were not deterring people from the most brazen misbehavior. One foreign business adviser in Jakarta for decades has likened the corruption load to the annual migration of wildebeest across the Mara River in Kenya. Most get safely across in the rush, but a few who are exposed on the flanks fall to the lurking crocodiles—in this analogy, the KPK.

Pushing the demand for bribes and extorted payments are low official salaries and the widening income gaps that are all too visible in Indonesian cities. Decision-making processes within government agencies have grown complicated precisely in order to extract fees from outside customers and from colleagues. Efforts to speed up and make transparent the more routine processing of permits and documents succeed where online and other methods can be employed. Sharply increased budget allocations to core agencies, such as the Indonesian National Police and the Ministry of Finance, are still not raising salaries enough to remove the need for moonlighting in second jobs or the temptation of corruption among the 5 million state-sector employees.

Five years after Sri Mulyani carried out a sweeping replacement of corrupt personnel in the finance ministry's income tax and customs departments, tax officers were still soliciting bribes to reduce exorbitant opening tax assessments from big foreign companies. New recruits to the noncommissioned ranks of the police were still expected to pay some Rp 50 million ($4,100) for acceptance, to commence a job that paid just Rp 250,000 ($21) a month—below the poverty line—for the first six years. The fee for entry to the officer cadre was much higher. In August 2013, Sofian Effendi, from the Independent Team for Bureaucracy Reform, an activist group, estimated that, on average, a candidate for a civil service position had to pay Rp 150 million ($12,500) to be accepted.

Governors, bupatis, and mayors used these payments to recoup election expenses and to fund patronage. Karyono Wibowo of the Indonesian Public Institute, a think tank, said running for mayor or bupati could cost around Rp 5 billion ($416,000), depending on the region's economic strength. Running for provincial governor could cost above Rp 100 billion ($832,000). Between 1999 and mid-2013, 298 governors, bupati, and city mayors (from the nation's thirty-three provinces and nearly 500 regions and municipalities) were jailed for corruption.

Each year 170,000 new state employees are recruited. The new civil service recruits, having paid so much for their jobs, in turn squeeze their clients or accept bribes, according to Emerson Yuntho of the activist group Indonesia Corruption Watch: "They will start to do whatever it takes to get their money back. And once they enjoy the easy money, they will continue to accept bribes or stolen state money."*

Johan Budi, the KPK's public spokesman, argues that low salaries are not the only factor, or even the main one. He points to the stream of high-income officials coming before the courts for corruption. In August, for example, Budi's agency arrested the head of the oil and gas ministry's agency in charge of sales of surplus production to the state's refining capacity, Rudi Rubiandini, as he received a $600,000 payment from agents of a Singapore oil trading firm. "Rudi would be on a salary of Rp 200 million [$18,000] or more per month. How much is enough?" Budi asked. A good argument, but public conjecture was that Rudi, previously a professor of petroleum engineering at the Bandung Institute of Technology, was perhaps simply a naive newcomer to a wider fundraising network within the ministry, known as the "oil mafia."

Along with continued detection and law enforcement, and more transparent processes in government, a significant drop in corruption probably depends on a steady reduction in the size of the bureaucracy, a large proportion of which is idle for much of its working day anyway, accompanied by a rise in productivity and salary levels based on promotion by merit. That might be funded either by improved revenues or by part of the proceeds from cuts in subsidies for goods consumed mostly by higher-income groups. Planning for such a bold reform was delegated to Boediono in Yudhoyono's second term but was abandoned as too hard.

At the KPK, Johan Budi admits the anticorruption fight will be "a never-ending story." Meanwhile, any foreign investor will find it hard to avoid demands for payments from a baffling multiplicity of gatekeepers. Under Suharto, big and medium business at least knew who had to be satisfied: the doors then opened, and appeals could be made against any obstacles. Now their executives also remain at risk from police and the legal mafia, who insert themselves into commercial, environmental, and labor disputes, and extort money

---

*Yuli, Krisna, Novy Lumanauw & Robertus Wardi, "Paying the Price for a Slack Civil Service," *The Jakarta Globe,* August 29, 2013.

by putting staff in cells. The smaller the enterprise, the bigger the risk, but the Chevron case shows that size alone brings no immunity.

Indonesians are less and less accepting of the idea that corruption is part of their culture. Dozens of nongovernmental organizations, such as Indonesia Corruption Watch and Transparency International, are publicizing cases of malfeasance at the local and regional levels, bringing them to national attention, sometimes at great risk to their activists. The media relentlessly publicize investigations and trials. The quick rise of the "cleanskin" politician Joko Widodo from mayor of a small city to governor of the capital—and successful presidential candidate—shows that there is a hunger among the Indonesian public for honesty and moderation on the part of their leaders.

11

THE EASTERN MARGIN

THE OFFICIAL CROSSING BETWEEN SOUTHEAST ASIA AND THE SOUTH PACIFIC IS AT A place called Skouw, on the north coast of New Guinea. From the nearest big town to the west, Jayapura, it's reached by a two-hour drive that starts around spectacular bays and hills and ends in a straight run through thick jungle. At Skouw there is a collection of customs and immigration buildings and beyond them an archway notifying you of your exit from Indonesian territory. On a rise a bit further on, the jungle has been cut back, yielding glimpses of a blue sea to the left and green mountains to the right. A wire mesh fence marks the start of Papua New Guinea. A sign declares it a nation guided by Jesus Christ. Another, in Tok Pisin, urges care against HIV infection: *Lukautim yu, yet lukautim famili.*

Asymmetries abound. On the Indonesian approaches are the base camps and forward posts of an army battalion, one of four kept along the border with Papua New Guinea, on rotation from other parts of Indonesia. Indonesian officials and army officers drive around in new-model luxury four-wheel drives. On the Papua New Guinean side, at Vanimo, the nearest town, is a single company drawn from one of the only two battalions in the entire Papua New

Guinea defense force. The company's forward deployment is a platoon of a dozen soldiers, stationed at the village of Wutung, near the border post. The official vehicles are basic Toyota Land Cruisers with bench seats.

Although Papua New Guinea has only 7.2 million people, compared to the 240 million of Indonesia, its border post flies a more diverse array of flags: the national flag, with its bird of paradise and the Southern Cross, flaps above the flags of the country's twenty provinces. Along the Indonesian perimeter every flagpole hoists the same emblem: the red and white of the Negara Kesatuan Republic Indonesia. In this "unitary state," symbols of regional loyalties are seen as a threat, even if they are tolerated for the time being at the other end of the archipelago in Aceh.

The border itself—the result of Dutch, German, and British officials far away in Europe drawing a line down the 141st meridian of longitude on a map in the late nineteenth century—is not much of a barrier. Every day, hundreds of people walk from Papua New Guinea through the Skouw border post into Indonesia, flashing a local identity card, so they can tend food gardens on their traditional lands or buy household supplies at cheaper prices than in Vanimo's shops, while many Indonesian peddlers cross the other way.

Further south, the border's line has few markers or fences. People cross it along tracks worn by bare feet over thousands of years. Among them, from time to time, are armed rebels from the Organisasi Papua Merdeka (OPM, Free Papua Movement), which opposes Indonesian rule over the western half of the island of New Guinea. There has been little to prevent them evading Indonesian army attacks or regrouping, and they find plenty of cover in the rugged terrain and thick jungle. A cross border raid in 1984 by a Kopassus unit, led by Prabowo Subianto, ended without result in a logistical debacle.

Thousands of civilians have also fled into Papua New Guinea over recent decades, escaping fierce sweeps by the Indonesian military. Over 10,000 remain in camps along the border between the central Star Mountains and the Torres Strait, and a smaller number around Vanimo near the north coast. The OPM still fights on, deep inside the Indonesian half of the island. The fiercest of four splinter groups is led by a man named Goliat Tabuni (after the Biblical giant, Goliath), who claims to be supreme commander of all.

When the cross border road was finished in 2006, Papuan New Guineans joked nervously about the "invasion highway." Their consul general in Jayapura was confidentially briefing US diplomats that the Indonesian military was supporting illegal logging by two companies at Wewak (far from the border, including with unauthorized flights), that it was importing cannabis for distribution within Indonesia, and that it was selling "red cards," the permits supposed to be restricted to local border communities.

Recently, though, the array of Indonesian troops along the border has looked more superfluous than ever. The Indonesian authorities have adopted a soft-power approach toward their Melanesian neighbors. An annual "fun run," in which hundreds of young people from both sides compete in a ten-kilometer race across the border, started in 2011. Indonesia is offering to hook up Vanimo and other towns along Papua New Guinea's north coast to its power grid, at rates presumably linked to its highly subsidized domestic energy prices, though the offer is being looked at warily as giving Jakarta too much leverage.

At the diplomatic level, the Indonesian foreign minister, Marty Natalegawa, initiated overtures in 2013 to the Melanesian Spearhead Group, a regional grouping in the southwest Pacific. The grouping and its members were being invited to visit Papua and see developments for themselves. Jakarta counts its two largest members, Papua New Guinea and Fiji, as being reconciled to Papua's inclusion in Indonesia. Two smaller ones, Vanuatu and the Kanak representation from French-ruled New Caledonia, are sympathetic to the Papuan separatist cause, with Vanuatu the sole government in the world that is trying to put it back on the UN agenda. The Solomon Islands, the fifth member state, is seen as wavering, but in mid-2013 it sent a delegation on an all-expenses-paid inspection.

Yet the gates to Indonesia's Papua are hardly being thrown open. Entry by foreigners is tightly controlled. A "clearinghouse" of officials from the Ministries of Foreign Affairs, Defense, and Home Affairs and from the police and the intelligence agencies meets every Thursday in Jakarta to vet applications from diplomats, journalists, aid agencies, and activist groups to visit Papua. Some are repeatedly knocked back for years. Inside Papua, the BIN, the police, and the military command have agents tracking the meetings of such approved visitors, as well as looking out for unapproved reporters and investigators who might have slipped in among the smallish flow of adventure tourists. Officials weakly defend the policy as necessary because of journalists and activists who will report atrocities and "genocide," regardless of what they actually see.

In 2006 this "intel" network quickly caught up with two Americans from an NGO called Land Is Life, who innocently came in on tourist visas after being invited at short notice to a conference held by an indigenous rights body, the Dewan Adat Papua (DAP, Papua Traditional Council). They were detained, taken back to Jakarta, and then expelled. As the then American ambassador, Lynn Pascoe, commented in a cable to Washington, rather than letting the pair attend the completely legal event and draw their own conclusions about the conditions in Papua, the Indonesian government had "reinforced its image as a repressive and paranoid regime, at least as far as Papua is concerned. We assume that the two Land Is Life staffers' experiences will spread among Papua watchers in the NGO community and on Capitol Hill." In October 2013, this writer gained approval for a four-day visit just to the Papuan provincial capital, Jayapura, but was denied clearance to visit the towns of Wamena, Merauke, and Timika for reasons that were not explained.

Despite some visible successes in stonewalling and dissipating the pro-independence "Papuan Spring" that had flowered after Suharto's fall, the ten-year presidency of Susilo Bambang Yudhoyono was ending with only slightly increased confidence about the loyalty of Papuans to Indonesia. Indonesians, or at least the political class in Jakarta, still seemed unwilling or unable to apply the lessons of their own independence struggle to the Papuans: their knowledge that a deep sense of subordination and historical injustice can't be bought off easily with lectures about lagging capabilities or economic promises and ornamental political institutions.

The fire is still smoldering, says Neles Tebay, a widely respected Catholic priest in Jayapura who has been urging a dialogue to address these fundamental grievances. "The call for independence is like smoke from a fire," he says, sitting in the garden of the theological college he runs close to Papua's Cenderawasih (Bird of Paradise) University, a perennial hot spot of protest against Indonesian rule; the slogan "Free West Papua" is daubed on several walls. "To dispel the smoke, you have to kill the fire."

THE FIRE WAS LIT in 1944 when the Dutch regained control over Western New Guinea in the wake of General Douglas MacArthur's island-hopping campaign toward the Philippines. As the historian Pieter Drooglever has recounted (in a book commissioned by the Dutch government in 2000, as Papua's accession to Indonesia came under intense challenge), the modern world came late to the territory. Its fringes had been touched sporadically by traders, explorers, and scientists. The Netherlands' East Indies government set up its first administrative centers around the coast in 1898, not having much hope of economic return. The idea was guardianship, the goal to "turn savages into people," as one of the first resident commissioners put it. The work proceeded steadily, augmented by intensified missionary work by Protestant churches along the north coast and by Catholics in the south.

Then came the cataclysm of the Japanese sweep through the island in 1942, leaving the Dutch and their allies with only a toehold around Merauke in the southwest. Unlike in many other parts of the Indies, the Japanese found no friendly nationalist movement to foster. When they freed a restive local leader named Stephanus Simopyaref from a Dutch jail in Biak, he set up a movement called Amerika-Babo (New America) under a flag similar to the Stars and Stripes: a single star on a red field, adjacent to horizontal blue and white stripes. The Japanese killed Simopyaref, but his flag eventually became the emblem of Papuan resistance, known as the Bintang Kejora (Morning Star).

Then came the Americans themselves, who used many local workers to build vast bases in the main town, Hollandia (as Jayapura was then named), and a long airstrip on Biak island. They accidentally penetrated the highlands when a joyriding flight of twenty-four airmen and nurses in May 1945 crashed in the Baliem valley. The three survivors were plucked out of the valley in a glider, which was retrieved in a "live capture" by a low-flying tug aircraft. The Americans, and the Japanese before them, were a stunning vision of modernity and power for those Papuans who saw them. The sight of African Americans in technical roles showed that this modernity did not necessarily exclude them.

A strong-willed Dutch commissioner, greatly taken with the Melanesian world, persuaded his political masters to make an exceptional case of New Guinea as they fought and negotiated with the Indonesian nationalists between 1945 and 1949. They were persuaded by the argument that the Papuans had a very low level of development, an entirely different "national character" from the Indonesians, and little or no Indonesian nationalistic sentiment; indeed, the Papuans were suspicious of the "Amberi," as they referred to the Malay race, even though the Malay language was becoming the territory's lingua franca. "A supplementary argument," wrote Drooglever, "was that the Indonesia-born Dutch would be able to have their own place in the tropical sun here, even after the Dutch flag had ceased to fly over the rest of the archipelago."

The territory was put to the side when the final transfer of power over the rest of the Indies came in December 1949, its disposition to be decided by negotiation within a year. Talks got nowhere. The Dutch felt they had agreement on transitional rule until western New Guinea was ready to decide its future under UN auspices. While the Papuans felt no tug of Indonesian nationalism, the pre-1942 exile of so many of their freedom fighters to Boven Digul and an even harsher prison camp at Tanah Merah reinforced the idea of an Indonesia that stretched "from Sabang to Merauke"—in other words, from the northern tip of Sumatra to the farthest corner of western New Guinea—as a central one for the Indonesian leadership. The idea of cultural difference cut no ice: Indonesia already had plenty of part Melanesians in places such as Ambon and Timor. "Unity in Diversity" allowed respectful space for all. The option of a halfway house within Indonesia had all but vanished when the nation dumped its Dutch-inspired federal structure six months after the 1949 transfer of sovereignty.

The two sides were set on a collision course. For seventeen years from 1945, the Dutch put effort and funds into training Papuans as administrators, teachers, medical staff, and technicians, and eventually about 4,000 were employed in middle- and low-ranking government jobs. "The Papuan world of 1962 differed radically from that of 1950, let alone 1900," Drooglever summarized. "Broad development had taken place and a small but high calibre upper class had been formed, who would, if given the chance, be able to lead society as a whole in the long term."

Meanwhile, the breakdown of talks in 1956 led Sukarno to step up his anticolonialism crusade, with the appropriation of Dutch property throughout the archipelago. The point of no return came in 1961 when the Dutch foreign minister, Joseph Luns, proposed a UN-supervised plebiscite in 1970. A legislature, the New Guinea Council, was installed, and on December 1 that year, the Bintang Kejora flag and an anthem were made the territory's emblems. The "Luns Plan" won a majority vote at the UN General Assembly, but not the two-thirds required for it to become a ruling. Nevertheless, it was promptly approved by the new Papuan legislature.

Sukarno responded that same December by setting up a *trikora* (threefold) command: to thwart the creation of a "puppet state," to plant the red and white flag in Papua, and to prepare for national mobilization. General Suharto was appointed to lead the campaign. Within a month, a significant naval clash occurred, with the Dutch sinking Indonesian torpedo boats that were heading for the territory, and in 1962 small Indonesian paratroop units were dropped into the jungles—although they didn't encounter any of the popular support they expected. The arrival of the Dutch navy's aircraft carrier meant that, for the time being, the Indonesians were outgunned.

Drooglever's archival searches unearthed a gloomy intelligence assessment that the arrival of massive Soviet and American military equipment for the Indonesia forces meant Jakarta would soon have the capability to land large forces in New Guinea. The new US administration of John F. Kennedy also saw itself on the losing side of Cold War competition for influence in Jakarta, if Washington continued to support the Dutch. The US diplomat Elsworth Bunker pulled the rug from under The Hague, and allies, such as Australia, duly stepped back. In an agreement signed in New York in August 1962, the Dutch agreed to a UN interregnum of seven months, starting on October 1 that year, with the territory to be handed over to Indonesian administration on May 1, 1963. However, they won the inclusion of an article providing for an act of self-determination—"in accordance with international practice"—in which all adult Papuans had the right to participate. Further provisions required UN officials to remain in New Guinea to prepare for an act of self-determination by the end of 1969, and Indonesia to guarantee freedom of speech, movement, and assembly for the Papuans.

Almost all these stipulations were abused, a British researcher, John Saltford, found in his own archival exploration in 2003. Indonesia refused to allow UN officials to remain; as the UN eventually reported, the Indonesian administration "exercised at all times a tight political control over the population." Infused with a sense of triumph, Indonesian military personnel were the dominating component of the new occupation of a territory renamed Irian Jaya (meaning "Victorious Irian"; the origins of the name "Irian" are unclear). As Drooglever told the US Congress in 2010:

> In the beginning at least, they enjoyed taking over a comfortable colonial administration. The typewriters, the hospital equipment, and other elements of the basic infrastructure were taken away. Jobs of the Papuan elite were taken over, the education system graded down, and the civil society of West Papua slipped down the road toward greater misery. After General Soeharto became president of Indonesia, the new minister of foreign affairs, Adam Malik, visited the territory. Malik was shocked by the desolation he found there. The Javanese civil servants had robbed the country blind. Embitterment reigned everywhere, in the words of this Indonesian minister on his return to Jakarta.

The displaced Papuan elite seethed with a sense of betrayal by the world community, which was worsened by the arrogant and harsh treatment meted out by Indonesian soldiers and officials. Several Papuans went into exile, including Nicholas Jouwe, the vice chairman of the former New Guinea Council.

In July 1965 rebellion broke out, with raisings of the Morning Star flag in several places and attacks on any Indonesian personnel who tried to prevent them. The newly formed OPM mounted its first big attack, with 400 fighters seizing an army barracks in Manokwari and taking control of the town for several days. The reaction was the first of several large-scale army sweeps, which intensified as the act of self-determination approached in 1969. One of the biggest was mounted after General Sarwo Edhie Wibowo, who had led the Special Forces in the massacres of communists across Java and Bali in 1965–66, became the regional commander in 1967, with the mission of securing a vote for Indonesia. According to a recent investigation by Jakarta's own National Commission on Human Rights (known as Komnas-HAM), Operasi Wibawa (Operation Authority) saw 6,200 troops parachuted and landed into several inland regions, supported by strafing from the air, with "hundreds" of lives lost among the local peoples. A longer campaign called Operasi Tumpas (Operation Destroy) ran from 1967 to 1970 in three districts, resulting in "mass killings."

With this reign of terror in the background, Suharto assigned the task of organizing the Act of Free Choice itself to his trusted assistant Ali Murtopo and his Opsus unit, after publicly warning that a vote to leave Indonesia would be "treason." It was decided that because of the lack of political sophistication among the Papuans and logistical difficulties, a "one man, one vote" system would be inappropriate; indeed, the New York agreement did not contain the words "plebiscite" or "referendum." Instead, the system chosen by Jakarta would be *musyawarah*, described as a "process of consultation" that would lead to the formation of consensus, although the New York agreement authorized this process only for the decision on the method of the self-determination act, in which *all* adult Papuans were to be able to take part.

The United Nations returned only a year before the ballot, with Bolivian diplomat Fernando Ortiz-Sanz and sixteen other officials deployed. Their efforts to hold a ballot at least in the coastal areas were pushed aside. In the event, between July 14 and August 4, 1969, while the world was transfixed by the first moon landing, the Opsus team chose 1,022 representatives from around the territory, who were rendered compliant by threats and bribery and kept in isolation while they rehearsed their unanimous "acclamation" to stay with Indonesia. Ortiz-Sanz duly reported that the procedure had been carried out "in accordance with Indonesian practice" (rather than "international" or the United Nations' own standards), a fudge that, despite the worries of some African member states, the General Assembly voted to approve. Only two years later, in 1971, Opsus was actively running the Papuan part of national elections—in which, miraculously, Papuans were now qualified and able to vote.

The OPM continued its resistance, as an amorphous organization that kept splintering and reforming under a succession of leaders, and encompassed both armed activities in remote areas and underground politics in the towns. Among the earliest of its military leaders was Seth Rumkoren, an educated man from Biak who had initially joined the Indonesian army before defecting to the jungle, where he made a unilateral declaration of independence in July

1971. With just a few score firearms, the OPM's fighting wing managed only limited ambushes, kidnappings, and hit-and-run attacks, and mostly stayed close to the Papua New Guinea border. Even so, it provoked a series of nine major counterinsurgency and sweeping operations through to the end of the New Order, sending waves of refugees into Papua New Guinea.

The largest of these was Operation Koteka (named after the penis gourd worn by highland men) in 1977–78 under regional commander Imam Munandar, which saw thousands of troops deployed into the villages of the Baliem valley, the Jayawijaya mountains to the east, to the suspected OPM headquarters just south of Jayapura, and to the area around the Freeport mine (after an OPM group cut the slurry pipeline). The Komnas-HAM investigation found widespread killings of hundreds of suspected OPM supporters and other civilians, torture "without concern about sex or age," and cases of Papuans being forced to dig their own graves before being shot. A Hong Kong–based volunteer organization, the Asian Human Rights Commission, said in October 2013 that it had identified 4,146 of those killed, in fourteen districts across the central highlands. Many had been killed by ground units after being rounded up and tortured, some by machine-gunning, rockets, or napalm bombs from OV-10 Bronco aircraft and helicopters. Further partial collaboration has come from the Baptist missions active in the region and from Australian Air Force personnel who were temporarily based at Wamena's airport while conducting a mapping project.

Meanwhile, the process of making Papua and its people Indonesian quickened, as did the extraction of its natural resources. The American mining company Freeport had reached its agreement with Jakarta on its gold and copper mine at Ertzberg two years before the vote and had evidently not been worried by any political risk. By 1973 it was extracting ore from an outcrop 3,500 meters above sea level, bringing it by aerial tramway to a crushing mill and township at an altitude of 2,750 meters, and then sending a concentrate in slurry form down a pipeline that crossed 116 kilometers of jungle and swamp to the coast. Within two years the operation was yielding huge profits for Freeport's shareholders and a large flow of tax receipts for Jakarta.

In 1988, with the Ertzberg deposit reduced to an open pit two kilometers wide, Freeport announced that its activity would shift to the even larger Grasberg ore body, which contained the world's largest known gold deposit (an estimated 91.4 tons), as well as 32 million tons of copper, with estimates of its value running to $80 billion. With the fiftieth anniversary of the company's mining permit approaching in 2017, Jakarta's politicians started agitating for a bigger share for the state. Amid rioting in 2009 by illegal miners, who were extracting remnant gold from the mine's dumps of waste rock, Freeport executives privately accused political figures, such as Amien Rais and even unnamed Saudi-financed Salafists, of stirring up trouble as part of a shakedown.

Logging also got underway, supervised and taxed informally by the military, while significant oilfields were opened around the "Bird's Head" extremity in the west. Eventually, in the first decade of the new century, the large-scale Tangguh liquefied natural gas field, operated by BP in Bintuni Bay, started exporting to China.

In early 1969 Suharto had announced a lavish long-term development program to make up for the earlier looting, but the beneficiaries were largely the migrants who began to flood in from other parts of Indonesia, either as "spontaneous" self-starters from places like Makassar or the quarter-million participants in the government's transmigration scheme to reduce population pressures and poverty in Java and Bali. While the Papuan population grew at a moderate annual rate of 1.84 percent, rising from 887,000 in 1971 to 1.5 million in 2000, the migrant population grew from 36,000 in 1971 to 708,000 in 2000, an annual growth rate of 10.8 percent. At that point, the Central Statistics Bureau stopped making the indigenous-migrant breakdown because it was becoming embarrassing; in the 2010 census, it simply reported a total population of 3.61 million. Extrapolating from the previous three decades of respective growth rates, the Australian scholar Jim Elmslie has calculated that the Papuan population would be 47.9 to 49.6 percent of the total. Papuans have become a minority in their own land.

Migrants from outside Papua now make up two-thirds or more of the population in Jayapura and many other big towns. In Jayapura the migrants have most of the jobs in formal-sector commerce: the shops and restaurants, the taxis and ojek (motorcycle taxis), the hotels, the security posts. Papuans appear at dusk, laying out offerings of *pinang* (betel nut) on pavements and boxes. Papuan women sell vegetables and fish in a night market while their men play cards. In the administration, the elected political jobs are largely now filled by Papuans, but in the ranks of senior and middle officialdom there are many non-Papuans.

The condition of the bulk of the ethnic Papuans, located in the hinterlands, is still reported to be miserably poor, half a century after the start of Indonesian rule. In 2013 the Jayapura branch of Komnas-HAM was reporting scores of deaths during the year from starvation and treatable diseases. Like neighboring Papua New Guinea, Papua has a serious HIV/AIDS epidemic, spread in the African pattern by heterosexual encounters with prostitutes, combined with poor hygiene. Preventive campaigns have been inhibited by the unwillingness of some religious authorities to accept the reality of widespread casual sex. Outside the large towns, the extension of education and health services is undercut by the absenteeism of staff. In Wamena in 2006, a visiting US embassy team could find no one manning the civilian government offices. Anecdotal reports say Wamena is swarming with unaccompanied minors, billeted with relatives and clan affiliates, sent by parents desperate for them to get an education.

Large-scale army operations tapered off from the mid-1980s and were replaced by a murkier kind of small-unit warfare that used semiclandestine special forces and local paramilitaries, some of them masquerading as OPM groups. Yet the memory of past mass killings, the high rate of mortal illness and food shortages, the perceived tokenism of cultural representation, and the steady displacement by migration and plantation projects have combined to maintain the Papuans' sense of "slow genocide"—an uncomfortable accusation for the more perceptive senior government officials.

Through the 1980s and 1990s, until the fall of Suharto, a growing number of highly educated Papuans tried balancing a form of cultural politics with engagement in the institutions, professions, and businesses created under the New Order's development orientation. But they also supplied their martyrs. Arnold Ap, an anthropologist at the ethnological museum at the Cenderawasih University (which is filled with the marvelous collection of artifacts assembled by Michael Rockefeller before his 1962 disappearance in Papua's southern jungles), led a cultural revival movement through traditional music. He was killed while in detention in 1984. Outbreaks of reckless messianism continued to grip the Papuans periodically. In 1988 Thomas

Wanggai, the holder of an American doctorate and degrees from Japan, unfurled the Morning Star flag and declared independence at a football stadium in Jayapura. Sentenced to twenty years for subversion, he died in a Jakarta jail in 1996. The return of his body set off widespread rioting and destruction around Jayapura.

As Suharto's grip weakened in 1997 and ended in May 1998, repressed Papuan sentiment was set to explode, as it did in East Timor, but without the unified leadership already formed by the Timorese resistance groups. Eventually, a "Team of 100"—comprising intellectuals, religious figures, students, and members of the provincial legislature—went to see the new president, B. J. Habibie, in February 1999. Having already decided to let the Timorese have a plebiscite on their future, Habibie was shocked to learn that the Papuans were demanding the same thing and urged them to reconsider.

His replacement later in the year, Abdurrahman Wahid, had more to offer. Having come to experience the dawn of the new millennium in Indonesia's easternmost province, Wahid announced that the territory would be named "Papua" rather than "Irian Jaya," and promised it extensive autonomy within Indonesia. Wahid's announcement encouraged hopes at a Musyawarah Besar (*Mubes* for short, meaning "Grand Consultation"), attended by thousands of delegates in February 2000 to discuss the "correction of history." This, in turn, led to the calling of a "second" Papuan People's Congress (regarded as the successor to a meeting in 1961 under Dutch auspices) at the end of May 2000.

To lead its executive, known as the Papuan Presidium, the congress chose a political figure, Theys Eluay, whose career suggested opportunism. In the 1960s he had helped the Indonesian military track down and eliminate oppositionists, and he had then voted for Indonesia as one of the 1,022 handpicked delegates in the Act of Free Choice. His shift toward the pro-independence camp had been a recent development; even while declaring himself the "Great Leader of the Papuan People" and forming his own security force of young volunteers, he still maintained close contact with the Indonesian security apparatus.

By this time, according to reports said to be based on a leaked document, the military was moving to subvert Wahid's conciliatory policies, stepping up its maneuvers to decapitate the Papuan movement with a version of the militia violence used in East Timor the year before. When Wahid was impeached and replaced by Megawati Sukarnoputri in July 2001, the plan was put into action.

A Kopassus unit invited Eluay to a dinner at its base near Jayapura. On his way home, he was escorted by Kopassus soldiers who had been ordered by their unit commander to talk Eluay out of making his planned declaration of independence on December 1, the anniversary of the 1961 unfurling of the Papuan flag. With Eluay insisting that mere autonomy was a lost cause, an enraged private soldier leaned forward and strangled him from behind. A following vehicle took the soldiers back to camp and Eluay's body was left in the car for police to discover.

The uproar following Eluay's death forced a court-martial, which was held in distant Surabaya in early 2003. It sentenced seven Kopassus officers and soldiers, including the three backseat passengers and their unit commanders, to jail for terms ranging between two years and three and a half years. It was not until 2013, a decade later, that Komnas-HAM in Jayapura managed to get a copy of the court finding to pass on to Eluay's family. Whether the Kopassus soldiers actually served their sentences, or in what circumstances, the human rights agency cannot say. Among their colleagues, they were regarded as having carried out their patriotic duty. The man who was the army chief in 2003, Riyamizard Ryacudu, declared that "for me, they are heroes because the person they killed was a rebel leader." Eluay's young driver, Aristoteles Masoka, disappeared and is presumed to have been murdered that same night. The soldiers claimed he ran off into the night.

BY THE TIME ELUAY WAS MURDERED, the Indonesian legislature had passed a special autonomy law (abbreviated as *Otsus* in Indonesian) for Papua. A panel of eminent Papuan personalities had sent a draft proposal for the law to the MPR in April 2003. When the central government sent its version to the MPR later, it looked similar: the provincial governor still had to be an indigenous Papuan; the province's share of mining royalties was still 80 percent, and of oil and gas taxes 70 percent; there was the creation of a Papuan People's Council, which would protect traditional customs; and the creation of new provinces had to be approved by both the provincial legislature and the MRP.

Yet it had been significantly watered down. There was no right to self-determination if a special historical commission found the 1969 process illegal; there was no regional police force; the Papuans had no control over inward migration, apart from a veto over any further official transmigration; a regional flag could have no connotations of sovereignty (ruling out the Bintang Kejora); and there were many more caveats on the transfer of powers. Nor did the law come into force immediately: this and many delegations of powers awaited enabling decrees and regulation. As the Australian scholar Richard Chauvel wrote, Otsus had become a battleground between the "old" authoritarian Indonesia and the "new" Indonesia of the reform and democracy era. The law itself expressed the more accommodating new Indonesia; its implementation, the old.

Before it came into force, Megawati signed a decree in January 2003 that split Papua into two new provinces, West Irian Jaya and Central Irian Jaya, in what was officially described as a process of *pemekaran* (flowering). It was a stunning act of bad faith that resonates to this day, seen as a classic divide-and-rule effort pushed by the intelligence community in Jakarta. "The damage the division did to Jakarta-Papua relations, let alone the idea within the Papuan elite that autonomy was an acceptable alternative to independence, is incalculable," commented Sidney Jones, a leading analyst of Indonesian security conflicts.

The westernmost province came into being, but the central one was put aside after fierce local protest. The Papuan governor, Jaap Solossa, supported a legal challenge to the division in the new constitutional court. The court ruled in November 2004 that the decision to create West Irian Jaya had indeed been unconstitutional, but since it was already in operation, it should be allowed to continue. Yudhoyono, who had recently become president, was happy to accept this convenient compromise. A Papuan former one-star general in the marine corps, and later an official in the BIN, Abraham Atururi, became governor of this new province, which was confusingly renamed "West Papua." Yudhoyono vowed to grant special autonomy to the two provinces, with a focus on improving the welfare of Papuans and using political rather than military means to solve problems.

Nonetheless, Otsus began inauspiciously and was suspect from the start among the Papuans. It was not long before ordinary Papuans and their leaders began wondering aloud what had changed. The flow of extra revenues seemed to stop among the portly politicians and senior officials of the two provinces and the ever-expanding number of districts. Many spent an inordinate amount of their time traveling lavishly outside the provinces, holding conferences, and equipping themselves with vehicles and other perquisites of office.

Dissidence and the repression of perceived challenges to Indonesian sovereignty continued. In 2005 a Papuan leader named Filip Karma earned a fifteen-year jail term for raising the Morning Star flag. As we have seen, in 2006 a boatload of dissidents, including a son of Thomas Wanggai, crossed the Torres Strait to seek political asylum in Australia, causing a serious diplomatic crisis and setting off a new security crackdown inside Papua.

Later that year, at a resettlement camp for Papuans inland from the Fly River in Papua New Guinea, this writer met Paulus Samkakay, a young activist from Merauke whose story seemed to epitomize Indonesia's policy failure to that point. His late father, Boneffasius Samkakay, was one of the 1,022 delegates chosen for the Act of Free Choice in 1969. Paulus showed me the certificates of appreciation given to his father by Suharto and General Wibowo. But the son had joined protests against Indonesian rule as soon as he reached adulthood, earning a spell of detention, and when the Papuan Spring erupted in 1998, he became an organizer of students and dock workers in Merauke.

Later, his activities were closely surveilled, and after the Torres Strait crossing, he too decided to try to reach Australia, by walking along the coast and finding a canoe to cross. He succeeded but was promptly returned by Australian officials to Papua New Guinea, where his wife and two surviving children waited, their youngest having died during the jungle trek. Not surprisingly, his bitterness was intense. "I came to the land of the kangaroo with big hopes," Samkakay told me, his eyes filling with angry tears.

For the 2,500 Papuans placed in dispersed clusters of self-built houses at the same place, East Awin, the remoteness of their surroundings signified the disinterest of neighboring countries and the world in their struggle. To reach the area required an expensive flight to the little town of Kiunga, a two-hour trip up the Fly River, and then a three-hour truck ride through axle-deep mud, and finally a twelve-kilometer walk when the road became impassable for normal vehicles. The flat, green scrubland and the lowering clouds varied little. The place appeared to have been chosen to be out of sight, out of contact. The exile must have seemed endless.

The people's hope was kept up with hymns and unfurlings of the Bintang Kejora flag, while the forced togetherness of such groupings—which included people from many of Papua's tribes— might in fact have been creating a bit of the unity that had eluded the resistance. An older woman, Afonsina Hambring, who had spent three years in the jungle with her husband, an OPM commander, before crossing the border in 1988, was taking a group from the women's association she leads out to do repairs on the road. "Every second we pray that God will start a war to change us," she said. "To make us one. Let's not get to the position of East Timor, fighting against each other."

Two strands of politics continued inside Papua—three, if the armed struggle by remaining OPM bands is counted. One was the nonviolent campaign for independence, or at least for some recognition of Papuan sovereignty and the right to a more convincing act of self-determination. That continues but has been dogged by division of effort between several organizations, one of the biggest among them the National Committee for West Papua (known by its Indonesian initials as KNPB). A second Mubes was convened by the newly formed Papuan People's Council in June 2010. The gathering symbolically "returned" the special autonomy law to Jakarta, called for tighter restrictions on inward migration, and demanded a new referendum.

Open demonstrations in support of these goals, especially the referendum, continue at the various anniversaries of events of the 1960s—most notably, the December 1 declaration of Papuan sovereignty under the Dutch and the May 1 arrival of the Indonesian administration. They are marked by small-scale violence, often with fatalities on both sides, as police try to prevent the flying of the Papuan flag. Then comes a trickle of cases through the courts, with judges handing out stiff sentences for sedition and assault. In one case, when a defendant retracted a confession he claimed had been made under torture, the judge ordered him to be charged with perjury.

In the structure of the Indonesian state, by contrast, the Papuans are being flooded by politics. What was just one province with ten kabupaten (districts) and municipalities in 1999 had by 2013 become two provinces with forty-two districts and townships. In August 2013 the relevant committee in the national parliament approved a plan to create three more provinces and twenty-two more districts, although Yudhoyono has been resisting any further provincial division, as has the Papuan provincial government and the Papuan People's Council, whose consent is now required under the Otsus law. But already the pemekaran process has created a revolving class of about 1,000 elected politicians, drawn in many cases by access to the Otsus flow of revenue, while the bureaucratic ranks have grown from 37,000 in 2000 to around 115,000. It is a staggering drain on financial resources and is dispersing the limited talent. The push continues to create more subregional governments because of automatic funding arrangements for them. Since these transfers are based on population figures, there is an incentive to inflate the number of inhabitants. Not surprisingly, many of the regional administrations in Papua are ranked as Indonesia's worst performers in delivering services.

The creation of the new districts in the interior tipped the balance of electoral politics in Papua away from the coastal and island people of the north coast and toward those of the highlands, embodied in the stocky figure of Lukas Enembe, who ousted his longtime coastal rival Barbabas Suebu to become governor in January 2013. With the electoral rolls apparently inflated by 30 percent more than the estimated number of voters, authorities had increasingly set them aside and resorted to a system known as *noken*, after the string bag traditionally used by village women to carry supplies, babies, and piglets. It allows community leaders to allocate all their votes in a block, supposedly after the widespread formation of a consensus. In this environment, Enembe won a landslide of votes. (The noken system was outlawed by authorities running the 2014 national elections, though its use in local ballots may still stand.)

Out of the fifty-six members of the provincial legislature, thirty are now highlanders. The mountain people pride themselves on being more practical and ready to work hard, because of their precarious traditional livelihood, which is based on cultivation—in contrast to that of the coastal people, who, they say, only have to pick fruit from trees and put a line or net into the sea. Whether this results in more effective governance or a version of the sometimes negative "big man" politics of the Papua New Guinea highlands remains to be seen.

For his part, Enembe is anxious to be viewed as an achiever. At a late-night meeting in Jayapura in October 2013, he addressed a visiting delegation from the national parliament about a $200-million-a-year scheme to build 6,000 kilometers of roads into the interior, including the long-envisaged trans-Papua highway linking the north and south coasts, through mountain ranges up to 4,500 meters high. "This will help our people living in remote areas, those left behind, to get out from poverty and underdevelopment," he told this writer later that night, at the provincial government building on Jayapura's waterfront. "It will let their produce be marketed outside. Now they can't do that, because there's no infrastructure access. They have to take flight to do that."

Enembe insists he is "Indonesian and proud of it." His voters would not necessarily feel a contradiction in taking part in elections under Indonesia's auspices and simultaneously hoping for the right to secede. A more bizarre ambivalence came in the first election held in the new district of Puncak, which was reminiscent of Papua New Guinean politics at their worst. A man from the Dani tribe named Elvis Tabuni registered as a candidate for bupati, representing the Gerakan Indonesia Raya party (Gerindra, Great Indonesia Movement), but a man from the rival Damal tribe, Simon Alom, tried to list for the same party. When his registration was rejected, his supporters attacked with stones and arrows. After twenty-three people had died, including four from police firing, the two sides brought in more muscle. Simon enlisted fellow clansmen from a shadowy militia group, Satgas Rajawali (Eagle Task Force), run by Kopassus in the 1990s to fight the OPM. In response, Elvis called in the OPM group led by Goliat Tabuni. Six more died before lavish compensation payments achieved a ceasefire, allowing the vote to go ahead in February 2013. When Elvis Tabuni lost the election to a third figure, Wellem Wandik, he again apparently called on Goliat Tabuni to intervene, who obliged with an attack on three Indonesian army outposts, killing eight soldiers and four civilians. Despite an appeal by Elvis, Wandik was confirmed as the new bupati.

Goliat Tabuni's group, operating in the mountains of the deep interior, is the most aggressive of the four main bands of the OPM, whose armed members might not number more than 200. Some are

more bandits than guerrillas, says Tito Karnavian, the former head
of the Indonesia National Police antiterrorist squad Detachment 88,
who became police chief of the region covering the two Papua provinces in August 2012. He cites a group in the Paniai lakes region that
had abducted and raped a group of schoolgirls and then demanded
ransom.

Since mid-2006 the police have taken charge of security inside
Papua, including the fight against the OPM, as consequence of the
earlier separation of the police from the armed forces. The military
presence is still substantial, according to military sources in Jakarta:
about 13,000 troops, including the four battalions (2,500 soldiers in
total) and an undeclared detachment of 100 to 200 Kopassus members. Tito insists that their role is border protection and civil aid, not
offensive operations. "I see no role for the military in the use of a
hard approach," he said in an interview at his Jayapura headquarters.

The force got off to a shaky start. In mid-June 2006 a battalion of the Mobile Brigade (known as *Brimob*), a force of infantry-
like police, was assigned from Jakarta to take over protection of the
Freeport mine from an army battalion, a service that had earned the
military many millions of dollars in payments. The Brimob troopers
were soon found to be taking bribes from the thousands of illegal
gold miners working the mine's tailings. One of their officers was
seen trying to break into a store of gold concentrates using a hijacked
bulldozer. Things improved with the unit's replacement by a locally
based battalion after six months.

In December that year, the police showed themselves to be perhaps more effective than the military at tackling the OPM and more
sensitive to local feelings. Using mobile phone intercepts, Tito's Detachment 88 tracked and killed a local OPM leader named Kelly
Kwalik, who was responsible for a string of fatal attacks against
foreign and local personnel at Freeport. The police then held back as
Kwalik's body was draped in the Morning Star flag, for viewing by
his many local supporters and clan members before burial.

In his first year heading Papua's police, Tito says he has set
out to steadily raise the proportion of indigenous officers in the
14,000-strong force from the present 30 to 40 percent to at least 50
percent. Meanwhile, the best Papuan officers are being given preference in sensitive commands, with locals heading the Mobile Brigade
and the districts of Jayapura, Wamena, and Mimika. "In hot places

I put Papuans," Tito says. "To make sure that there is no issue of human rights or genocide. Maybe in 1977, when I read that report, but today there is no [such] fact."

Tito has also called on the New Zealand and Dutch police forces to advise on so-called community policing, which he hopes will further shift the police mind-set from a military approach to a law-enforcement one. The police chief has also applied a version of the "softly, softly" deradicalization approach of his former antiterror command. In early 2013 he secretly hosted the leader of one of the smaller OPM groups—a man from the nearby Keerom district—at his home in Jayapura, after earlier providing medical assistance for the man's family, though without achieving any immediate change in thinking.

Busting police corruption remains the police chief's other big task. The 14,000 police in Papua have a budget of only $8.8 million. Their fuel ration is seven liters a day per vehicle. By contrast, a middle-ranking police officer arrested in May 2013 at Sorong for smuggling fuel oil and illegally cut hardwood was found to have had $132 million flowing through his bank accounts, with payoffs to thirty-three colleagues. There was outrage when this officer was acquitted of all the major corruption charges by a court and given only a two-year sentence for illegal logging. The widespread suspicion that military and police officers permit or actually run logging and other illegal activities on an even wider scale throughout Papua has only been deepened by the controls placed on outside monitors.

The gap between the politics of the Indonesian state and those of the Papuan resistance remains like a wildly flowing highland river, a formidable crossing. Yet a few lines have been thrown across. The young activist who had fled Merauke into Papua New Guinea, Paulus Samkakay, returned to his hometown. By 2014 a man of this name was prominent in local newspapers as head of a group called Tim Enam (Team Six) and was standing for the regional assembly. I wanted to confirm whether it was the same person I had met in East Awin and, if so, to find out about this new chapter in his life and what had led him to abandon the life of exile. But the "clearing house" vetoed my request to visit Merauke. E-mails to potential local intermediaries went unanswered. Finally, a telephone call got through to one of Samkakay's relatives; on a connection cutting in and out, he confirmed it was indeed the same Paulus Samkakay.

Efforts to open a "dialogue" since the 2010 "return" of the special autonomy law, meanwhile, have had little result beyond some vague commitments in Jakarta. The theologian Neles Tebay, an articulate man born in a highland village in 1964 who went on to earn a doctorate at the Vatican, says the word "dialogue" carried a suspicion in Jakarta of signifying a willingness to discuss sovereignty. He insists it is unconditional.

At first, the only receptive listener in Jakarta was Jusuf Kalla, the patron of the Aceh peace accord. Then a wider range of parliamentarians and opinion leaders agreed it was worth a try, since a hardline approach was making no headway. In late 2011 and early 2012, President Yudhoyono declared a willingness for dialogue, nominating Vice President Boediono as a contact and two figures involved in the Aceh peace process, the diplomat Farid Hussein and the retired general Bambang Dharmono, to open contacts with the OPM and to coordinate Papua's development, respectively. In 2013 Yudhoyono also received the elderly founder of the Papuan resistance, Nicholas Jouwe, who was allowed to return for a visit home from Holland after forty years in exile.

But who should speak for the Papuans? The existing laws on political parties allow no formation of a purely regional party, except in Aceh. In this absence, candidates run under the banners of national parties. The resistance is fragmented. Tebay told Indonesia's leaders it was no use simply talking to such Papuan figures as the governors, who had already declared themselves for Indonesia. The dialogue had to be with the unreconciled.

Over 2010–11, a Papuan peace conference met and discussed who should start the dialogue. It decided that those who could talk freely and without fear were the exiled spokespeople. The conference nominated the Vanuatu-based John Otto Ondawame, Rex Rumakiek in Australia, Octavianus Mote in the United States, Benny Wenda in Britain, and Leonie Tangama in the Netherlands. The group is thought to have met twice since but has made no known approaches to the Indonesian government or received any from it. In late 2013 Tebay felt that time had run out for Yudhoyono to achieve anything in the remaining months of his presidency. With the 2014 elections looming, Papua had receded from thinking in Jakarta. "It is far away, not just in geographic distance but in their minds," he said. "Indonesia stops at Makassar."

Toward the end of Yudhoyono's two permitted terms and on the president's invitation, the two Papua governors forwarded drafts for a better administrative system, to be called *Otsus-Plus*. They proposed several important measures to protect and nurture the indigenous Papuans. The governors should have more control over private-sector activity, including involvement in renegotiating the Freeport contract. Papuan leaders should be given carriage of Indonesia's participation in Pacific regional forums. The national and provincial governments should work to remove illiteracy within a set time, starting by making schooling free and compulsory up to junior high school, with policies to make sure teachers stayed at their jobs.

Most importantly, the draft by West Papua governor Atururi urged restriction of the right of non-Papuans to settle in the two provinces: they should come as temporary workers. Papuans should be guaranteed half of all employment, and maternal and infant welfare policies should be improved to build the indigenous population. Inside Papua, the reception was tepid: the proposals did not address the fundamental question of the region's place in Indonesia, students said; political prisoners declared they would reject the clemency urged by Enembe, on the same grounds. By contrast, in Jakarta the ideas were seen as dangerously bold. With the original Otsus still not fully implemented, Otsus-Plus would be left for a new president to consider after the 2014 elections.

FOR A WHILE, IT SEEMED that the international understandings that had helped Indonesia gain and retain control of Papua were being modified. One was the Cold War rivalry that had made Indonesia such a prize. Another was the conflation of self-determination with decolonization, making colonial boundaries the rule for independent successor states, no matter how arbitrarily they were drawn. Failure of government is becoming a factor for questioning sovereignty in international law.

Since the early 1990s, there have been several cases of self-determination outside decolonization, notes Osaka University's Akihisa Matsuo. Kosovo was one breakaway state. "The protection of people in Kosovo apparently had more weight than the territorial integrity of Serbia," Matsuo says. In response, Russia, Serbia's ally, sought the detachment of South Ossetia and Abkhazia from Georgia. More recently came the separation of South Sudan from

Khartoum's rule. "The history of Sudan seems to suggest that lack or low level of integration, natural or historical, between areas ruled by the same colonial power can be a reason for the establishing of a separate state," Matsuo says. The case of East Timor effectively created a precedent for a population under Indonesian sovereignty to ask the MPR for secession. In theory, Papua could become a reasonably self-sustaining independent state. As Jim Elmslie calculated from 2010 figures on the gross domestic regional product for its two provinces and their population, per capita GDP was $3,510, which was far above the Indonesian average of $2,452 and more than twice that of Papua New Guinea.

The moment for such thinking to pry Papua loose may have passed at the turn of this new century, however, when the New Order lay discredited and the Papuans had a more unified voice. But then Indonesia became a key ally in the West's fight against jihadist terrorism. It became prominent among the emerging new economic powers and was then courted by Washington for cooperation in the strategic "pivot" to maintain its dominance in Southeast Asia. Its worrying neighbor in the south, Australia, meanwhile, became captive to its politicians' need for Indonesian assistance in limiting the flow of asylum seekers by boat. As Tito Karnavian puts it, "Indonesia has become a nation with bargaining power."

Still, Pieter Drooglever, the Dutch historian who turned over the poignant records of his own country's involvement in Papua, thinks Jakarta does have an interest in making an agreement with the Papuans. In a reflection on his book, he writes:

> Indonesia not only has a tradition of military and authoritarian rule, but also of cultured interaction and efforts to provide good government. We can only hope that the latter two aspects gain the upper hand. Finally, there is the consideration that the interests of Indonesia and the Papuans, because they are neighbours and have a shared history, are, in the main, the same. The two primary motives for establishing the administrative centres in 1898 were to secure the eastern border of the archipelago and to develop the Papuans and their country. These can still go together, by hook or by crook. A solution should be found that combines a better future for the Papuans with the proper regulation of the eastern border of Indonesia. It would, however,

appear to be difficult to combine an open window onto the Pacific with a grumbling, misunderstood and maltreated population on the Indonesian side of the 141st meridian.

Anthropologists Brigham Golden and S. Eben Kirksey also point out that *merdeka* (freedom) has a much fuzzier meaning for Papuans than just separate statehood, as Indonesian officialdom understands the word. It can mean freedom from poverty, from racial inferiority, and from the perceived stigma of their "primitive" past, as well as control over their land, food, and water.

There is a scope here for negotiating a way forward, if Jakarta can free itself for a while from its "unitary state" mantra and accept that, in many respects, it is already federal.

12

THE BURNING
QUESTION

IN THE MIDDLE OF 1997, AS A FOREIGN DEBT CRISIS IGNITED IN THAILAND AND SPREAD south to Indonesia and east to Korea, much of Southeast Asia found it hard to breathe. Fires raged through dried-out peat marshes in Kalimantan and Sumatra, through tropical forests and across semi-cleared lands. The smoke grew into a thick white shroud that covered the region, from the northwestern end of Sumatra, across the great archipelago to the Philippines and New Guinea. Visibility dropped to a few hundred meters. An airliner crashed into a mountain near Medan. Authorities in several countries warned their populations to stay indoors and wear face masks to screen carbon particles. A Rand Corporation study later found that the death rate for the elderly in Kuala Lumpur, the Malaysian capital, had jumped over 90 percent during the period. It seemed an apocalyptic end to an era in which growth and development had been put above all else.

The fires and the smoke lasted six months, until the monsoon rains arrived in November. But this was just the start. The haze from Indonesian fires became an annual dry-season phenomenon, reaching another peak of intensity in 2006. By then, it was becoming more than a regional nuisance and health hazard. The first report of the Intergovernmental Panel on Climate Change found that deforestation and forest degradation contributed 17 to 20 percent of global greenhouse gas emissions. Indonesia has the third-largest area of tropical forest of any country in the world, after Brazil and Congo. But it also has the fastest rate of deforestation of any country.

Indonesia is barely industrialized, by comparison with North America, Northeast Asia, or Europe. Yet the greenhouse gas emissions from its plunder of the forests, amounting to 80 percent of its national emissions, give it the invidious distinction of being the world's third-largest emitter, after the United States and China. The clearing of the forests and draining of the peat marshes in Indonesia, in which the fires were part of the process, became an international problem. For Susilo Bambang Yudhoyono, at the start of his presidency in late 2004, deforestation and climate change became a challenge. He set out to make Indonesia at once a responsible world citizen and a beneficiary of the new global carbon-trading economy that was starting to emerge.

Yudhoyono inherited a political class, a bureaucracy, and a business private sector largely impervious to all these concerns. The Indonesian constitution put "the land, the waters and the natural resources" of the country under the powers of the state, to be used for the greatest benefit of all the people. One of Suharto's earliest laws, in 1967, put all forests more specifically under state control. Over following years, he replaced the customary leadership of communities with a top-down system of appointments, from provincial governor to village head. Customary tenure of forests was thus pushed aside, along with the local representation that might have pursued ownership and land-use rights.

In 1982 the New Order mapped the 75 percent of the Indonesian land area classed as forest. Out of 144 million hectares, it marked 64.3 million as "production" forests. By then, as we have seen, the military had been given control over the allocation of forestry concessions and was collecting a large percentage from concessionaires. Suharto's business cronies, such as Bob Hasan, had made vast fortunes from the export of unprocessed logs and then cornered the production of plywood. In 1990 they were the leaders among nearly 600 concessionaires holding long-term leases over 60 million hectares of tropical forest.

In 1996 the ageing Suharto embarked on a new project aimed at maintaining his prized achievement of rice self-sufficiency. A

"Mega Rice Project" in the Kapuas region of Central Kalimantan saw drainage canals cut through a million hectares of swampy peat land and forest, drying them out. The scheme pushed aside Dayak communities that relied on the shifting cultivation of open ground and collection of rattan vines for furniture making. By the next year, the peat was oxidizing and emitting huge volumes of carbon dioxide, and combusting as fires spread into the ground from the burning of tree cover. Similar land-clearance programs were underway elsewhere. The 1997 haze originated from fires in twenty-three provinces. The Mega Rice Project was one of the follies stopped during the economic bailout of 1998. By then, though, about one-third of Indonesia's forest cover had been lost during the New Order period.

The process worsened in the years after Suharto resigned, as the New Order was reformed. Power shifted back from the central government to local authorities and a resurgent civil society. It was almost anarchy. Customary groups reasserted their rights to forest land, sometimes in conflict with other groups. Dayak communities expelled many of the settlers transplanted from Java and Madura under the Suharto government's *transmigrasi* program, which had aimed to export a rice-growing culture to the outer islands as well as to relieve population pressures. The Habibie government's law on regional autonomy gave the kabupaten the authority to "manage natural resources."

That same year, 1998, a new forestry law, replacing Suharto's 1967 law, reaffirmed the authority of the central Ministry of Forests over access to forests, allocation of land, and use of forest resources. But district governments went on issuing hundreds of logging concessions. In many cases, local officials brokered partnerships between the existing big timber companies and the communities who had been granted the new leases. The annual rate of deforestation doubled from 1 million hectares in 1999 to 2 million by 2003.

The scale of illegal logging—illegal as far as Jakarta was concerned, if not local authorities—was revealed in a series of raids by the national police in 2008. They seized nineteen ships at one small port, Ketapang in West Kalimantan, which were loaded with 12,000 logs of tropical hardwood for which there were no papers of origin. Another 32,000 logs were found being floated down the wide Kapuas River. This seizure in a short space of time suggested an extractive industry earning about $3.5 billion a year. Further sizeable shipments of hardwood came in other parts of Kalimantan, while smaller loads of high-value sandalwood and blackwood were intercepted in the eastern islands. But there was another industry that would mount an even bigger threat to Indonesia's natural forests.

IN THE EARLY PART of the twentieth century, planters cleared large areas of forest in what are now Indonesia and Malaysia for the bioresource of the new motoring age, rubber, from seedlings smuggled out of South America. In recent decades, however, a new kind of tree imported from West Africa and South America has transformed the landscape again in these two countries.

Palm oil is a staple ingredient of the packaged foods, toiletries, and cosmetics of the supermarket era: from bread and cookies to frozen chips, chocolate, lipstick, shampoo, and shaving cream. The palm grows in marginal soils under tropical sun and with high rainfall; within five years it yields heavy bunches of the reddish-yellow fruit from which the oil is extracted, which fetches up to $1,250 a ton at market peaks. With yields of up to four tons per hectare from a mature tree, the crop can be a valuable earner for a smallholder.

Many governments from Africa to the Southwest Pacific encouraged the development of smallholder plots, grouped around nucleus estates and processing plants, to spread the cash economy to their villagers. Yet the crop also offers a double benefit to the big timber companies: after getting an early profit from the large trees they clear on their concessions, they can replant the land with this quick-return tree crop instead of setting it aside for the decades required for forest regrowth. Consequently, Indonesia has seen some of its biggest conglomerates diversify from timber or pulp and paper production into palm oil, while many groups in completely unrelated fields have also taken over or developed plantations.

Indonesia's production of palm oil grew from less than 200,000 tons in the 1960s to about 27 million tons in 2013. It exported about 18 million tons of crude palm oil in 2012, earning $21.6 billion—and the government reaped $5.7 billion in export tax. With the trade balance and government budget squeezed by the rising net imports of petroleum, the government raised the mandatory proportion of biodiesel in subsidized fuel in 2013 and is promoting the extension of palm-oil plantations in Kalimantan, Sumatra, and Papua. Production is expected to rise to about 40 million tons a year by 2020.

The spread of palm-oil plantations threatens the livelihood of communities that live off the natural forests, especially where *adat* (customary) forms of ownership are unrecognized. In Sumatra, the oil palm threatens the survival of various animal species, including a rhinoceros and a sub-breed of tiger; in Kalimantan, the orangutan. The shrinking of the natural forest and replacement with monotonous lines of oil palm, the exclusion of traditional human communities, and the vanishing wildlife also reduce opportunities for forms of specialist tourism that might generate rewarding local employment. In 2005 the new Yudhoyono government encouraged an initiative that aimed to end the cutting of old-growth forest. Some of the bigger plantations joined a voluntary system known as "Certified Sustainable Palm Oil," which gave a label to oil that was produced according to certain environmental and social standards, and not from newly cleared land. For expanded planting, the industry was pointed toward an estimated 20 million hectares that had already been cleared in previous logging operations and was lying unused.

In 2011 Yudhoyono imposed a two-year moratorium on new forest exploitation permits and extended it for another two years in 2013. In theory, this set aside 64 million hectares of natural forest, while the government fine-tuned an ambitious new-age scheme to keep the forests and peatlands and make money out of them. Called the Reducing Emissions from Deforestation and Forest Degradation program (abbreviated to REDD+), the UN-sponsored scheme sees developing countries compensated if they preserve their carbon sinks, such as forests and swamps.

Jakarta embraced the idea with enthusiasm. In 2008 one group of environmentalists saw it earning between $2.5 billion and $4 billion a year. The government's council on climate change estimated it could bring in $15 billion a year by 2030. Foreign governments, including those of Norway and Australia, were among the aid donors that made pledges totaling $4 billion to get it started. In 2009, at a meeting of the Group of Twenty in Pittsburgh, Yudhoyono pledged to reduce Indonesia's greenhouse gas emissions by 26 percent by 2020; even a 41 percent reduction was possible, he said, with enough international support. Dozens of pilot schemes got underway, many of which saw entrepreneurs from the big cities putting themselves and their organizational skills between the residents of the forest and the central government, and taking some of the money flows.

In 2013, after six years of the REDD+ scheme, not a single carbon credit had been sold from Indonesia, notes one scholar, Abbie Carla Yunita. The Australian aid agency pulled out of the scheme it had been supporting in Kalimantan, while out of the $1 billion pledged by Norway, only $50 million had been disbursed. In many schemes, the question of who held the tenure of the land had not been resolved. With that being unclear, the ownership of the carbon rights was also uncertain.

The government was slow in producing a map of which forest areas must be protected and which might be exploited. The powerful Ministry of Forests chopped and changed the classification. One important area for a REDD+ scheme, the Katingan Peatland Restoration and Conservation Project, in Central Kalimantan, had its area cut in half from 203,000 hectares in 2013, making it unviable as a habitat for its estimated 4,000-strong orangutan population, on which ecotourism and other ventures depended. Logging and palm-oil companies went ahead clearing land under licenses given before Yudhoyono's moratorium in 2011.

In 2013 it was estimated that a further 5 million hectares of forest had been cleared since the president's announcement. Civil society groups were questioning the self-certification processes of the sustainable palm-oil scheme, arguing that certifiers selected and paid by the companies were glossing over practices that the scheme was supposed to eliminate. Only about 35 percent of palm-oil production was covered by the scheme; those outside it had no trouble finding buyers.

Some local communities, or at least local exploiters, have resisted restoration schemes for devastated lands. The canals that had drained the peatlands have become waterways and are sometimes used to transport timber cut in small sawmills. Remedying the land means blocking these canals so that water soaks into the land and raises the water table closer to the surface. In 2013 the actor Harrison Ford came to Indonesia to front a documentary film on deforestation; he was horrified at the land clearing that was happening within the boundaries of national parks, including the vast Tesso Nilo lowland park in Riau province, home of a dwindling band of Sumatran wild elephants. Encroachments have taken about one-third of its area, with seventeen companies and 584 small cultivators growing palm oil for sale to mills located around the park's periphery, according to a World Wildlife Fund report in mid-2013. In mid-2014, an authoritative study by a former senior Indonesian forestry official Belinda Arunarwati Margono and colleagues at South Dakota University found that the rate of deforestation was increasing and was twice the rate reported by the government. Some 6 million hectares of primary forest was cleared between 2000 and 2012, the rate of clearance rising by 47,600 ha a year. In 2012, Indonesia lost 840,000 ha of forest, compared with 460,000 ha cleared in Brazil (where the jungle area is four times greater).

In June 2013 the annual haze set in again severely. Satellites picked up dozens of "hot spots" in Sumatra from fires set to clear land, despite a total ban by Jakarta on this method. Singapore declared a "very hazardous" level of air pollution from smoke particles. Recriminations broke out between Indonesia and Singapore and Malaysia, though it emerged that some of the plantation companies accused of encouraging land clearances by fire were domiciled in these neighboring countries.

The picture is a familiar one: good intentions and policies at the top undermined by a lack of enforcement capacity on the ground and by the corruption of the agencies supposed to monitor and guard the forests. Still, the approach cannot be written off. Government agencies are working on a uniform map to delineate which forests are protected and are developing a protocol for "free, prior, and informed consent" by local communities. In May 2013 the constitutional court ruled on an appeal by indigenous community support groups that "customary forests" could no longer be classified as state forests. Potentially, this provides a legal basis for about 40 million people to regain control over their traditional lands. Yudhoyono's government worked on timber certification agreements with the European Union and other markets, although illegal timber still leaked out to China through Malaysia and Papua New Guinea.

The slow start to the REDD+ scheme might turn out to be a blessing. Had the global carbon market really taken off before ownership of the carbon rights were sorted, the outer islands of Indonesia might have seen another rush of land-grabbing by big corporations and the politically connected. But collecting and distributing compensation from the international market will not be enough, warns a well-known writer on the environment, Chandra Kirana. Indigenous communities will need to be engaged in exploiting their forests in sustainable ways: by setting up ecotourism ventures, by taking some high-value timber for specific products, and by harvesting foods, spices, beverages, and fibers.

Palm oil and other plantation crops are not the only threat to the forest cover. Across Kalimantan, as we have seen, the coal-mining industry has scarred the landscape with open-cut pits and access roads. Samarinda, the capital of East Kalimantan, is ringed by seventy mines and depleted workings filled with acidic water. Only in a minority of the 12,000 coal-mining concessions across Indonesia are attempts made to restore land.

The collection of revenue by regional governments is opaque. Rather than an unforeseen by-product of political decentralization, this was the result of a conscious policy to have a fragmented coal industry that allowed easy entry by new domestic entrepreneurs and that kept out the big international mining companies. In a revealing remark, a senior official at the Ministry of Energy and Natural Resources told the American embassy in December 2007 (in a reference to the 35-million-tons-a-year Kaltim Prima Coal): "There will be no more KPCs." The Indonesian government preferred ten companies producing 5 million tons a year than one producing 50 million. The official shrugged off the loss of revenue and environmental protection this would involve. "Indonesia would be better off if we had kept mining large-scale," says environmentalist Chandra Kirana. "In the name of nationalism we have actually thrown away our resources for the benefit of a very few."

An even smaller-scale mining boom is also having adverse effects. Across the islands, up to 3 million people are estimated to be making a living from sluicing alluvial sands for gold without any permits or supervision. Often they strip forest to get to the layer of gold-bearing sands underneath. Close to the giant Freeport mine in Papua, thousands of "illegal" miners sift through discarded rock for gold traces. Typically, these small miners mix mercury into their slurry, where it amalgamates with the gold. Officially, Indonesia imported only 7.9 tons of mercury in 2011 for industrial and medical use. One estimate, using export figures from trade partners, put the actual import level around that time at 280 tons a year. The mercury would have been smuggled from Malaysia and Singapore and paid for from the proceeds of the gold that was smuggled out. Miners or gold dealers would then use blowtorches to vaporize the mercury from the globules of amalgam. The result is extremely high concentrations of mercury in the bodies of the miners and people living nearby, in the river fish on which many inland communities depend, and in the marine life chain downriver and out to sea. Sometimes cyanide is used to help dissolve the mercury, resulting in the methyl mercury that caused the Minamata poisoning in Japan. The combination of uncontrolled deforestation and mercury contamination is particularly severe on local livelihoods in the western side of Kalimantan, which has no coal reserves to compensate for falling forestry employment and rising health problems.

FOR THE MAJORITY OF INDONESIANS, however, these problems are out in the jungles and islands. In 1977 the economist Sumitro Djojohadikusumo, then Suharto's minister for research, saw an "island-city" in the making on Java and Madura. Indonesia's population was then 142 million, which he believed would rise to 250 million by the end of the twentieth century. Population growth was slower than Sumitro predicted, thanks in part to the New Order's family-planning program. By 2013, it was still just under 250 million; demographers see it rising to 290 million by midcentury, before the ageing profile and decline seen in other Southeast Asian countries sets in. Still, it remains the fourth-most populous country in the world, and 58 percent of its people live on Java and Madura. That is, about 145 million live on a land area only slightly larger than that of New York State, or 60 percent of the area of Australia's state of Victoria.

About 53 percent of Indonesians now live in urban environments. That may have stopped or slowed the clearing of Java's remaining forest cover, which has been all too evident in the rising incidence of rainy-season flooding and dry-season droughts in recent decades, caused by the felling of trees in the watersheds for timber and firewood or open land for planting. As we have seen, the process is being reversed in some areas, notably with the planting of teak along the barren Gunung Kidul range, southeast of Yogyakarta. More and more inhabitants now live in the cities along the Java Sea coast, where dwellings are made of industrial materials and household energy comes from a grid or a gas canister. Java remains a remarkably green and beautiful landscape, but more and more of the rice paddies on its urban fringes are being turned over to housing and factories.

The largest urban conglomeration is around Jakarta. The 2010 census put the resident population of the national capital district at 9.5 million. Yet the surrounding cities of Bekasi, Tangerang, Depok, and Bogor are linked dormitory and industrial centers. Up to 4 million workers commute into Jakarta from places as far out as Sukabumi, on the southern side of West Java's mountains. The population is remarkably stoic, even cheerful, for what would elsewhere be regarded as an urban nightmare.

The encroachment of housing on the uplands and mountain slopes to the south of the city has lessened the landscape's capacity to retain the monsoon rains, which arrive each November and remain for several months. The network of drainage canals into the Java Sea, built by the Dutch, is now clogged with silt and rubbish. Even the preliminary downpours of the rainy season can bring the entire city to a halt, with flash flooding of road intersections. Conversely, water shortages occur during the midyear dry season, as about 40 percent of the capital district's population relies on groundwater wells for their household water.

Much of the groundwater and reticulated city water is highly contaminated. The Citarum River—which flows for 160 kilometers from near the West Java provincial capital, Bandung, to the Java Sea through Jakarta—has long been listed by international environmental institutions as among the world's top ten pollution concentrations. Textile, footwear, and garment factories near its source and metal industries along its banks pour in untreated waste that contains toxic chemicals and heavy metals. Households add untreated sewage and rubbish, the latter piling up in vast floating masses behind bridges and weirs.

Despite this, about 28 million people depend on its waters, in one way or another, from source to sea. The river provides about 80 percent of the surface water tapped for Jakarta's water supply; millions wash themselves and their clothes in it as well. They are put at risk of skin diseases, cancers, and toxic metal accumulation. The government launched a $3.5-billion cleanup program in 2009, with a $500-million loan coming from the Asian Development Bank over fifteen years. Five years later, the river is still listed among the world's worst pollution spots.

Another twenty-nine rivers around Indonesia are listed by the government as being highly polluted with chemicals and bacterial agents, including human waste. In 2013 about 68 percent of the Indonesian population had access to improved sanitation systems, but a World Bank study found that poor sanitation was still costing the equivalent of about 2.3 percent of gross domestic product from losses of economic output for health and environmental reasons. Less than 5 percent of sludge from septic tanks and about 1 percent of household waste water was treated, and about 14 percent of urban dwellers still had to defecate in open spaces.

Air quality is another environmental issue in the cities. The major cities of Jakarta, Surabaya, and Medan have fewer than thirty days in total of clean air during the year. Unleaded petrol was mandated in Jakarta, Cirebon, Bali, and Batam from around 2001 but took time to come into widespread use. In 2005 a study of school-age children in Bandung found that two-thirds had lead content in their blood that was well above World Health Organization standards. Unleaded petrol was mandated in the city the following year, and significant improvement in bloodstream lead levels was noticed within two years. Even with unleaded fuel, the vast number of cars and motorcycles has created a persistently high level of sulfur dioxide, carbon monoxide, and particle pollution in the cities. Lagging investment in public transport has boosted the people's reliance on private vehicles. Commuting times into Jakarta from outlying towns are measured in hours for those not able to access the limited surface rail network. Some workers choose to spend their evenings in shopping malls, cooking their own meals in special kitchens, and take only an hour or two getting home rather than the four hours the commute would last straight after work. The Jakarta city administration started plans for a mass rapid transit system in 1980; it was not until 2013 that it signed the first contracts for construction. Meanwhile, it adopted palliative measures, including dedicated bus lanes, the conversion of buses to natural gas fuel, and a monorail line that was abandoned partway through construction.

It was not simply a shortage of financial resources that held back solutions to these urban environmental problems. International agencies were ready to offer large-scale funding but were frustrated by the lack of coordination and drive among the city and central government agencies. Contradictory policies abounded, notably in the promotion of so-called green cars (smaller vehicles with relatively low-emission engines, costing under $10,000) in 2013 through lower sales taxes. Indonesia has often had well-conceived and bold ideas at the top, but they have been confounded by inept administration or subverted by vested interests on the ground.

Another source of resistance was the widespread feeling that the advanced industrial nations were now preaching what they had not practiced during their years of rapid growth. At a seminar on the environment organized by Sumitro in the late 1970s, the late nuclear physicist Edward Teller gained a spontaneous round of applause from Indonesian officials when he declared that the worst kind of pollution was "the pollution of poverty."

Four decades later, a source of great hope is the flourishing, all over Indonesia, of civil society organizations that are concerned with the environment and customary land rights. They have stood up when prickly officialdom denied visas to activists from international environmental groups; they have investigated conflicts in the remotest parts of the archipelago, sometimes at great physical risk; and they have publicized their findings against hugely powerful interests. Environmentalism has now become a thoroughly indigenous concern.

13

FROM SBY
TO JOKOWI

ABOUT A YEAR BEFORE THE 2014 ELECTIONS, A NEW STICKER APPEARED ON THE BACKS of cars and motorbikes in Yogyakarta. It has a picture of a smiling Suharto. *"Piye Le Kabare?"* the Javanese-language caption asks. *"Isih Penak Jamanku To?"* ("How are you doing? Wasn't it better in my time?") At Suharto's birthplace, the village of Kemusuk, on the outskirts of the city, a new museum opened with innovative visual displays about the high points of his career. It quickly became a thriving spot for domestic tourists, who were delivered in busloads. The museum has a small mosque attached. By contrast, the sprawling Suharto family house around the corner, built near the humble cottage of his birth, is decorated with images of Semar and other wayang characters. A servant proudly shows a spring where the young Suharto used to meditate. A large *pendopo* (pavilion) contains the reinterred remains of his two maternal forebears who were renowned *kyai* (holy men) in Javanese mysticism. Aspiring political candidates come here to meditate in the hope of imbibing some of the wahyu (authority) of the Suharto line.

At the end of the presidency of Susilo Bambang Yudhoyono, a decade widely seen as one that would "consolidate democracy" and launch Indonesia on a path to a more important global status in the twenty-first century, at least some in Suharto's home region sensed that a nascent nostalgia for strong government was waiting to be harvested. It was based on a filtered view of an era slipping back into the past, one of which 60 million Indonesians of voting age in 2014 had no clear memory.

This was enabled by a widespread feeling that Yudhoyono had been, if not a failure, a disappointment. Three years into his first term, there was already a strong feeling in elite circles that he had "squandered" the mandate of his convincing victory over Megawati Sukarnoputri in the 2004 runoff, part of the country's first direct presidential election. Nevertheless, in the 2009 election he had been so popular that he defeated Megawati in the first round with 60.8 percent of the vote; the PD, newly formed as a personal vehicle for his candidacy in 2004, became the biggest party in the DPR, its share of seats rising from 10 to 30 percent. With an even bigger mandate, no reelection to worry about in 2014, and the liberal-minded econo-mist Boediono as his vice president, Yudhoyono was positioned to make the reforms that would put Indonesia's fearful past behind it and enable the nation to confidently seize the opportunities of the new century. Instead, his second term was a litany of hesitation and retreat in the face of pressure.

Returned to power in 2009, Yudhoyono convened a three-day "national summit" with business, academic, and regional govern-ment representatives to review shortcomings of governance. Then he ordered his new cabinet to prepare a "100-day plan" to make early use of the mandate and set priorities in some fifteen areas. First on his list was smashing the "legal mafias," which had just shown their baleful power in the conspiracy of police and prosecutors to frame two commissioners of the anticorruption agency. Other pri-orities included the revitalization of domestic defense industries to reduce dependence on foreign-supplied equipment; better coordina-tion of the police, intelligence, military, and social-religious agencies in overcoming terrorism; increasing the electricity supply; expand-ing food production; better land-use planning and controls to meet climate-change commitments; more investment in infrastructure; incentives for small enterprises; extending health insurance; and im-proving education.

Even before the one hundred days were up, however, the gov-ernment's momentum had dissipated and its attention been diverted by the Bank Century controversy, whipped up in the DPR by the Golkar faction, ostensibly one of Yudhoyono's partners. As we have seen, the controversy led to the sacrifice in 2010 of one of his most highly regarded ministers, Sri Mulyani Indrawati. The government failed to apply an automatic adjustment to fuel prices, leading to periodic political crises over price hikes to prevent the ballooning of subsidies. An inordinate amount of revenue continues to flow to this form of "middle-class welfare," instead of to measures such as the abolition of school fees in the upper secondary years or the financing of Yudhoyono's ambitious health insurance scheme, launched in 2014.

As well, powerful ministries continued to subvert or contradict government policies, diverting more resources to nationalist symbols and deterring new foreign investment by applying conditions that mandated increased local equity and processing. Growth of formal jobs lagged behind the economic growth rate, and the informal sector actually started growing again as a proportion of workforce activity. An official survey in 2013 found that 37.2 percent of children under five had stunted growth, a slight increase from 2007.

Military reform halted when Yudhoyono took over. The territorial role was maintained, diverting resources from improving Indonesia's external defense capability and perpetuating many corrupt and predatory moneymaking activities. Yudhoyono dragged his heels on the official divestment of military businesses, and it was carried out in a less than transparent manner, with some enterprises transferred to civilian proxies and the auditor in charge openly saying that the territorial role helped keep the military involved in illegal business. The military retained jurisdiction over its personnel for offenses against civilian law. Courts-martial jailed soldiers who were involved in shootings and murders, notably in the Theys Eluay and Cebongan prison cases, but for much shorter terms than civilian courts would have awarded.

Yudhoyono maintained impunity for military personnel who were involved in past human rights abuses and indeed kept some figures in high government positions, such as the defense department head Syafrie Syamsuddin (who was persona non grata in the United States over incidents in East Timor) and his cabinet secretary for some years, Sudi Silalahi (widely seen as an organizer of the Laskar Jihad militia, which had joined interreligious fighting in Ambon and

Poso). This impunity stretched down to the lowliest members of the civilian militias raised in East Timor, as was clear from the immense pressure Yudhoyono placed on Dili to have Martenus Bere released in 2009. The acquittal of the retired general Muchdi Purwopranjono over the murder of the human rights activist Munir Said Thalib left unexplored the higher levels of the conspiracy within the BIN.

If nostalgia for the Suharto era has some political currency in 2014, Yudhoyono must bear some responsibility. He did not come out to question the mythology of the New Order. Toward the end of his presidency, he paid homage on October 1 at the Crocodile Hole, where the story of communist treachery is enshrined.

In 2012 came a moment in which Yudhoyono could grapple with the legacy of the 1965–66 massacres. His government's own Human Rights Commission concluded a three-year investigation that found that the PKI massacres warranted redress. Survivors and family members of the victims emerged from the shadows to tell their stories to the media. Possibly influenced by the Australian prime minister Kevin Rudd's moving apology to his country's indigenous people in 2010, Yudhoyono floated the idea of an apology for the massacres, balanced by the inclusion of the shooting of Muslim demonstrators at Tanjung Priok in 1984 and the abduction and sniper shooting of students in 1998. His legal adviser Albert Hasibuan said he had been charged with drafting the apology.

As it happened, that was the last that was heard about it. Yudhoyono's military colleagues and the Muslim parties in his coalition persuaded him to drop the idea. It can be assumed that his wife and her family were also defensive: Sarwo Edhie Wibowo, the president's father-in-law, was the general who had set off the massacres in his sweep across Java and Bali at the head of the Special Forces. The desultory investigation of the former first family's moneymaking ended with Suharto's death in 2008.

The issue would not go away, however, reemerging with the release of the chilling documentary film *The Act of Killing* in the United States at the end of 2012. The Indonesian magazine *Tempo* collected book-length material detailing mass execution after mass execution across Java in 1965–66, with the leading perpetrators coming from the Pemuda Ansor, the youth wing of the NU.

An example was given to Yudhoyono by the mayor of a small city in Central Sulawesi. As a sixteen-year-old in 1965, Rusdi Mastura had been delegated by his teachers to join those who were guarding three local PKI committee members. Men had come to take the prisoners away one night. When Rusdi became mayor of Palu, he started inquiries into their fate. Witnesses came forward. They had been taken by the Palu army garrison outside town to a prepared grave and shot. In March 2013 Rusdi stood up at Palu's town hall and issued a public apology, promising help with health and education to the bereaved families and to build a memorial to the killings.

Yudhoyono's retreat was further shown up in September 2013 when the Dutch ambassador issued a public apology for the killing of up to 5,000 villagers in South Sulawesi around the end of 1946 by Dutch commandos under Captain Raymond "Turk" Westerling and handed compensation to the surviving families of the victims. A month after the Dutch apology, some families of the PKI dead and former political prisoners gathered in Yogyakarta. They were attacked and dispersed by vigilantes who called themselves the Indonesian Anti-Communist Front. "It is legal for us to kill them, just like when we killed PKI members in the past," the leader of the attackers proclaimed to reporters. The police stood by.

But it was over issues of religious tolerance that Yudhoyono has disappointed the most, at least among more secular Indonesians, educated women, and minorities. He gave unprecedented deference to the MUI, raising it to an almost judicial status. The decision to adopt restrictions on the proselytizing freedom of the Ahmadiyah sect in 2008, in response to the MUI's urging of a ban, gave the signal (no doubt unintended) for repeated attacks on Ahmadiyah communities and places of worship (of which about fifty remain closed).

A 1969 regulation on the building of places of worship was tightened in 2006, giving more power to surrounding communities to veto new constructions. Since then, about 600 churches either built or under construction have been closed or demolished. Yudhoyono's government has not enforced court orders permitting church projects to go ahead. Even a Supreme Court order allowing a congregation to enter the Yasmin church in Bogor, just outside the capital, was not enough for the national police to be ordered to protect worshippers from a local Muslim group that was blocking their access.

The forces of orthodoxy later moved on to the Shia community among the Muslim ummat, a minority in Indonesia, although in some eyes the traditionalist Sunni followers of NU also veer close to Shiism. Yudhoyono's religious affairs minister suggested to displaced Ahmadiyah and Shia communities that the solution to their problems lay in converting to the mainstream. His home affairs minister praised the FPI as a potential national asset. Yudhoyono himself tended to speak more of the sentiments of the majority than of the rights and freedoms of the minorities.

Toward the end of Yudhoyono's presidency, moves were afoot to rein in some of the democratic and constitutional reforms that had applied since he took office. When direct personal criticism cut, his circle floated the idea of reinstating the presidential lèse-majesté law struck down by the constitutional court. In 2013 his party tabled a draft amendment to the election law that would end the direct election of bupati and city mayors, in the third tier of government. Such elections were wasteful of funds, encouraged corruption, and were often accompanied by violence, the bill's supporters argued. Instead, the executives would be appointed by a vote of the district legislature, a process that critics saw as bringing back an even murkier process and blocking the rise of independent reformist candidates. The Ministry of Home Affairs appeared to be on a collision course with the population of Aceh over the use of the former GAM flag as the province's emblem. The drift toward splitting Papua into more provinces was unaddressed in proposals for enhanced Otsus (special autonomy) laws that were passed on to Yudhoyono's successor.

All this added up to a presidential style that was widely seen as unduly passive even by Javanese standards, which value caution, quietness, and compromise. His critics said Yudhoyono acted "more like a referee" or "led from behind." "We have a president, but do we have a leader?" asked the senior journalist August Parengkuan. The Aceh peace settlement might not have happened if the vice president, Jusuf Kalla, had not exceeded his authority. Reporting its talks with several of the president's advisers in 2008, the US embassy said that the "thinking general" had a firm grasp of the issues coming before his cabinet and often spoke at length and listened to everyone in the room but would tend to conclude without issuing instructions or summing up. He was forgiving of incompetence and intent on maintaining harmony. In the Ahmadiyah decision, Yudhoyono overruled nine of his advisers and accepted the single voice of the MUI, telling his staff he needed to retain the support of conservative Muslims and to save the face of three ministers who had made public promises of some sort of decree.

The president's former military colleagues, such as Agus Widjojo, say that no one should have been surprised at this. "That is SBY," Widjojo says. Another former colleague, the retired general T. B. Silalahi, who became a presidential adviser, told the Americans in 2008 that Yudhoyono had been the "golden boy" of his military academy class, graduating as its medal winner, and had been promoted quickly and "protected from controversy throughout his career." As a battalion commander in Timor, Yudhoyono had been kept at headquarters in Dili, and as second in command of the Jakarta garrison in 1996, he had remained disconnected from the infamous attack on Megawati's party headquarters, Silalahi was quoted as saying. As we have seen, he steered through the turmoil of 1998 and the violence of 1999 in Timor on Wiranto's staff without any taint being attached to him. Indeed, Silalahi claimed, Yudhoyono had supported students and "worked with moderates to ease Suharto out of power."

Behind the Javanese reticence, some saw an individual diffidence in Yudhoyono. The son of a modest-income priyayi family in a small town in East Java, he married into the family of the illustrious General Wibowo and has often seemed more like the adoptive son of that family than the self-made career soldier that his academic and service records describe. His intellectualism and extensive foreign exposure—at American military colleges and universities, at courses in Malaysia and Europe, and in the UN peacekeeping mission in Bosnia—may have estranged him from his nationalist military colleagues, who were steeped in brutal domestic counterinsurgency campaigns, or he may have felt they did.

But his wariness would have been encouraged by the precarious calm of Jakarta politics when he won office and the weakness of his backing, aside from the popular mandate. His Partai Demokrat had no deep base or great sources of funding and had to get its legislation through the DPR political casino. Powerful military rivals looked on, envious and contemptuous that a "thinking general" should overtake them. They and the political party leaders had the ability to whip up demonstrations and scandals in the DPR. The example of Wahid's impeachment was all too recent. Fears of a military takeover took a long while to recede, as the alarm over the 2006 coup in Bangkok indicated.

Although these excuses were wearing thin by the second term, some of the criticism of Yudhoyono failed to appreciate the nature of politics and leadership in a democratic system of checks and balances. The powers of the presidency had been greatly limited by the reforms of 1998–2004, and those of the parliament, the judiciary, the provinces, and the regions greatly enhanced. The role of the military as the enforcer of the president's policies had ended. The capacity of the police to win public trust or enforce the law had not yet grown. Extremist voices and unscrupulous cabals had less to fear.

To his credit, Yudhoyono supported the work of the KPK, the anticorruption commission, and its special linked courts, even when their investigations and prosecutions struck deep into his own party over the Hambalang sports complex scandal; by 2013 they seemed to have shattered his hopes of leaving a strong PD, one able to field a successor. He also identified himself closely with the effort to preserve Indonesia's forest cover through the REDD+ schemes, an initiative that persists, despite the many obstacles it has faced. Suggestions of special laws to protect the president from personal criticism were not taken up in legislative attempts, and Indonesia's remarkable media freedom came to be uncontested and largely uncontrolled, except through ownership strings. In short, Yudhoyono presided over a decade of unprecedented peace and prosperity in Indonesia, and although religious minorities suffered from the tyranny of the majority in places, Yudhoyono himself embodied a new kind of educated, worldly moderation in politics and religion.

IF THERE WAS ONE CONTENDER to replace Yudhoyono and remedy his legacy of "indecision," it was Prabowo Subianto. That the former Kopassus commander and former son-in-law of Suharto could emerge from the darker side of the past and become a serious challenger showed the failure of the reform-era leaders—Yudhoyono in particular—to address the brutal side of the New Order, assign accountability, and draw the historic lessons.

As we have seen, Prabowo carried a huge weight of suspicion arising from many incidents during his military career. He was a ferocious and successful proponent of the vicious counterinsurgency war in East Timor from the late 1970s. In August 1983 a ceasefire between the Indonesian army and the Falantil guerrillas under José Xanana Gusmão broke down at an area called Kraras. Timorese auxiliaries suddenly turned on a unit of Indonesian combat engineers—for shooting local men and molesting a woman, according to some accounts—and killed sixteen. The army sent in a battalion, scattering the population into the bush. At the end of August, Prabowo arrived with a Kopassus task force and began operations around Kraras. In early September soldiers selected thirty-two civilians, two for each dead soldier, and executed them.

The provincial governor at the time, Mario Carrascalao, later wrote in his memoirs that the East Timor military commander, Colonel Rujito, told him such reprisals were army policy. Some accounts put Prabowo on the spot and in charge of the executions; he has not given a clear account of his activities in Timor around that time. As part of his antiguerilla activities, Prabowo fostered Timorese irregular fighters; some of them later moved to Jakarta as street criminals for political hire. One was Hercules Rozario Marshal, who became a "godfather" of extortion in the capital for decades and who set up a movement to support Gerindra, with Prabowo as head of its advisory board.

Earlier in 1983, Prabowo and his Kopassus unit prepared to arrest the then army commander, Benny Murdani, and other senior generals for an alleged plot against Suharto. More senior Kopassus officers disarmed the unit, and the defense minister, General Mohammed Jusuf, later found Prabowo's suspicions to be wide of the truth. By then, Prabowo had married Suharto's daughter Titiek. He was moved sideways into the Kostrad command, not returning to Kopassus until 1995, when he was given three rapid promotions ahead of his peers. In 1997–98, Kopassus personnel under his command formed a hit squad called Tim Mawar (Team Rose), which abducted and tortured nine student leaders and democracy activists.

The influence of Prabowo has also been seen in a rash of media disinformation that blamed the economic crisis on the machinations of the United States, the IMF, Jewish international financiers, and unpatriotic Sino-Indonesian tycoons. It was noted that Prabowo had been cultivating an Islamist audience through the hardline Dewan Dakwah Islamiyah Indonesia (Islamic Propagation Council of Indonesia) and several of his more devout military colleagues. One senior ethnic Chinese business figure, Sofyan Wanandi, has said Prabowo accused "Chinese Catholics" of trying to topple Suharto by taking their capital out of the country. Prabowo had told Wanandi he was ready "to drive all the Chinese out of the country even if that sets the economy back twenty or thirty years."

In March 1998 Suharto promoted Prabowo to the Kostrad command, putting him in charge of most of the army troops ready for rapid action, including Kopassus. We have seen how, later in 1998, he attempted to overawe the newly installed replacement president, B. J. Habibie, the day after Suharto's resignation; how the new administration court-martialed and jailed several of the Kopassus officers and soldiers belonging to Tim Mawar; and how a military "honor board" then expelled Prabowo from the army.

The most specific allegation against Prabowo derives from the Tim Mawar abuses. The senior-most Kopassus officer sent to court-martial and jailed over the abductions was only a major, Bambang Kristiono. He insisted it was all his initiative, done without informing his superiors. Prabowo accepted only command responsibility and claimed that, having been cashiered from the army, he had paid the penalty. His brother, the businessman Hashim Djojohadiku-sumo, even suggested that the abducted activists should be grateful for being returned alive.

As for the irregular forces Prabowo raised and unleashed in Timor, he has argued that local militias and self-defense forces were part of Indonesian military doctrine and common to any counterinsurgency campaign. "That's what the Americans found out in Iraq," he told one interviewer in 2009. He drew another analogy with the Iraq campaign, comparing the Tim Mawar case to the American abuse of prisoners at Abu Ghraib and Guantanamo Bay. What was a human rights abuse for one regime was "extraordinary rendition" for another. Prabowo has scoffed at the allegations he was commencing a coup d'état, in the style of Suharto's gradual moves against Sukarno, when he confronted Habibie in May 1998. With the thirty-four battalions of Kostrad behind him, who could have stopped him if he had wanted to seize power?

Drummed out of the army and divorced from Titiek Suharto, Prabowo spent two years in the political wilderness—appropriately, in the Biblical setting of Jordan, whose King Abdullah was an old friend from the days of their military training together in the United States. He then returned to Indonesia; his brother Hashim had restored his fortune through the sale of the Kazakhstan oilfield, and with his help Prabowo acquired a pulp and paper business from the jailed Bob Hasan and later moved into coal-mining leases, palm oil, and fisheries. His home base became a high-security ranch at Hambalang, in the foothills just outside Jakarta.

In 2004 Prabowo contested internal elections in Golkar to choose the party's presidential candidate, coming last; his old army foe Wiranto was the winner. Prabowo decided he needed his own machine. That year he won election as chairman of the largely dormant Indonesian Farmers' Association, his modern campaign tactics and funding overwhelming his rivals, and through the organization he connected with voters across Java, in particular. Prabowo also became leader of the association that promoted *pencak silat,* a form of martial arts similar to jujitsu in the Malay culture, and later of an association of traders.

In 2008 he resigned from Golkar and established Gerindra, declaring himself its candidate for president. At the 2009 elections, the party gained only 4.5 percent of the vote and twenty-six seats in the 560-member parliament, far below the threshold required to nominate Prabowo as a presidential candidate. He negotiated a written pact with Megawati Sukarnoputri: he joined her campaign as her vice presidential candidate; in return, she and her PDI-P would give him and Gerindra top billing in an alliance for the 2014 elections. The pair were trounced at the 2009 presidential election, winning 27 percent of the first-round vote, compared to Yudhoyono's 60.8 percent.

Over the following five years, Prabowo worked hard to clean up his credentials and build grassroots support, helped by a lavish advertising campaign that he and his brother financed. Through the farmers' association, he signed up millions of members for Gerindra; he toured Java, telling villagers how they were falling behind in Indonesia's resources and commodities boom. He brought thousands selected as cadres for live-in training at his Hambalang ranch. All had to deposit their mobile phones and other devices and devote themselves for three or four days to mastering the Gerindra platform brochure and door-knocking techniques.

Prabowo studied the campaign of Barack Obama and became the leading user of social media among Indonesia's politicians. He also hired a number of American political campaign managers, principally the controversial publicist and film-maker Rob Allyn, to apply more sophisticated and differentiated messaging than had been hitherto seen in the country's politics. To educated audiences, at home and overseas, he delivered statistics-heavy speeches pointing to a future in which depleting natural resources and a growing population would meet in a great disappointment of hopes. Nearly half the money circulating in Indonesia was in Jakarta, and almost 40 percent more in other large cities. No wonder Indonesia's Gini coefficient was showing greater inequality. Where others, such as Yudhoyono, blamed the weaknesses of government on corruption, Prabowo reversed the linkage: corruption and inefficiency derived from weak government.

One great source of weakness he saw was the proliferation of autonomous governments since 1998: where China had one autonomous body on average for each 42 million of its population and India one for each 34 million, Indonesia had one for every 484,000 people. With thirty-three provinces and 502 kabupaten and municipalities, Indonesia had created "gross inefficiencies" for itself. By the end of 2012, Prabowo pointed out, seventeen serving or former provincial governors and 138 bupati or mayors were in jail, facing trial or under investigation for corruption. Even local election campaigns were costing a thousand times the monthly salary of a bupati: how could that be recouped except by milking official funds?

Prabowo set out a "big push strategy" to ramp up food and biofuel production from new estates, to invest in more infrastructure and social services, and to "simplify and increase the efficiency of all executive, legislative and judicative institutions." To encapsulate his vision of a prosperous and respected Indonesia, Prabowo was wont to cite the Kopassus motto, "*Siapa Berani Menang*"—a translation of the motto of Britain's Special Air Services Regiment: "Who Dares Wins." As the 2014 elections approached, opinion polls by Indonesian media organizations showed Prabowo to be among the top two or three preferences for president. A very young electorate, it seemed, had no memory of, or concern for, Prabowo's past and liked the machismo he projected.

Human rights issues, however, continued to cast a shadow over Prabowo in elite circles and internationally. The 1998 military "honor council" had not been a trial, and he had been dismissed from the army not for the abductions but for "disobeying orders."

In 2000 Prabowo became the first person barred from entering the United States under the International Convention against Torture and other Cruel, Inhuman or Degrading Treatment or Punishment. Other governments of signatory countries feared that they might be obliged to allow prosecution over the Tim Mawar abductions, should Prabowo enter their territory.

In Indonesia, Prabowo tried to allay grievances by recruiting three of the nine acknowledged abduction and torture victims as candidates and campaign staff. But he also employed the former leader of the Tim Mawar, Major Bambang Kristiono, after he completed his jail term. Human rights organizations began questioning the fate of thirteen activists who had disappeared in 1997–98; Prabowo has denied any knowledge of them. Some suggest they may have been eliminated by the Jakarta military garrison, then under the command of Syafrie Syamsuddin (later the head of the defense department under Yudhoyono, and also persona non grata in the United States).

As much as any specific human rights cases, however, many of Prabowo's former army colleagues and civilian contemporaries worried about his personality. To them, his 1983 attempt to arrest General Benny Murdani and the events of 1998 indicated an impulsive character prone to acting on conspiracy theories. Some were even reminded of Adolf Hitler's use of his 1933 election gains to create a totalitarian state, suggesting that Prabowo was using populist support to recentralize power in the presidency.

The candidate himself worked to allay these fears. On the personality question, Prabowo was said to retain a professional "anger manager" on his staff. The very public conversion of his brother Hashim to an evangelical version of Christianity also sent conciliatory signals to the Chinese community and other predominantly Christian groups. Whereas other secular parties were setting up Muslim wings, Gerindra took the unusual step of starting an affiliate Christian association, with Hashim as its head. Prabowo himself vowed to get the contentious Yasmin church in Bogor built as soon as he was elected.

The brothers also made efforts to improve Prabowo's standing in Washington, endowing a chair in Southeast Asian affairs at the Centre for Strategic and International Studies, named after their father. A group called Business Executives for National Security—led by a wealthy mining executive, Stanley Weiss—promoted Prabowo as the potential Lee Kuan Yew of Indonesia, which might then emulate Singapore's rise out of developing-country status.

IN 2012 PRABOWO AT ONCE showed off his political clout and created an immense obstacle for himself. The governorship of the national capital was coming up for election. Prabowo persuaded Megawati to bring in the popular mayor of the central Java city of Solo, Joko Widodo, as her party's candidate. Widodo would face the Golkar incumbent, Fauzi Bowo, who was notorious for his huge payments to smaller parties to win their support.

A carpenter's son, Widodo grew up in a house with woven bamboo walls, in a squatter settlement along a river bank in Solo, from which his father also ran a lumber business. Widodo did well at state schools and gained entrance to the prestigious Gajah Mada University in Yogyakarta, where he gained a degree in forestry engineering. After work in forestry concessions in Aceh, he returned to Solo and started up his own furniture making business, which made products for both domestic sales and export. Widodo had been mayor of Solo since 2005. Becoming known affectionately as "Jokowi," he had protected its ancient buildings and historical precincts, cleaned up its parks and streets, and restored it as a cultural and tourism center. The city's image as a recent host of Islamic extremists, centered on the Ngruki pesantren, had receded. Although he belonged to the PDI-P (his father was an avid follower of Sukarno and made pilgrimages to the first president's grave in Blitar), Widodo had managed to avoid the label of "politician." Skinny, modest, and prone to on-the-spot inspections and public encounters (known in Javanese as *blusukan*), he was seen as "one of us" by the Indonesian public, and not one of the political class.

Prabowo teamed him up with a seasoned regional politician from his own Gerindra party, Basuki Tjahaja Purnama—usually known by his Hakka-language nickname, "Ahok"—an ethnic Chinese former bupati on the tin-mining island of Belitung. The Gerindra cadres set to work, taking a detailed manifesto for city improvement around the capital's neighborhoods. The combination of the down-to-earth Jokowi, Javanese and Muslim, and the blunt-speaking Ahok, ethnic Chinese and Christian, swept to victory, signaling a more inclusive mentality in a city that had a long tradition of backing Islamic parties and the Golkar machine.

Within a year, Widodo was so popular that calls mounted for Megawati to stand aside and make him her party's candidate for president. Opinion polls showed him significantly ahead of the next most popular figure, Prabowo. Inside the PDI-P, the push for Widodo came from the realization that Megawati was unlikely to win the presidency herself; he was the only chance to get the party back into power. Moreover, he was so popular that numerous candidates could expect to win seats in legislatures on his coattails, without the usual campaign expenditure. Outside the party, it was a case both of Widodo's own popularity and, for some, of the appeal of someone who could defeat Prabowo. Despite his perceived disregard for political guile, however, Widodo paid careful homage to entrenched power groups. On the day of the scandal of the murderous raid on Yogyakarta's Cebongan prison by vengeful Kopassus soldiers, the Jakarta governor made a call at the Kopassus headquarters on the fringe of the capital—a gesture of support.

Megawati herself was reluctant to step back from the leadership. She had a strong sense of the party as the home of Sukarnoism. Would that family legacy disappear once Widodo took the leadership? While not rejecting Widodo as a possibility, she kept her options open until late in the run-up to the April 2014 parliamentary elections. Disguising his ambitions, Widodo held back from pushing the question for fear of offending her pride. Her followers floated the idea of Widodo serving an apprenticeship as her vice president. This offered Megawati a good prospect of the presidential election win that had eluded her three times before. For his part, an increasingly testy Prabowo tried to hold Megawati to her agreement of 2009. Her entourage could only vaguely remember the piece of paper. When they did recall it, they said it had lapsed because the Megawati-Prabowo team had lost in 2009.

Prabowo's second line of argument was that Widodo had won Jakarta because of Gerindra's initiative and campaign support. He had also promised the people of Jakarta to serve them for five years; he needed to show results from his governorship and would still be young enough to contest the presidency in 2019. All Prabowo's effort and all the funding poured by himself and Hashim into Gerindra

since 2008 (about $500 million in total, some of his supporters esti-
mated) depended, it seemed, on Widodo's sense of his obligations, as
well as on Megawati's stubborn pride.

Early in 2014, however, Megawati recognized what the opinion
polls were saying and decided to hand the presidential candidacy
to Widodo. The tactical question then arose: when to announce it?
Going public too early, Megawati feared, would make her legislative
candidates and party campaign managers too complacent. Widodo
and his advisers argued that continued suspense would reduce the
effectiveness of his contribution to the PDI-P campaign. Megawati
held out until the eve of the official three-week campaign period before revealing that Widodo had been anointed to carry forward the
Sukarno heritage.

Other parties and candidates trailed behind these two leading
camps. In Golkar, the business magnate Aburizal Bakrie held control of the party machine and insisted he would run as its presidential candidate. He had won the party chairmanship in 2009 and
had gotten himself nominated in a process that denied others the
opportunity to put themselves forward for selection. Free advertising on his group's two television channels and the publicity spinoff
from owning several football clubs projected "Ical" (his preferred
nickname) as a down-to-earth pragmatist who could get Indonesia
moving.

Bakrie's standing in the opinion polls languished, however. At
Sidoarjo in East Java stood an effigy of him wearing a yellow Golkar
campaign shirt, on the vast field of mud spilling from his company's
exploration well. The ongoing dispute in London with other shareholders in the Bumi coal enterprise suggested a business group that
was veering from one loan crisis to another, with Bakrie perhaps out
to use Golkar's political power to keep the government agencies off
his back.

No alternatives to Bakrie stood out as potential election winners.
The former vice president and party chairman, Jusuf Kalla, had been
knocked out in the first-round vote in 2009 when he stood as Golkar
candidate with the ex-general Wiranto as his running mate. By 2014
his peacemaking in the eastern islands and Aceh was many years
ago, and Kalla himself—turning 72 in May 2014—was regarded as
too old for the youthful electorate. Scandal-tarnished figures from
the New Order were visible elsewhere in the party's senior hierarchy.

Golkar, it was said, was a party that eats its young. And did it really need the presidency? Holding a consistent 20 percent or so of the vote and the parliamentary seats throughout the reform era, Golkar was highly useful, if not essential, for getting any difficult policy into application. Bargaining was what politics was all about.

Divided according to the different religious aliran (streams), wracked internally by personality disputes, and hit by various scandals, the Muslim parties also seemed set to remain in supporting roles. The PKS, or Prosperous Justice Party, which had once seemed the rising star in Indonesian politics, had sunk in public esteem after the unseemly multiple marriages of its top leaders and the involvement of some of them in the massive beef import corruption case, in which former party president Lutfi Hasan Ishaaq received a sixteen-year jail sentence in December 2013. The other three main Muslim parties—the PAN, under Yudhoyono's senior minister Hatta Rajasa, the PKB, which was squabbling over Abdurrahman Wahid's legacy, and the PPP, led by Yudhoyono's contentious religious affairs minister Suryadharma Ali—were useful allies rather than serious contenders for majority support.

The steady Islamization of Indonesian society was reassuring for believers, who could look at parties that had ideas about improving their livelihoods and welfare. Their leaders were potential running mates for secular candidates. Nominations to run in the presidential election also required the backing of 20 percent of the parliamentary membership elected three months earlier (or 25 percent of the popular vote). The Muslim parties could help lift a candidate over this threshold—hence Yudhoyono's careful inclusion of them all in his governing coalition, rewarded by ministerial positions. Prabowo, too, seemed alert to this contingency, with his longtime ally and controversial former Kopassus colleague Muchdi Purwoprandjono leaving Gerindra to join the PPP in 2011.

In the election for the DPR held on April 9, 2014 no party emerged with a very clear claim on power. The PDI-P gained the biggest vote, 18.95 per cent, but not quite yielding the 20 per cent of seats needed to nominate a presidential candidate on its own, and showing the effects of Widodo's delayed anointment. Golkar won 14.75 per cent and Gerindra 11.81 per cent. These three parties were thus in the running to form coalitions around them for a presidential tilt. Yudhoyono's Partai Demokrat won 10.19 per cent but lacked a

magnetic candidate to succeed him. The Muslim parties faired surprisingly well: The NU-based PKB at 9.04 per cent, the Muhammad-
iyah-linked PAN at 7.59 per cent, the PPP at 6.53 per cent and the
Muslim Brotherhood-influenced PKS at 6.79 per cent (the latter con-
founding predictions that its scandals might result in failure to reach
the 3.5 per cent threshold to win DPR seats). Along with two secular
parties led by rejected Golkar aspirants, retired general Wiranto's
Hanura at 5.26 percent and media tycoon Surya Paloh's NasDem
(National Democrat) at 6.72 percent, these second-echelon parties
were candidates for courtship in the presidential dance.

With the Democrats tied to Yudhoyono's weak legacy, and Golkar locked to a widely disliked leader in Bakrie, the presidential
competition got down to a two-candidate race. A combination of
horse-trading and fervent Islamic appeal gained Prabowo the support of PAN, after he chose its Hatta Rajasa as running mate, and
the PKS, with the PPP also signing up, despite an internal revolt
against its leader, Suryadharma Ali (by then sacked as religious affairs minister and facing corruption investigations). Prabowo also
evoked New Order nostalgia for "firm" government in his overtures
to Golkar, which eventually succumbed. This gave him, at least
while he looked a potential winner, the backing of nearly 60 per cent
of the DPR membership, a vital source of support for a president in a
system lacking a US-style presidential veto over legislation. Widodo's
main support outside the PDI-P came from the PKB, from Paloh's
NasDem, and from a clutch of former army generals with deep dis-
trust of Prabowo. These included Wiranto, who brought in his Hanura party, former Jakarta governor Sutiyoso, who had a small party
of his own, and Luhut Panjaitan, by then an influential businessman.
But from looking like a cakewalk for Widodo, in polling early in the
year, the competition narrowed to the point where a month before
the election, some polling institutions linked to interests fearful of
Prabowo withheld their findings.

The theme of politics as SBY's presidency drew to an end was the
kind of government Indonesia needed after a decade of perceived in-
decisiveness. Prabowo made much of the scandals emerging among
provincial and regional governments, suggesting that a tightening
of Jakarta's control was the remedy. Yudhoyono's own party was
floating a draft law to abolish direct elections of bupati and mayors.
In official speeches, especially by military leaders, the term *Negara*

Kesatuan (Unitary State) was increasingly attached to *Republik Indonesia,* which had sufficed until the reform period.

Prabowo ramped up this theme, launching his campaign with a mass rally at a Jakarta football stadium at which he arrived by helicopter and then, wearing knee-high boots, rode a chestnut horse around the perimeter along ranks of young men in red-and-white uniforms. Here and in other speeches in the Indonesian language, he railed against the "thieves" who were stealing Indonesia's wealth or selling out to foreign interests, and made conspicuous Koranic references. To those with long memories, it looked like protesting too much: Prabowo was the son of the economist whose pupils had re-opened Indonesia to foreign investment and who at one time had been on the CIA payroll; his mother was a Christian from Manado, and his father from the aristocratic priyayi class known for its Hindu leanings; Prabowo himself had been educated outside Indonesia. Yet with 30 per cent of the 188 million eligible voters aged between 17 and 29, many had no memory of all this, nor of the old human rights cases. As the campaign drew on, Prabowo appealed to authoritarian as well as nationalistic yearnings. In one speech ten days ahead of the July 9 vote, he spoke favorably of "a return to the 1945 Constitution" (the charter that conferred wide emergency powers on the president in the desperate days after Japan's surrender (and of decision-making by consensus rather than majority vote. The floating of this idea deepened fears that a victorious Prabowo would set about undoing all the democratic reforms since the fall of his ex-father-in-law in 1998. Even further, Prabowo's campaign consciously tried to awaken millenarian hopes among the Javanese: his campaign workers handed out 50,000 rupiah banknotes with a stamp proclaiming him as the *ratu adil,* the "just ruler" expected in Javanese tradition to appear and come to the rescue when dynasties declined and disorder ruled.

There was a darker side to the campaign too, recalling the "birther" smear against Barack Obama. An unregistered tabloid newspaper appeared six weeks ahead of the vote, showing a fake marriage certificate purporting to show Joko Widodo was a Christian and of Chinese parentage. The newspaper was circulated around mosques and Islamic schools, evidently using a mailing list held at the Ministry of Religious Affairs, which was allocated to the PPP in Yudhoyono's government, a party by then allied to Prabowo. An

official in the periphery of Yudhoyono's advisory circle was identified as the publisher. This crude smear, playing to ethnic and religious prejudice, was patently false, but Widodo felt obliged to make
his own Islamic faith more conspicuous (including by a quick *umroh*
or short pilgrimage to Mecca just ahead of the vote).

The generals on Widodo's side threw back what seemed to be
rather more truthful negatives on Prabowo's part. They said that as
his seniors, they had seen military records which allegedly included
adverse psychological assessments; Prabowo had been held back a
year in the military academy for indiscipline; he had mounted the
coup attempt against the army command in 1983; his dismissal in
1998 had been for authorizing the Tim Mawar abductions.

Nonetheless, the Jokowi campaign started weakly. It was badly
organized, with the candidate's daily scheduled hopelessly overloaded, so that local support groups were left carrying expenses
when he failed to show up and busloads of reporters were trapped in
traffic trying to reach venues. A coherent policy document appeared
only five days before the vote. The campaign pitch was mild, emphasizing the candidate's simple lifestyle, modest upbringing, and reputation for honesty. The slogan was "Jokowi is us." Widodo used the
word *publik* (the public, emphasizing citizenry with rights) rather the
rakyat (the people, suggesting a passive mass) that Prabowo tended
to employ. Prabowo evoked an agrarian dream of vast new agricultural zones in the outer islands keeping the bellies of the *rakyat* full,
harking back to Suharto's drive for self-sufficiency in rice; Widodo
talked of smarter consumption of resources. Both spoke of promoting domestic enterprise and keeping foreign investors in their place.
Where Prabowo offered a more *tegas* (firm) leadership that would
take the necessary decisions, Widodo talked of administrative systems to take discretion out of the hands of politicians and officials,
at least in routine transactions, and to involve the public in consul-
tations ahead of major decisions. At least initially, Widodo looked
like an ingénue wandering onto the national political stage. Some
Javanese compared this to the episode *Petruk Dadi Ratu* (Petruk
becomes king) inserted into wayang (traditional theatre) versions
of the Hindu epic, the *Mahabharata*. In this, the thin one of four
clownish figures picks up a talisman of power accidentally dropped
by a powerful warrior and becomes king, with comic and chaotic
results. Yet as the campaign wore on, centered on five televised

debates, Widodo showed more firmness in his grasp of policy issues, while Prabowo noticeably moderated his vehemence, apparently out of fear his strident appeal could evoke fear rather than respect. The vice-presidential candidates were also influential. On Prabowo's side Hatta Rajasa delivered a welter of figures on demand. Widodo had meanwhile resisted pressures to enlist Megawati's daughter Puan Maharani as running mate; instead he enlisted Jusuf Kalla. On television, the former vice-president put in some telling blows, including a jibe at the various "mafias" represented in a Prabowo coalition supposed to be resolute against *kebocoran* (leakage) of state funds.

The election became a stark choice between two kinds of leadership. As one businessman and writer in Surabaya, Johannes Nugroho, put it: "Prabowo embodies the quasi-feudal Indonesia in which leaders emerge from 'lineage' families such as his, the continuity of tradition and privilege of the ruling class. His brand of power is paternalism in its highest form. In complete contrasts Joko Widodo is a self-made businessman who ventured into politics, whose ancestry is no different from that of most Indonesians. Yet this is the essence of his mass appeal. Jokowi is the Indonesian Dream in the making." Another election watcher in the East Java city, political scientist Suka Widodo, saw it as contest of old and new political styles. "In Java, there is a belief that the leader has to be impressive, handing out benefits," he said. "By contrast Jokowi is asking for volunteers and donations from the voters, instead of handing out money to the people. Prabowo looks the part."

If Prabowo drew on some of the George W. Bush campaign methods, Widodo's campaign adopted part of the Barack Obama model in 2008. Large numbers of young volunteers turned out to campaign and monitor officialdom. This became critical in the count which began immediately after some 134 million of the 188 million eligible Indonesians voted on July 9, the largest one-day election so far held anywhere. The potential for bribery with so-called *uang saksi* [witness money] or straight-out intimidation of officials making the first count at 460,000 voting stations across the archipelago was a real worry. That these counts were then aggregated through five stages before the final result was tallied by the *Komisi Pemilu Umum* [KPU, General Election Commission] in Jakarta on July 22 increased the risk of interference. But "crowd-sourcing" brought thousands of young netizens into play as a safeguard: they photographed voting tallies with their smartphones and relayed them to ad hoc networks like Kawal Pemilu [Guard the Election], set up by a young Singapore-based technology graduate, Ainun Najib, and a clutch of tech-savvy friends.

The long wait between the vote and the official count was tense for Indonesia. Early estimates by most private polling institutions, based on samples, showed Widodo with a lead. Prabowo's camp produced their own forecasts from somewhat less credible groups. On the eve of the announcement, Prabowo appeared to announce his withdrawal from the election, claiming systemic cheating in the count; his headquarters called for a massing of supporters outside the KPU for the announcement; it appeared to some analysts that the expected loser might create unrest. Yudhoyono was concerned enough to sack his army chief, General Budiman, that night. Reports of the army's village-level monitors, the sergeants known as babinsa, making the rounds of households to urge votes for Prabowo had been widespread. The military had a strong stake in the election, hoping Prabowo would wrestle back anti-terrorism and internal security responsibility from the police if he won.

But support was melting away from Prabowo. His running mate, Hatta Rajasa, failed to appear with him at press conferences, and his chief legal adviser resigned. The result confirmed Widodo had won with 53.15 per cent of the vote, a margin of some 8.5 million votes too big for a challenge in the Constitutional Court to disqualify. The Jokowi era was about to begin. In his victory speech, delivered late that night from the deck of a traditional wooden ship docked in Sunda Kelapa, Jakarta's old port, Widodo declared a duty to show that "politics is full of fun, that there is happiness in politics, that there is goodness in politics, and that politics is a liberation" and that Indonesia's "long-lost voluntarism is now back with a new spirit."

His authority would face challenges from within and without. While the nation was distracted by the tense election, the new parliament had cunningly changed many of the rules concerning its membership. The DPR speakership no longer went to the party which had the largest number of seats in the customary way but would now be appointed by majority vote, meaning the PDI-P could not expect the key role for Megawati's daughter, Puan Maharani. Corruption investigations against DPR members could be stayed indefinitely by the president, instead of the previous maximum of 30 days. A powerful audit committee was abolished, and wider authority given to DPR members to "suggest" spending on projects in their districts.

However Prabowo's majority support in the parliamentary ranks started to fracture too. Moves began in Golkar to oust Bakrie as chairman and bring this party of deal-makers back into alignment with its former leader now returning to the vice-presidency, Jusuf Kalla. Yudhoyono's Democrats were also moving towards the emerging new government.

Widodo's other rival power center was Megawati. Her presidency had begun with the murder of Theys Eluay in Papua and ended with the poisoning of the human rights advocate Munir, with the return to an attempted military solution in Aceh in between. Numerous former generals, some with sinister records of political violence, remained embedded in the PDI-P, and were no doubt keen on positions of power. This group could be a brake on further military reform. As president also, Megawati had turned against the decentralization she had earlier supported (except in the divide-and-rule case of Papua).

Yet Widodo himself is a product of political devolution, and his achievements in Solo show its better side. Some provinces had become notorious for the corrupt political dynasties that emerged since the reforms—notably Banten, in the industry. But apart from Widodo's record in Solo, which has been maintained by his former deputy mayor and now successor F. X. Hadi Rudyatmo, there are many other success stories. In the Jembrana regency, on the western side of Bali, an academic turned bupati named I Gede Winasa introduced touch-screen voting machines for local elections and biometric time clocks to keep bureaucrats at work, and extended free education and health services. In the northern Sulawesi province of Gorontalo, a Muslim region carved out of the mostly Christian province of Manado in 2001, the first governor, Fadel Mohammad, set out to run his government like a "chief executive officer," introducing more salary incentives for officials, abolishing such perks of office as personally assigned cars, introducing information technology, and sending staff to management courses at leading universities. Alex Noerdin, who was elected governor of South Sumatra in 2008, was able to reorganize the province's finances to extend free education through to the senior high school year.

At his *Jawa Pos* media group in Surabaya, proprietor Dahlan Iskan set up the Institute for Pro-Autonomy in 2001, and began evaluating all the regional governments in East Java. The newspaper continues to publish an annual ranking of their performance. Within a few years, the survey was influencing elections. In the Bojonegoro regency, a negative evaluation by the institute outweighed the endorsement of the incumbent bupati by two influential kyai (religious leaders), and he was thrown out. Local budgets used to be shrouded in secrecy; now they are made available online and dissected by the institute's analysts.

In the Blitar regency, a network of public health clinics published a schedule of services and standards of staff behavior, an initiative copied across East Java. In Surabaya municipality, the government introduced online registration for places at public schools to avoid favoritism, with examination scores the basis for selection to the most sought-after senior high schools. The institute has extended its surveys to several other provinces in Java, Sulawesi, and Kalimantan. Rohman Budijanto, its director, admits there is a "Jakarta syndrome" that tends to deride regional autonomy, while ignoring the scandals besetting the central government (where the parliament is routinely cited as the most corrupt institution in public opinion surveys). The autonomous regional governments continue as wells of creativity in Indonesian governance, he says. "It is impossible for us to re-centralise power in Jakarta."

The quality of performance by a region's government is generally in inverse proportion to its natural resource wealth, it has to be said. The electoral laws also serve to maintain the Jakarta syndrome. Local political parties are banned, except in the special case of Aceh under the 2005 peace agreement. Everywhere else, parties must have a nationwide organization to run in the national elections. They must win at least 3.5 percent of the vote to gain any representation at all in the national parliament. The system so far has been weighted against the rise of local heroes outside the existing parties. Given the corruption within these parties, there is still a risk that people will become disillusioned with democracy. A new political movement requires the harnessing of a broad-based social network that is already in existence. The case of the PKS was one example. Another emerging force is that of organized urban labor, which is showing its muscle with mass strikes and demonstrations to win increases in minimum wages.

One figure gaining a national profile is Said Iqbal, president of the Konfederasi Serikat Pekerja Indonesia (Confederation of Indonesian Trade Unions), who has a master's degree in engineering. The distinctive flavor of contemporary trade unionism came out one evening at his headquarters in the down-market Cililitan district on the eastern side of Jakarta. Tens of thousands of his members had swarmed into the center of the city that day, stopping all movement, to demand a wage rise. Iqbal and his colleagues broke off an interview to make their evening prayers facing Mecca. The New Order regarded independent trade unions as nascent communism; repressing them became a large part of the duty of army garrisons as factories spread in the 1980s. This repressive policy gained notoriety with the 1993 abduction, rape, and murder of the activist Marsinah after a protest at a factory in East Java. Educated, devout, and using the label *pekerja* (a classless term for "worker"), rather than the name *buruh* (laborer), once favored by the PKI, the trade unions are considering the formation of a political party. Such an Indonesian labor party would be a counterpoint to the big-business representation in Golkar and other existing parties.

As Indonesia faced the 2014 elections, the constitutional court signaled a further evolution of the country's democracy, in the direction of openness. It had sat for ten months on its judgment in a case arguing for simultaneous elections of the president and parliament, to prevent the bargaining and extempore coalition formation that was occurring between the separate elections. The court accepted this argument, effectively abolishing the requirement for presidential candidates to have the support of 20 percent of the DPR membership or members representing 25 percent of the electorate. However, to prevent "chaos and legal uncertainty," it deferred application of its ruling until the elections of 2019. Why the court had not published the decision promptly in March 2013, in time to be applied in 2014, remained shrouded in judicial mystique. But looking forward, it pointed to coalitions and policies being formed behind presidential candidates well ahead of elections, instead of in the final weeks of campaigning. It also strengthened the hand of Widodo, who would have the option of standing for re-election in 2019 without the support of the PDI-P or the Sukarno dynasty if his personal popularity remains high.

As the Yudhoyono decade came to its end, Indonesians were taking lessons from the failure of a democratic experiment in a nation with which they were often compared. While watching Egypt's overthrow of a long-running military-backed dictatorship, similar in many ways to the New Order, and its return to martial law two years later amid chaos, Indonesians counted their blessings. Their military had not returned to the barracks and frontiers but had abandoned a direct role in politics. Their political parties were diverse and were required to compromise and work together. A plurality of political institutions allowed creative thinking as well as malfeasance, but both sides of the picture were exposed in a remarkably open society. Indonesia under SBY had not done its theoretical best, but nor was it doing badly.

14

INDONESIA IN THE WORLD

Nature has ordained that Indonesia, lying between two continents—the Asian mainland and Australia—and washed by the waters of two vast oceans—the Indian and the Pacific—must maintain intercourse with lands stretching in a great circle around it. From time immemorial, it has had relationships with all of them, varied as they are. Its position at the very heart of a network of communications has for centuries made the archipelago a halting place for all races and a staging base in international travel.

WHEN IN APRIL 1953, SOON AFTER INDONESIA'S INDEPENDENCE, THE COUNTRY'S FIRST vice president, Mohammad Hatta, wrote these words in his essay "Indonesia's Foreign Policy," published for an international audience in the journal *Foreign Affairs,* he was articulating an approach that would remain remarkably consistent throughout the six decades that followed. Only eight years after a global war had raged through its islands, Hatta saw Indonesia as occupying a benign geographic and diplomatic position. The American navy controlled the Pacific Ocean on one side; the British navy, the Indian Ocean on the other. Neither power had any evil intent toward the new republic. "On the contrary, they are desirous of seeing Indonesia remain independent and become prosperous," Hatta wrote. "Are they not the very people who hold that the infiltration of Communism can be prevented only by raising the economic level of the masses?"

The two big communist powers, meanwhile, were too far away to threaten Indonesia. The new nation could therefore concentrate on its own development, without being forced to line up with either side in the Cold War. It was not neutralism: Indonesia would not ignore the great international issues of the day but would take a stance based on its own evaluation of rights and wrongs, in a foreign policy that came to be abbreviated as "free and active." As Hatta put it: "Our Republic will rally to or support every effort within the framework of the United Nations to do away with, or at least grind off, the sharpness of the controversy between the two trends or blocs, so as to ward off as much as possible the cropping up of a large-scale conflict that may set off a third world war."

To emphasize his determination not to be counted in any big power's bloc but rather to seek a middle path, President Sukarno convened his famous Afro-Asian summit in Bandung in 1955, laying the ground for the foundation of the Non-Aligned Movement in 1961.

Many tides have flown through the archipelago since then. Hatta himself resigned a year after Bandung, in quiet protest at Sukarno's autocratic tendencies and his partnership with Indonesia's communist party. The United States intervened with covert support for the PRRI/Permesta rebellion. The Soviet Union supplied arms to Sukarno's government, and the People's Republic of China ideological support to the communists. By 1965 Sukarno was proclaiming a "Jakarta–Phnom Penh–Beijing–Pyongyang Axis"; the Americans and British were feverishly prodding the army to overthrow him and suppress the communists.

The New Order cut Indonesia off from China. But it kept diplomatic ties with Moscow, Havana, Hanoi, and Pyongyang, as well as with the Eastern European nations then under communist rule. Nor did Suharto openly embrace the United States, though he accepted its economic and limited military support. His regime was not popular in the Non-Aligned Movement. Supporters of Salvador Allende wrote "Jakarta" on walls in Chile after Augusto Pinochet's coup. Some Africans felt solidarity with the Papuans; others with the Timorese, former subjects, like themselves, of the Portuguese empire.

Suharto was mortified when, in 1996, the visiting South African president Nelson Mandela asked to visit the jailed Timorese guerrilla leader, José Xanana Gusmão. Yet Suharto never veered away from formal insistence on remaining nonaligned.

In 1975 the elderly Hatta was still summing up Jakarta's foreign policy as "*mendayung antara dua karang*" ("rowing between two reefs"). That year, as communist forces achieved victory in the South Vietnam and Cambodia conflicts, the reaction of Suharto and other anticommunist leaders in the region was not to rush behind America's skirts (the Nixon doctrine had already told allies in Asia to boost their own defenses before expecting any help). Instead, Suharto and the leaders of Thailand, Malaysia, Singapore, and the Philippines decided to tighten cooperation within their Association of Southeast Asian Nations (ASEAN). As the American position in Indochina worsened in 1971, it had already declared Southeast Asia a "zone of peace, freedom and neutrality."

ASEAN became and continues to be the inner ring of the "great circle" of countries in Indonesia's world. Progressively expanded to a membership of ten countries, with the inclusion of Brunei, Vietnam, Cambodia, Laos, and Myanmar (Burma), the regional association is the hub for alignment of trade, diplomatic, and social policies. In 1992 ASEAN began gradually applying a regional free-trade agreement, aimed at eliminating tariffs on all traded items originating within the group by 2015. As the largest member by population and economic size, Indonesia now sets the pace for the grouping and hosts its headquarters. Under the New Order, however, Indonesia tended to be the slowest ship in the convoy, especially on anything that another member might consider interference in domestic affairs, such as human rights standards. Postreform, Jakarta has been much more activist: for example, it urged Myanmar's military to follow the contemporary Indonesian example rather than the Suharto-era one.

ASEAN also became the center of an emerging regional "architecture" in Asia. Indonesia headed off pressure from the former Malaysian prime minister Mahathir Mohamad for a strong linkage with East Asian countries in a turn away from the West. In 2005, helped by a new leader in Malaysia, Indonesia was influential in establishing the East Asia Summit, now an annual meeting of the ten ASEAN leaders with those of Australia, China, India, Japan,

New Zealand, South Korea, the United States, and Russia. The summit, whose member countries comprise 55 percent of the world population and 56 percent of total world gross domestic product, remains the main Asian forum for discussion of economic and security issues.

ASEAN rejects the idea of military cooperation on a regional basis, although several member states have bilateral training and exercises between their defense forces. Malaysia and Singapore belong to the Five Power Defence Arrangements, set up with Britain, Australia, and New Zealand in the 1960s; it is still a mechanism for joint exercises, particularly in air defense. Thailand and the Philippines have defense treaties with the United States, while Singapore has less formal but close defense and intelligence relationships with the United States and Australia. Indonesia maintains a studied detachment, balancing its sources of military equipment between American, Russian, and European suppliers, and is wary of any arrangement that might be construed as a military pact.

It has a prickly relationship with Australia. Most of Indonesia's political and military leadership experienced the humiliation of withdrawal from East Timor in 1999, leaving it to an Australian-led stabilization force, whatever their thoughts about the wisdom of the 1975–76 annexation and the subsequent occupation. In 2006 a group of Papuan independence activists crossed the Torres Strait in a small boat to claim political asylum in Australia; that set off a diplomatic crisis in which Yudhoyono recalled his ambassador from Canberra. Canberra signed a hastily drafted treaty stating its recognition of Indonesian sovereignty in Papua, but the relationship remains hostage to events in Papua that might set off anti-Jakarta protests in Australia or provoke the flight of more refugees.

Repairing the "neglected" relationship with Indonesia has become a regular refrain of incoming governments in Canberra. The new conservative government of Prime Minister Tony Abbott came to power in September 2013 declaring that its foreign policy would focus on "Jakarta, not Geneva," and that ties with Indonesia were Australia's "most important foreign relationship." It turned out that this did not mean the closest or friendliest relationship, however, but simply the one that required the most work to keep civil.

The 2010 WikiLeaks disclosures had embarrassed the United States in its dealings with Jakarta. In 2013 the trove of US National

Security Agency material released by the whistle-blowing computer specialist Edward Snowden exposed Australian as well as American intelligence gathering in Indonesia. The leaked reports said both countries monitored local mobile telephone conversations from facilities within their embassies in Jakarta and elsewhere. A document from the Australian Signals Directorate, the electronic espionage arm of Canberra's defense department, reported on a program in 2011 to intercept the mobile phones of Yudhoyono and his wife, as well as those of several senior ministers. Abbott declined to give an apology of any kind. He caused further offense by insisting such spying was partly to protect Indonesia itself. The backlash saw interruptions to the cattle trade and to cooperation in combatting human trafficking. The leaks emphasized to Indonesians that Australia's "inner circle" was still based on its postwar intelligence pact with other English-speaking countries: the so-called UK-USA Agreement, or "Five Eyes" pact, between the United States, Britain, Canada, Australia, and New Zealand.

When Australia was not raising hackles in Jakarta, the country most likely to offend was, oddly enough, the one most similar in language and culture. Indonesians resented the superior attitudes found among Malaysians, well ahead in average income. Reports came back of harsh treatment of Indonesian domestic workers by their Malaysian employers and the forced repatriation of millions of Indonesians working illegally in the country. The inclusion of Javanese dances in Malaysia's cultural repertoire brought angry charges of false appropriation.

Disputes have been running since the 1950s over the ownership of islands and seabed resources in the sea adjacent to the Malaysia-Indonesia border on the eastern side of Kalimantan. In 2002 the International Court of Justice upheld Malaysia's claims to two small islands, Sipadan and Ligitan. The two governments now wrangle over the seabed boundary, which straddles a potentially huge oil and gas field known as the Ambalat block on the Indonesian side. Incursions by navy patrol boats and the construction of lighthouses have led to tense confrontations and at least one ramming incident.

Being able to match Malaysia in the air and on the sea became one of the unvoiced reasons for Indonesia to acquire advanced weaponry; in 2013 some of its newly acquired Sukhoi-30 fighters were stationed in Makassar in order to be close to the disputed area. If

ASEAN deliberations often seemed to be more aimed at building personal relationships than achieving any immediate outcomes, keeping disputes like this under control was partly the reason.

In an echo of its Cold War position, Indonesia tried to avoid lining up on either side in the new strategic rivalry that was building between China and the United States. As much as it wanted to welcome back the American president Barack Obama, who spent part of his childhood in Jakarta, Indonesia's government was sniffy about Obama's announcement in November 2011 of a strategic "pivot" into Southeast Asia and the Indian Ocean, particularly his plan to rotate a US Marine Corps strike force through Australian bases in Darwin each year, close to Indonesia's restive eastern provinces. But it could not help tilting one way.

Suharto had resumed relations with Beijing in 1990. In the new century, Chinese banks and enterprises began investing heavily in Indonesia's infrastructure and resources sector, and Sino-Indonesian businesses invested deeply in their ancestral homeland. Yet China's abrasive grab for resources, such as coal and timber, often ignoring customs procedures, gave it a predatory character. Its official uptake of Indonesian exports was 11.4 percent of the total in 2012, lagging behind that of the largest market, Japan, at 16 percent. With imports, the China-Japan balance was roughly reversed. In 2013 the Chinese ambassador in Jakarta was complaining privately to diplomatic colleagues about perceived snubs from Indonesian leaders and officials. China's assertion of territorial and resource rights in the South China Sea also touched on Indonesia's claims. It had no islands or reefs in dispute, unlike Vietnam and the Philippines. But Beijing's famous "nine-dash line" on its map of the sea, denoting its claim to maritime resources down to its southern and western areas, cut into Indonesia's exclusive economic zone.

In November 2013 the Indonesian air force held a large-scale exercise around the Natuna Islands, Indonesia's territorial outpost in the South China Sea. In March 2014 its navy was due to hold a similar defense exercise, which was clearly aimed at sending a message to China. The Chinese navy preceded this with an unusual exercise in which a flotilla of warships returning from the Middle East diverted south through the Sunda Strait, cruised eastward off the south coasts of Java and Bali, and then headed north through the Lombok and Makassar Straits—all a perfectly legal maneuver under the law of the sea and duly notified to Indonesia, but a show of naval reach nonetheless.

Under the "free and active" rubric, Indonesia's diplomats pursue an active role in multilateral forums. Indonesia keeps nearly 2,000 military personnel attached to UN peacekeeping missions in Darfur and South Sudan, Lebanon, the Congo, Haiti, Liberia, and the Philippines and has declared its willingness to join any mission set up in Syria. Frowning on interventions outside a direct UN mandate, it opposed the American-led campaigns in Afghanistan and Iraq.

Although Indonesia is an assiduous member of the Organisation of the Islamic Conference, its position as the largest Muslim nation by population is not matched by its authority on religious or Middle East political questions. It remains a receiver of wisdom from the Arab world, rather than a messenger of multireligious tolerance. Its lack of formal diplomatic relations with Israel limits its influence on the Palestinian question; its offer of help in mediating the tension over Iran's nuclear program was not taken up by either Tehran or Israel and the West. Its pressure on Myanmar's junta amounted to quiet jawboning and waiting for a change of mind, rather than applying sanctions or exclusions with ASEAN. In short, Indonesia's diplomacy is long on so-called soft power and short on application of "hard power" sanctions or force.

This was realistic enough in ambition. Indonesia's 6 percent average growth during much of Yudhoyono's presidency took its economy past $1 trillion in size. If this growth is sustained, Indonesia will enter the list of the world's ten biggest economies in a decade or so. Several studies by banks and rating agencies suggested a $9 trillion economy by 2030, which would make it the sixth-largest economy after China, the United States, India, Brazil, and Japan. The fashionable concept of the "BRIC" emerging economies (Brazil, Russia, India, China) expanded to include Indonesia, before growth faltered and deficits blew out in several of these countries. If many Indonesians came to assume that finally their nation was about to come into its destiny as a great power, wiser heads among them were pointing out that much better performance in economic policy and delivery would be required.

The identity of the Indonesian republic wrapped around this economy also still seems to be in formation. Will the educated strata left by the European Enlightenment continue to grow and prevail over the authoritarian mentality bequeathed by the harder side of colonial power and the Japanese occupation? Will diversity flourish, or will the "unitary state" draw power back to the center? Will the competition of market-based capitalism eventually overwhelm the cooperative impulse that is still so embedded in Indonesian thinking on the right pathways of commerce? Will the syncretic cultures of Java, Bali, and other proud ethnicities resist the "Arabization" that is infiltrating the nation through heightened religious devotion?

As the republic moves through its second half century, these questions remain. Perhaps, in the "staging place for all races" between two great oceans that Hatta wrote about in 1953, it is characteristic of the nation to leave them open.

ACKNOWLEDGMENTS

TO LIST THE FELLOW JOURNALISTS, THE ACADEMICS, THE POLITICIANS, THE OFFICIALS, the diplomats, and others who have helped me over the course of my working life to understand Indonesia—or at least to think I understand it—would require a book in itself. Many contributed unknowingly in encounters and gatherings over recent years to the background of this book. But as I put together this snapshot of Indonesia as it moves through the second decade of this century, the following individuals responded promptly and helpfully.

Peter McCawley, Christopher Manning, Asep Suryahadi, Satrio Budihardjo Joedono, and Bambang Ismawan were my guides through economic issues. James Castle, Gene Galbraith, Shoeb Zainuddin, Patrick Alexander, Henry Heinz, Donald Greenlees, Geoffrey Gold, Christopher Flanagan, and Daniel Horan were informed and wise advisers in the labyrinth of commerce and resource extraction. In Australia, Marcus Meitzner, David Reeve, Tim Lindsey, Adrian Vickers, and Vanessa Stearman were ready reference points on political and social trends, as were, in Jakarta, the old hands Tim Scott and Dennis Heffernan, while Agus Widjojo spoke frankly about military reform.

In Surabaya, Leak Kustiya, the editor in chief of *Jawa Pos*, took a day to show me around this vibrant city, while Rohman Budijanto and his team at the media group's Institut Pro-Otomi briefed me on regional government. As always, my journalist friends in Jakarta were superbly informed and lucid. Among them, Sabam Siagian, Ati Nurbaiti, Warief Djajanto Basorie, John McBeth, Yuli Ismartono, Lin Neumann, Michael Bachelard, Karuni Rompies, and Otje

Soedioto gave me their insights and opened their contact books. Dewi Fortuna Anwar, Adi Sasono, and Ilham Habibie gave me their time to discuss the role of Muslim intellectuals. Andreas Harsono, of Human Rights Watch, and Sidney Jones, of the Institute for Policy Analysis of Conflict, briefed me on human rights issues, as did Sayid Iqbal and Simon Field on the role of organized labor. On environmental questions, particular help came from Muslim Rasyid, of Jikalahari, and Susanto Kurniawan, of the Elang Foundation, both in Pekanbaru, and from Chandra Kirana, of Daemeter in Bogor. Damien Kingsbury gave me introductions to Mohammed Nur Djuli and Shadia Mahaban, who told me their gripping stories of the Aceh conflict and peace process. In Jayapura, the governor of Papua, Lukas Anambe, gave me a long midnight interview at the end of a busy day. The Papua region police chief, Tito Karnavian, gave me a long and frank briefing on security issues, while valuable insights on Papuan sentiment came from Neles Tebay, Paul Mambrasar, Manfred Naa, and Frits Ramandey. In Sydney, Peter King and Jim Elmslie helped with the latest scholarship on this troubled region.

Rizal Sukma organized a room and a visiting fellowship for me at the Centre for Strategic and International Studies in Jakarta, which became my base for research. Three of the founders of the CSIS—Harry Tjan Silalahi, Jusuf Wanandi, and Klara Juwono—were as informed, incisive, and outspoken as they were during my first years in Indonesia. Lina Alexandra deftly organized the logistics of my CSIS stay between her own research. I thank them all.

At the Australian National University, Andrew MacIntyre and Andrew Walker at the College of Asia and the Pacific allowed me the flexibility to mix my book research with writing and editing, and I was supported by James Giggacher and Belinda Cranston of the college's media unit. Nadjib Riphat Kesoema, Indonesia's ambassador in Canberra, Gary R. M. Jusuf, consul general in Sydney, and their staff were helpful in making arrangements, as were Siti Sofia Sudarma and her team at the Information and Media Directorate at the Ministry of Foreign Affairs in Jakarta. Ambassador Greg Moriarty and his staff at the Australian embassy were also most supportive. Julian Welch, my editor at Black Inc., worked with great skill while the rest of Australia was enjoying the summer break; his editing and suggestions resulted in a much improved book. My wife,

Penny, held the fort at home in Sydney during my long absences on research trips, and I thank her too.

The accuracy of all the content of this book and responsibility for any errors remain at the feet of the author, however, and it is always wise to recall the old Jakarta saying: "Anyone who thinks he understands the situation is sadly mistaken."

NOTES ON SOURCES

CHAPTER 1: NUSANTARA

Onghokham ideas on "Mooi Indie" (Beautiful Indies) are discussed in David Reeve et al. (eds.) *Onze Ong: Onghokham Dalam Kenangan*, Komunitas Bambu, 2007. The references to the writings of M. C. Ricklefs come from his panoramic *A History of Modern Indonesia, ca. 1300 to the present*, 4th edition, Palgrave and Stanford University Press, 2008; Benedict Anderson's comment from his essay, "The idea of power in Javanese Culture," in Claire Holt (ed.) *Culture and Politics in Indonesia*, Cornell U.P., 1972; Herbert Feith's observations from *The Decline of Constitutional Democracy in Indonesia*, Cornell U.P., 1962.

CHAPTER 2: THE CROCODILE HOLE

Clifford Geertz put his theory about the cultivation of Java in *Agricultural Involution: The Processes of Ecological Change in Indonesia*, University of California Press, 1963. The cited comment by Harry J. Benda comes from his 1964 essay "Democracy in Indonesia," that by David Levine from his 1969 essay "History and Social Structure in the Study of Contemporary Indonesia," and that by Herbert Feith from his "History, Theory and Indonesian Politics: A Reply to Harry J. Benda," published in 1965. These three articles are included in Benedict Anderson & Audrey Kahin (eds.) *Interpreting Indonesian Politics: Thirteen Contributions to the Debate*, Cornell Modern Indonesia Project, 1982, republished by Equinox (Singapore) 2010. The account of the September 30 Movement and its immediate effects draws from Harold Crouch, *The Army and Politics in Indonesia*, Cornell, 1978; John Roose, *Pretext for Mass Murder: The September 30th Movement and Suharto's Coup d'Etat in Indonesia*, University of Wisconsin Press, 2006; Bradley R. Simpson, *Economists with Guns: Authoritarian Development and U.S.-Indonesian Relations, 1960-1968*, Stanford U.P. 2008; Jusuf Wanandi, *Shades of Grey: A Political Memoir of Modern Indonesia 1965-1998*, Equinox, 2012; Kurniawan et al., *Pengakuan Algojo 1965* [Admitting the 1965 Slaughter], Tempo Publishing, 2013.

CHAPTER 3: THE NEW ORDER

Ruth T. McVey made the cited comparison in her 1977 essay "The *Beamtenstaat* in Indonesia," also in Benedict Anderson & Audrey Kahin (eds.) *Interpreting Indonesian Politics* cited above. The Sawito affair (including Ali Murtopo's remark) was examined by the magazine *Tempo* in its issues of October 16, 1976, August 13, 1977, and November 19, 1977. Radius Prawiro made the remark about B. J. Habibie's aircraft project to Raphael Pura, correspondent of *The Asian Wall Street Journal*; the late president Suharto wrote Sultan Hamengkubuwono IX out of the Yogyakarta clash of March 1, 1949, and also admitted approval of the "mysterious killings" of alleged criminals in his autobiography *Soeharto: Pikiran, Ucapan dan Tindakan Saya*, Citra Lamtoro Gung Persada, 1989. The chapter draws on the author's *Suharto's Indonesia*, CollinsFontana, 1980, and University of Hawaii Press, 1981, for the early New Order years, and Adam Schwarz, *A Nation in Waiting: Indonesia in the 1990s*, Westview Press, 1994, and updated editions in 1999 and 2004 which carried the story through to Suharto's fall and just beyond. Angus McIntyre's *The Indonesian Presidency*, Rowman & Littlefield, 2005, provided many insights into the cultural and psychological factors behind the careers of Sukarno, Suharto and Megawati Sukarnoputri.

CHAPTER 4: REFORMASI

The account of B. J. Habibie's presidency draws on his autobiography *Detik-detik Yang Menentukan* [*Decisive Moments*], Ilthabi Rekatama, 2006; R. E. Elson's paper "Engineering from within: Habibie the man and Indonesia's reformasi," for the Johns Hopkins School of Advanced International Studies conference on "Indonesia's reformasi: reflections on the Habibie era," March 26-27, 2007; Endy M. Bayuni, "How Soeharto schemed and Habibie botched it," *The Jakarta Post*, October 9, 2006; Wimar Witoelar, "The Lady or the Tiger, or Habibie guesses wrong," www.perspektif.net, October 9, 2006; "Wiranto's Game Plan," cover story *Tempo* [English edition] No. 06/VII/Oct 10–16, 2006; "Coup D'etat!," cover story *Tempo* [English edition] No. 05/VII/Oct 03–09, 2006; author's interview with Adi Sasono, August 29, 2013. *Tempo*, September 18-24, 2000, reported the remark of Ali Alatas on the Santa Cruz massacre. The Wikileaks cache of State Department cables includes former US ambassador Cameron Hume report of Habibie's account of his last words with Suharto. Angus McIntyre's insightful *The Indonesian Presidency* greatly helped the passages on the Abdurrahman Wahid and Megawati Sukarnoputri presidencies.

CHAPTER 5: TSUNAMI

This story of the Aceh conflict and the peace settlement quotes extensively from the author's interviews in Banda Aceh with Shadia Mahaban and Mohammed Nur Djuli in May 2013. Anthony Reid (ed.), *Verandah of Violence: The Background to the Aceh Problem*, National University of Singapore Press, 2006, was an immensely useful source on the history of the region and origins of the revolt. The cited comment by Reid comes from his fascinating introduction and chapter on the Dutch colonial impact. The Indonesian side of the Helsinki peace negotiations is recounted in Hamid Awaluddin (Tim Scott trans.), *Peace in Aceh*, Centre for Strategic and International Studies, Jakarta, 2009.

CHAPTER 6: BEYOND DWIFUNGSI

The remarks by retired army general Agus Widjojo come from an interview by the author in August 2013. The State Department cables published by Wikileaks were an invaluable source on developments in Indonesian military affairs and the thinking of military leaders up until 2010; all references to US Embassy reports come from this material. Otherwise, quoted comments come from contemporary reports in *The Jakarta Post, The Jakarta Globe,* or *Tempo* magazine. The remark by Prabowo Subianto about the lack of written orders in the Indonesian military was quoted by Ken Conboy in *Kopassus: Inside Indonesia's Special Forces,* Equinox, 2003. The passage on the separation of the military from business activity was helped by the Human Rights Watch report "Unkept Promise; Failure to End Military Business Activity in Indonesia," January 12, 2010 and Lex Reiffel and Jaleswari Pramodhawardani, *Out of Business and on Budget: the challenge of military financing in Indonesia,* Brookings Institution, Washington DC, 2007. Background on the military and its doctrines comes in Marcus Mietzner, *Military Politics, Islam, and the State in Indonesia: from turbulent transition to democratic consolidation,* ISEAS (Singapore), 2009, and Jun Honna, *Military Politics and Democratization in Indonesia,* Routledge, 2003. The comments by the 1970 military academy class came in Sudrajat et al, *Mengawali Integrasi Mengusung Reformasi: Pengabdian Alumni Akabri Pertama 1970,* Kata Hasta Pusaka, Jakarta 2012.

CHAPTER 7: SUPREME COMMODITY

Anecdotal material on the coal-mining boom in Kalimantan came from interviews during 2013 with industry figures who asked to be kept anonymous. Wahyu Dhyatmika, Khaidir Rahman, SG Wibisono, Firman Hidayat, "The Coal Capitalists," *Tempo Interaktif,* August 16, 2012, gave further biographical material on the new coal barons. The portrait of the impoverished past of Srihardjo came from David Penny & Masri Singarimbun, *Population and Poverty in Indonesia: Some Economic Arithmetic from Srihardjo,* Cornell University, Department of Agricultural Economics, 1973. The picture of the more comfortable present came from a visit with Christopher Manning in September 2013. Asep Suryahadi of the SMERU Research Institute, and Satrio Budihardjo Joedono, emeritus professor of economics at the University of Indonesia, gave interviews from which the quoted remarks are taken. J. K. Galbraith's paradigm came of course from *The Affluent Society,* Houghton Mifflin, 1958. Manning's conclusions about the effect of minimum wage rises came in "A Robust Wage Campaign in 2013," *The Jakarta Post,* June 4, 2013. Vikram Nehru wrote about the conflict between the macro-economic managers and the departmental nationalists in "Manufacturing in India and Indonesia: performance and policies," *Bulletin of Indonesian Economic Studies (BIES),* Vol. 49, Issue No.1 2013. Hadi Soesastro's remark is recalled in Hal Hill & Mari Elka Pangestu, "M. Hadi Soesastro: Indonesian Public Intellectual, Asia Pacific Visionary," *BIES* Vol. 46, Issue No. 2, 2010.

CHAPTER 8: CAPITAL

For views on the entrepreneurship dilemma see Gustav F. Papanek (ed.), *The Indonesian Economy,* Praeger, 1980, and "The *Pribumi* entrepreneurs of Bali and Central Java (or, How not to help Indigenous enterprise)," *BIES,* Vol. 42, No. 1, 2006. The observations on the Bank Central Asia are based partly on an interview with a senior manager who asked not to be named. The recovery of major New Order business conglomerates from the 1997-98 financial crisis is intensively covered in the State Department cables published by Wikileaks, as is the "mud volcano" set off in East Java by a Bakrie group company, and in international business newspapers. The account of the Bakrie-Rothschild dispute over Bumi Plc draws on reports in British and Indonesian newspapers: see notably reports in *The Daily Telegraph, The Financial Times,* and *The Economist* over 2009-2014.

CHAPTER 9: BETWEEN MECCA AND THE SOUTH SEA

The classic definition of religious *aliran* [streams] came in Clifford Geertz, *The Religion of Java,* Free Press, 1960. Background to this chapter came from the third volume of M. C. Ricklefs' history of Islam in Indonesia, *Islamisation and its Opponents in Java c. 1930 to the Present,* National University of Singapore Press, 2012, and from Solahudin (trans. Dave McRae), *The Roots of Terrorism in Indonesia: From Darul Islam to Jem'ah Islamiyah,* Cornell U.P., 2013. Yudi Latif's remarks came in a talk to the author and other members of an Australian media delegation to Jakarta in 2008, as did the comments on terrorism by a senior official of Densus 88, Indonesian National Police. Adi Sasono's and Shadia Mahaban's comments come from the 2013 interviews mentioned above. Abu Bakar Ba'asyir's remarks about Western tourists were heard and videotaped by Nathan Franklin, then a Ph.D. candidate at Charles Darwin University, Australia, at Paciran, East Java in October 2007: see his account *Inside Indonesia* 92: Apr-Jun 2008.

CHAPTER 10: KORUPSI

The specific detail of the corruption cases in this chapter came from contemporary Indonesian press reports and from US Embassy cables in the Wikileaks cache. On public perceptions of corruption in the DPR (Parliament) see for example the 2013 Indonesia Network Election Survey http://nasional.sindonews.com/read/2013/09/05/12/779603/survei-ines-anggota-dpr-dicap-tukang-bohong. For the World Bank view see S. Lateef, et al; *Combating Corruption in Indonesia,* World Bank East Asia Poverty Reduction and Economic Management Unit, 2003; and Anti-Corruption Resources Centre, "Causes of corruption in Indonesia," at www.U4.no. Satrio Budihardjo Joedono's comments and those of the KPK's Johan Budi came in interviews by the author. Further information and comments in this chapter came from business executives, investment consultants and academic legal figures who spoke on condition they not be identified.

CHAPTER 11: THE EASTERN MARGIN

US ambassador Lynn Pascoe's cable was disclosed by Wikileaks. Quoted remarks by Lukas Enembe, Neles Tebay and Tito Karnavian come from interviews by the author in November 2013. Pieter Drooglever's comments come from *An Act of Free Choice: Decolonisation and the Right to Self-Determination in West Papua,* Oneworld Publications, Oxford and New York, 2009; from his

summary article accessible on http://resources.huygens.knaw.nl/indonesisch
ebetrekkingen1945-1969/DekolonisatieVanIndonesieEnHetZelfbeschikking
srechtVanDePapoea/papers_pdf/summary_afc and his testimony to the Asia,
the Pacific and the Global Environment Subcommittee, House Foreign Affairs
Committee, US Congress, September 22, 2010. Details of Operasi Wibawa and
other military sweeps came in *Warta HAM Papua* [News on Human Rights
Papua], Main Issue, Year VI, 2013, Komnas HAM [National Human Rights
Commission], Jayapura. Survivors of the Biak massacre testified at a "citizens
tribunal" held by the West Papua Project, Centre for Peace and Conflict Stud-
ies, University of Sydney, in July 2013. On the murder of Theys Eluay see Clin-
ton Fernandes, *Reluctant Indonesians: Australia, Indonesia and the Future of
West Papua,* Scribe, 2006. Papers presented at a conference "Comprehending
Papua" held by the West Papua Project at the University of Sydney, February
23-24, 2011, are also drawn upon: John Saltford, "Reflections on the New
York Agreement, the Act of Free Choice, and Developments Since"; Akihisa
Matsuno, "West Papua and the Changing Nature of Self-Determination"; S.
Eben Kirksey, "Reclaiming the Messianic Promise"; Richard Chauvel, "Policy
Failure and Political Impasse: Papua and Jakarta a decade after the 'Papuan
Spring"; Jim Elmslie, "West Papuan Demographic Transition and the 2010 In-
donesian Census: 'Slow Motion Genocide' or not?" The comments by Sidney
Jones came in an interview with the author, and in her reports for the Institute
for Policy Analysis of Conflict, Jakarta: "Carving Up Papua: More Districts,
More trouble," October 9, 2013; "*Otsus Plus:* The Debate over Enhanced Spe-
cial Autonomy for Papua," November 25, 2013; "Papua update: The latest on
Otsus Plus," February 27, 2014. The author interviewed Paulus Samkakay and
Alfonsina Hambring at the East Awin settlement, Papua New Guinea, in 2006.
For the diverse interpretations of "merdeka" [freedom] in Papua, see S. Eben
Kirksey, *From Cannibal to Terrorist: State Violence, Indigenous Resistance
and Representation in West Papua,* M.Phil. thesis, Oxford University, 2002,
and Brigham Golden, "Political Millenarianism and the Economy of Conflict:
Reflections on Papua by an Activist Anthropologist," *Asia Source,* 23 June,
2003, http://www.asiasource.org/asip/papua_golden.cfm and their subsequent
writings.

CHAPTER 12: THE BURNING QUESTION

On the 1997 haze see Rand Corp, *The Dangers of Smoke Haze: Mortality
in Malaysia from Indonesian Forest Fires,* http://www.rand.org/pubs/research
_briefs/RB5066/index1.html. Abbie Carla Yunita wrote about the REDD+
program in "Social safeguards and equity in forest governance: Lessons from
the Kalimantan Forest and Climate Partnership, Ulu Masen," B.A. honors thesis, Monash University, Melbourne, 2013. On the Tessa Nilo encroachment see
World Wildlife Fund Indonesia, *Palming Off a National Park,* June 2013. Information on the REDD+ scheme and efforts to delineate land ownership came
from an interview with environmentalist and writer Chandra Kirana in Bogor,
November 2013. See also "Indonesia's Constitutional Court returns customary forests to indigenous people," www.redd-monitor.org, May 17, 2013. On
the acceleration of deforestation see Belinda Arunarwati Margono, Peter V.
Potapov, Svetlana Turubanova, Fred Stolle & Matthew C. Hansen, "Primary
forest cover loss in Indonesia over 2000–2012," *Nature Climate Change,* published online June 29, 2014. On pollution in the Citarum River and mercury

residue in Kalimantan see Blacksmith Institute and Green Cross Switzerland, "Top Ten Toxic Threats in 2013: Cleanup, Progress and Ongoing Challenges" at www.worstpolluted.org. The campaign against lead pollution in Bandung comes from Nguyen Thi Kim Oanh (ed.), *Integrated Air Quality Management: Asian Case Studies,* CRC Press, 2013.

CHAPTER 13: FROM SBY TO JOKOWI

On SBY's "squandered" second mandate, see Greg Fealy, "Indonesian Politics in 2011: SBY's Incumbency and Democratic Regression," *BIES,* Vol. 47, Issue 3, 2011. The rise in stunted growth among children was found in the 2013 Riskesdas (Basic Health Research) report of the Ministry of Health, widely reported on December 7, 2013. The official report on the 1965-66 killings is *Komisi Nasional Hak Asasi Manusia [Komnas HAM], Republik Indonesia, Ringkasan Eksekutif Hasil Penyelidikan Tim Ad Hoc Penyelidikan Pelanggaran HAM Yang Berat Peristiwa 1965-1966,* July 23, 2012. An unofficial English translation of the summary is available on http://tapol.org/sites/default /files/sites/default/files/pdfs/Komnas HAM 1965 TAPOL translation.pdf. On the continued harassment of PKI survivors see Ati Nurbaiti, "Muscle testing of bullies amid dangerous state silence," *The Jakarta Post,* November 4, 2013; Bambang Muryanto and Bagus BT Saragih, "Resurgence in intimidation of families of 1965 purge victims," *The Jakarta Post,* October 29, 2013; "Hard-Liners Attack 1965-66 Purge Support Group," *The Jakarta Globe* October 28, 2013. On the short-lived presidential apology initiative see Rabby Pramudatama, "SBY to apologize for rights abuses," *The Jakarta Post,* April 26, 2012, and Katherine McGregor, "Mass Violence in the Transition From Sukarno to Suharto," *Global Dialogue* 15 (1), 2013. John Roosa wrote on the banning of the Indonesian translation of his book in "Book banning in Indonesia: A blast from the past," *The Jakarta Post,* January 13, 2010. On the proposal to end direct elections of provincial and regional chiefs, see Carlos Paath and Markus Junianto Sihaloho, "Indonesia Lobbies for End to Direct Elections in Regional Races," *The Jakarta Post,* December 4, 2013. August Parengkuan's comment was made to the visiting Australian media delegation in 2008. The US Embassy comment on Yudhoyono and that of General T. B. Silalahi are contained in the Wikileaks cache, Agus Widjojo's in his interview with the author. For a summary of material on the Kraras massacre in East Timor see http://hass .unsw.adfa.edu.au/timor_companion/the_1980s/massacres.php and Mario Carrascalao, *Timor Antes do Future,* Livraria Mau Huran (Dili), 2006. Sofyan Wanandi is quoted on the threat made by Prabowo in Schwarz, *op cit.* See also Tonny, "Prabowo and his anti-Chinese past?" on the Australian National University (ANU) New Mandala website, June 27, 2014. On Prabowo's justification of his past, during the 2009 elections, see Geoff Thompson, "The Farmer Wants a Country," ABC-TV Foreign Correspondent, transcript at http://www .abc.net.au/foreign/content/2009/s2532107.htm. The ex-generals who accused Prabowo of being unfit for the leadership were A.M. Hendropriyono, Wiranto, and Luhut Panjaitan: see Margareth S. Aritonang & Sita W. Dewi, "Gloves come off as campaign heats up," *The Jakarta Post,* June 5, 2014; "Wiranto: Prabowo Terbukti Terlibat Penculikan, Jangan Terjebak Istilah," Kompas.com, June 19,2014; Michael Bachelard, "Prabowo Subianto: will he be Indonesia's next president?" *The Age* (Melbourne) June 21, 2014. On Prabowo's election manifesto as it developed, see Emirza Adi Syailendra, "Indonesia's Prabowo

Subianto tests the water in Singapore," ANU East Asia Forum, October 6, 2012. Veteran investment consultant Dennis Heffernan made the "Golkar eats its young" comment to the author. A vivid running analysis of the 2014 election came in the "Indonesia Votes" stream of the ANU's New Mandala website, in particular these postings: Steven Sherlock, "House of Cards III," July 28, 2014; Liam Gammon, "We was robbed," July 24, 2014; Alex Arifianto, "Neutral no more," July 21, 2014; Justin Snyder, "Campaign finance, strategy and accounting," July 18, 2014; Roanne van Voorst, "Voting No. 1," July 15, 2014; Jacqui Baker, "Stand by your man," July 14, 2014; Edward Aspinall & Marcus Mietzner, "Prabowo's game plan," July 10, 2014 and "Don't be Fooled: Prabowo (still) wants to get rid of direct presidential elections," July 2, 2014; Greg Fealy, "Uneasy Alliance: Prabowo and the Islamic Parties," July 9, 2014; Rianne Subijanto, "Mixed Messages," July 3, 2014; Jeffrey A. Winters, "Jokowi and Prabowo Reflect a Decade of Frustrations with SBY," July 2, 2014; Ross Tapsell, "Anti-democratic? Prabowo's response," July 1, 2014; Edward Aspinall, "Indonesia's democracy is in danger," June 17, 2014; Tom Power, "Why were the polls wrong about Islamic parties?" April 15, 2014. Rob Allyn discussed his role in Prabowo's 2014 election campaign in "Every vote must be counted, every voice must be heard," posted on New Mandala, July 16, 2014. The comment by Johannes Nugroho was made in an email to the author, that by Suka Widodo in interview by the author. A transcript of Joko Widodo's victory speech was carried in *The Jakarta Post*, July 23, 2014. Rohman Budijanto made his comments in an interview at the Institut Pro-Otonomi, Surabaya, November 2013. On the changed election rules for the presidency in 2019, see Ina Parlina & Nurfika Osman, "Court rules one voting day in 2019," *The Jakarta Post*, January 24, 2014.

CHAPTER 14: INDONESIA IN THE WORLD

Mohammad Hatta's 1953 essay can be read on http://www.foreignaffairs.com/articles/71032/mohammad-hatta/indonesias-foreign-policy. On the Tony Abbott government's foreign policy see Michael Wesley, "In Australia it's now less about Geneva, more about Jakarta," September 10, 2013, on www.eastasiaforum.org. On the Edward Snowden leak about telephone interception see Mark Corcoran, "Decision to tap Susilo Bambang Yudhoyono's phone came in wake of Jakarta bombings that killed Australians," www.abc.net/news, November 18, 2013. The Chinese ambassador's comments were relayed in a confidential interview by the author with another senior envoy in Jakarta. The prediction that Indonesia would be the world's seventh biggest economy by 2030 comes in Raoul Oberman et al, *The Archipelago Economy: Unleashing Indonesia's Potential,* McKinsey Global Institute, September 2012.

INDEX